THE MAVERICK'S ROUNDUP

GWENNETH LEANE
AND
BRUCE LEANE

THE STORY OF ONE MAN'S JOURNEY FROM TOOLBOX TO PULPIT

PUBLISHER
Kylie Margaret Leane
kmlpublishing.com

COVER ART/DESIGN
Kylie Leane

© 2020 Gwenneth Leane
All rights reserved.

No portion of this publication may be
reproduced or transmitted,
in any form or by any means, without the
prior written permission of either copyright
owner or publisher of this book.

THE MAVERICK'S ROUNDUP
PUBLICATION HISTORY

Paperback Edition / January 2020
Gwenneth Leane and Bruce Leane
ISBN: 978-0-9944382-6-3

PRINTED IN AUSTRALIA

For information address:
gwen.leane@gmail.com

Gwenneth's Blog can be found online at:
Gwen's Goss
Bruce Leane can be found at:
The Maverick's Roundup Facebook Page

THE MAVERICK'S ROUNDUP

GWENNETH LEANE
BRUCE LEANE

GWENNETH & BRUCE LEANE

Acknowlegements

This roundup is a life of commitment by my wife and me as we answered God's call. It was an unconventional life but God stands behind commitment.

The area covered in South Australia was immense. We were involved in church services in over forty-five towns involving thousands of people from many different lifestyles weekly.

To you all I say may God richly bless you. We give you what the Lord has given to us. We have a policy to release people to serve the Lord that we know love and serve. I have not mentioned everybody that has contributed to my life and ministry in this roundup and I apologise but thank you for being a part of our journey who ever and where ever you are. Because of you this round up is possible.

I would like to thank Elizabeth Foster Bailey for her hard work in proof reading my story.

If anyone in reading this story would like to make contact, we would love to hear from you or drop in and say 'hello' if we have not gone to the maverick's heaven.

We celebrated our diamond-wedding anniversary in July 2012.

Email: gwen.leane@hotmail.com

Foreword

I wish to introduce to you one of my greatest friends. I have known Bruce for many years and have watched in awe his amazing achievements; his steadfast commitment to God and sharing the good news of Christ. His pioneering ability has taken him to some of the toughest places in this country where no one else was prepared to venture.

Bruce is a man of great passion and love for Christ and as you read his story, the challenge will be to build up your faith.

It gives me great honour to share these words with you. In my mind, Bruce is one of the pioneers of the gospel Australia has ever had. When no one was there, Bruce was there.

The Reverend Clifford Beard

Chapter One
The Call

The atmosphere, infused with the presence of God where anything could happen and it did. We four couples experienced surprise and later, a quiet awe. It was as if Acts Chapter Two was being re-enacted in the lounge room of our home; the moment played out exactly as in the original text from the Bible, 'A deep sense of awe was on them all…'

After a long silence, the group started to chat and Ron began to talk about his favourite subject, speaking in tongues.

'Ron, speaking in tongues is not for today.' I was ready to do battle for the truth as I saw it. No upstart was going to tell me what was truth and what was not.

'You read the scriptures,' Ron opened his Bible and read aloud from Acts and first Corinthians.

'Ron, that was only for Bible times.' I believed I was an authority as I had learnt that passage off by heart during my youth when I took Scripture Union exams.

'It's a load of poppycock and baloney.' I exclaimed emphatically.

My guests commented that they thought Ron's theory was the truth. I looked at Gwen; she was looking down at her Bible.

Suddenly I could not hear or speak. I was terrified, I thought I had had a stroke or a heart attack; however, my mind was still clear. Ron went on talking and reasoning about the scriptures. After a few minutes, I began to hear and speak again. I quickly and politely suggested that we halt our discussion and go home. No one was the wiser as to what happened to me. After the last goodbye, Gwen looked at me as if I had grown to heads.

'What happened to you? You went suddenly quiet,' she said.

'Something weird happened. I think it was God's way of speaking to me. He wanted to catch my attention and make me listen.'

'What do you think God is saying?'

'I don't know but I feel that what Ron was saying about speaking in tongues is true and I'm not going to argue about it anymore.'

'But that means that what we've been taught about these things hasn't been right?' Gwen was horrified.

'It looks a bit like that.' I too, was feeling as if the goal posts had suddenly moved without my knowing.

Ron and Margaret Inglis, newly married and recently arrived in Berri, had joined our group of praying friends. He was a sharp, young fellow from the city and had obtained a job as a refrigeration mechanic. The couple were members of the Christian Revival Crusade in Adelaide.

The pickers' quarters that we called home became a meeting place where we met with three other couples of like mind each week to pray for revival.

I had erected an add-on room next to our quarters as a lounge room. The lounge was an old style suite of two chairs and a sofa. I had bought it cheap because the springs were laughing at us.

'Honey, I've bought a lounge suite.'

'What! Where did you get it?' There was a note of hope in Gwen's voice, she had long dreamed of a nice lounge suite.

'I bought it at a sale.'

'What's it like?'

'Come and have a look, honey.' I proudly took her outside to show off my bargain. 'What do you think?'

Her face said it all. Disappointment, struggled with anger. She was very upset.

When my mum next came to visit us, she and Gwen got to work and reupholstered the suite with red damask material.

This suite now graced the little sitting room on the end of the shed. The springs still complained and took revenge by sticking into backsides when sat on. The suite was very bulky and took up most of the room but you do not need much room to pray.

Strange how a small insignificant incident becomes part of the fabric of a momentous change of thought and direction in life as the lounge suite did at that time, but that is how God prepared me for my calling.

Chapter Two
We Follow The Call

Two Aboriginal men called on the Boss soon after my experience of 'being struck dumb' by the Lord. It was unusual for Aboriginal people of that era to visit white people and seek their help.

'Mr Chapple, we are planning a mission out in the scrub at Winkie and would like to borrow some sweatboxes to make a stage. We were told that you might be willing to lend some.' Sweatboxes were large, shallow boxes used for handling dried fruit.

'So long as you bring them back, I don't see any problem,' the Boss said.

The word 'mission' had my ears flapping.

'Can you help us shift the boxes out to the mission site,' one of the men asked. The Boss turned to me,

'Bruce, take the old truck and load up some boxes and take them out.'

'Follow us and we'll show you where to go,' the Aboriginal men said. I followed them to a patch of mallee scrub beyond the Winkie settlement, there were people running everywhere and soon I was involved as well.

'Put the boxes under that bough shelter. They will make a good stage and soundshell.' I did as directed.

'What is everyone going to sit on?' Curious, I looked around surely they would find seats from somewhere. People could not just sit on the ground or stand up.

'There's plenty of good red earth to sit on, anyway, we'll put some bags and hessian down to sit on,' the leader of the group informed me.

'Can you help run this bundle of hessian around those posts to make a compound?' the leader approached me again.

This was not going to be the sort of mission that I knew to be mission. This was mission Aboriginal style.

Frank and Sylvia Graetz, Gwen and I, Ron and Margaret Inglis and others in our group decided to follow the mission. The evangelist was Mr. Dick Piety from Queensland. He and a team of indigenous Christian men and women had travelled down through to the Riverland, holding missions in all the Aboriginal camps along the way and picking fruit as they went. We were like cats on hot tin roofs with excitement.

Everyone knew him affectionately as Brother Dick. He turned out to be the ultimate storyteller with hundreds of stories of miracles performed by God from all over the eastern States. He travelled the Aboriginal Convention circuits held over Easter Holidays, as guest speaker. One of his great sayings was, 'the hanimals had more sense than the humans did, the hanimals went into the hark.'

As the week wore on Dick planned a special night, he called it a Tarry Meeting.

'What's a Tarry Meeting?' I asked Dick. I had never heard of such a meeting.

'It's a meeting where you pray and wait for the Holy Spirit to fill you just as in Acts Chapters 1 - 2. Then he read the words to me, 'Go tarry in Jerusalem until you become endued with power from on high.'

'Oh, I see.' I was not game to argue after my experience the week before with Ron.

Wild horses would not have kept me from that meeting. When I arrived, Ron met me at the entrance to the hessian compound,

'How are you tonight, Bruce?'

'It's not a matter of how I am; I'm here to be filled with the Spirit of God.'

He looked a bit startled. I had not told him of my experience.

The evening progressed with Dick giving us a short talk, and then we knelt to pray. Dick moved around laying hands on people who either knelt or sat praying. Before he reached me, the Lord had visited me. His presence fell over me like a light blanket and I became lost in his presence worshipping the Lord in tongues.

No one had ever told me how to speak in tongues and no one laid hands on me. God dealt with me personally. There was no pressure, no hype, just the quiet presence of God.

When Dick did reach me, I was lost in the presence of God and for the first time in my life, I had been touched with a miracle. I now had a prayer language.

I have never lost the quiet living presence of the Holy Spirit; or of continually filled with the power of God, it is like filling up the car with petrol every week. God had supplied the power factor, the Holy Spirit. The bowser has never run out.

The old rugged cross was now twice as precious to me. I'd found forgiveness, redemption, and salvation at its base, and was now charged with power and purpose.

The meetings at the compound of the Old Rugged Cross

continued for a couple of weeks and then Dick announced one Sunday after he had finished preaching,

'God has directed me to say to you that from now on Bruce will take charge. He and his family, Frank and his family are your leaders. They will love you; honour them. The Lord will bless you.'

We felt rudderless without Dick. We were living in a bubble of glory and without Dick; the whole group would break up.

It was a critical moment - would the people accept white men as their leaders? Would we white people be up to the challenge? It was a miracle! The people turned as one and looked at Frank and me, silently acknowledging us as their spiritual leaders, transferring their allegiance from Dick to Frank and me. It could only have been God inspired.

Dick was only partly right; Dora was the real spiritual mother of the people; she was a great woman of God.

Our calling was to support her, and do and go where she could not. On the other hand, we needed her to open doors into the camps that we were unable to do.

George and Dora Karpany had built a shanty and called it home on the riverbank across from the township of Berri. There were quite a number of humpies belonging to Aboriginal folk around Dora and George. Many of the riverbank groups were careful to separate themselves from white folk.

The camp is now the landing stage for a fleet of houseboats and the bridge that now spans the river at Berri towers over the area where many humpies once stood.

Dora maintained a Christian leadership role the whole of her life and became a very close friend over the coming years. In fact, she called us her son and daughter.

Her husband George, was a beanpole of a man, a strong big bodied man who commanded respect from both indigenous and non-indigenous, his bearing that of a king. He held boxing awards from World War 1.

Dora had an only child, Keith. He broke her heart repeatedly with his wayward living. Undaunted, she fostered many children who were abandoned or whose parents were unable to look after them. She brought them up as her own trying to give them a better start in life. Dora mothered many broken, outcast people, trying to lift them up and create within them personal pride.

You and I can never imagine what it cost her to be 'sold out' for Jesus unless you have lived in the camps as she did, surrounded by relatives and friends cadging food and money, alcohol flowing like the river outside her shack and relatives running brothels.

Almost none of the Aboriginal folk lived in regular housing at that time. Many hundreds of times, Gwen and I with our children and Frank and his family ate and drank with these people in their shacks. Built of unlined bare iron sheets, tacked up, old wood stoves standing alone, dirt floors covered with bits of old lino thrown out in the dumps - no bathroom or flushing toilet - these shacks though, were clean and tidy, tributes to ingeniousness.

Dick had 'thrown down the gauntlet' to us. Would we pick it up and lead the people?

We would be going against all tradition by becoming involved with indigenous people. Nobody in the non-indigenous community, at that time, ever mixed with the indigenous. Some very fine people who were hungry for love, acceptance and fellowship crossed our path and helped confirm our call.

The Call was here, staring me in the face, did I have what it takes to run with it? God did not ask for my Ministers' Credentials or at what Bible College I had studied at or if I had a PhD in indigenous affairs. Nor was it the glory of going overseas as a missionary or pastoring a rich respectable church. God was calling me just as I was.

The education I had longed for - that would deliver me from the dairy to serve God as a pastor drifted out of sight, over the hill and far away, when Dad enlisted in the Royal Australian Air Force then stationed in Papua New Guinea during the Second World War. There was my personal war with Asthma, leaving me feeling disadvantaged in the extreme.

Regardless of these setbacks, this was the moment God had been grooming me for - in the school of hard knocks. There was much to learn about the indigenous people but God was dealing with my heart and attitudes.

Because of all the new thoughts and ideas that were bombarding our minds, we were praying much. We were traversing an ocean without a map it seemed and prayer was our only recourse to the ear of God. That wife of mine spent a lot of time catching the ear of God. I kept busy preaching and visiting after work.

The Call was for me, and my family, to preach, teach and lead, and to become outcasts with these people. It was to lead broken, unrecognised indigenous people who did not trust anyone especially white people. The indigenous were not wanted and in the hope that they would go away were treated as though they did not exist or as non-people. No church I had ever attended seemed aware of the dreadful need of these Aboriginal people.

I was called to identify with them in their way of life just as Christ identified with us in our sin if he was to rescue us and lift us up to be the people God wanted.

Chapter Three
Picking Up The Challenge

'Life was never meant to be easy,' so Malcolm Fraser informed us. Surely, there could be easier ways to live it, I wondered, as the reality of my Call confronted me with scores of people just existing on the edge of society. Some were very warm and lovely people who loved us and who were just crying for some direction, recognition and friendship. Others did not want to know us and cold-shouldered us. There were those with a hostile and bitter spirit at their treatment and abused us.

I talked over our new direction with my Boss who knew me well by this time and knew that the block work would not suffer. He accepted that Gwen and I now had a different call on our life.

So the Leane family and the Graetz family approached the local Church of Christ to inform them tactfully that we were going to lead a new flock. We made it clear what our plans were we did not go behind anyone's back. Concerned, the pastor took me aside,

'Bruce, you are wrong to take your family and work amongst these people.'

'But this is where I've been called,' I tried to explain.

'But you aren't trained, and there is no mission or church behind you. How are you going to survive?

Why don't you get them to come here to this church?' He thought I was rushing into some dream without counting the cost.

'They will never come here because they can't dress well enough nor afford to. The other thing is they are too shy and scared. They just wouldn't fit.' I tried to make him understand.

He was upset two dedicated families would be leaving his flock. He had to try to dissuade us from something that to him was folly. Later several young Aboriginal couples married in the church.

By this time Aboriginal children were accepted into the Winkie School where our children attended so the change in our circumstances did not affect our children greatly, the Aboriginal people loved them.

Our church base for many years was the shanty George and Dora called home. Fred, George's brother and wife Janet, lived nearby and it quickly became the gathering place for the river people living in nearby settlements such as Lyrup, Monash, Winkie, Renmark and Barmera and down river to Swan Reach.

We saw a great lift in the general spirit of the people. Their shacks made spic and span for our visit and services on Sundays. We quickly became the bridge between the two cultures.

After morning service, there would be the smell of cooking fish on top of a wood-burning stove,

'The fish is cooked,' George would yell. He had been up early and caught some fish, cleaned and filleted them before the service. People would emerge from whatever corner into which they had slunk to feast on George's fish.

'How do you cook this fish, it melts in our mouth,' Gwen and Sylvia wanted to know.

'Just cook on top of the stove, not in a pan.' George explained.

'But doesn't it burn?'

'No not if the fire is right. All the fat from the fish is fried out of it not into it as happens when fried in a pan with fat,' George grinned. It was the best river cod and bream I ever tasted.

The Aboriginal dialect was almost a forgotten language and English the language used. There was a hidden language used when the people did not want anyone to know. A garbled mixture of English and dialect disguised conversations so that strangers were ignorant. Over time, we learnt to some extent, that hidden language.

The Aboriginal settlement being on the other side of the river meant that

to visit the settlement we needed to catch a punt. It was a bore because if there was a big queue of cars or the punt was on the other side it meant a long wait that wasted a lot of time. Sometimes George would row over in his boat and pick us up, then row us back. If I was alone and wanted to cross to the settlement, I wanted an easier way.

A brainstorm hit me that I needed surfboard. I built one three metres long by two thirds of a metre wide out of marine plywood. It was hollow to give it buoyancy. I used the Boss's shed at night, with a whole lot of doubtful advice from onlookers. Two students, young Christian men, Michael and Lou, employed as fruit pickers worked with me picking Apricots. They were trying to earn money to pay their university fees. They were all eyes and ears,

'It will never float,' Michael shook his head doubtfully.

'That's right,' agreed Lou, 'how can you make a surf

board without a plan?'

'Yes, why didn't you draw up a plan?' Michael wanted to know.

'Because the plan is in my head I don't need to put it on paper.'

The lads shook their heads in disbelief.

Launching day arrived,

'Where are you going to launch the board?' The boys wanted to know.

'Why do you want to know?' I grinned.

'We want to see you sink.' Lou had visions of saving a drowning man.

'I'm going down to Lake Bonny at Barmera to test it. Going to come?' I laughingly invited.

'Sure. We aren't going to miss this.'

I carried the board on the roof of the car. At the lake, I placed it in the water and it floated. 'Bet you can't paddle out around that buoy out there and back, fully dressed without getting wet,' Michael issued the challenge.

'Yeah, betcha,' agreed Lou with a smirk on his face.

'I betcha I can,' I knew these lads had some prank in mind. I would not stay dry if they had anything to do with it.

I rolled up my trouser legs and with the paddles; I started out around the buoy. I was nearly into shore when the two young scoundrels swam out to me and tipped me off.

'We owed you that one,' they laughed uproariously at my discomfort and so did my family. Throughout the day, the board was rowed, used as a diving board, sat on and people were tipped off. The surfboard was well tested and every one voted it the best surfboard ever. My point proven, I came home satisfied.

It also meant that I could now cross the river any time I

liked quickly and easily. I would place my Bible and books in front of me and paddle across.

The next obvious need was some sort of a mobile church so we did not have to use someone's home.

'I've been thinking about it." Frank said to me one day. 'I saw a marquee advertised the other day, about 4 metres by 4 metres. It was just the thing.' Frank looked at me to see what I would say.

'Sounds just the thing. We could put up the sides if there was a crowd or if it was cold and only a few people attending, leave the sides down.'

'We'd need a trailer though.' Frank was getting excited.

'Well, I know where I can get a trailer. But what would we sit on?' I too could see the possibilities.

'I've got some empty 4 gallon oil drums and some planks. Put the planks on the drums. That'd do?'

'Yes, after all we aren't in a flash church and need comfortable seating,' I said, 'What will we do for music, though?'

'I'm sure I could play an accordion. I am a trained musician; I have been to the Adelaide Conservatorium of Music. It would not be hard to play. I saw one advertised in the paper the other day if the people still have it, I will buy it. Besides, Dora has her button accordion as well.' Sylvia, Frank's wife added her two bob's worth to the planning. George backed up by clicking two spoons instead of bones to keep the beat. Sometimes someone might join playing on a guitar or gum leaves. When played properly the gum leaves sound much like a violin. Music became a great feature of our meetings; the people loved to sing and harmonise.

We talked the plan over with Dora, 'We are going to get a trailer and marquee, some planks and drums for seats and go and visit the camps, Dora. What do you think?'

'Oh, she breathed, ecstatically, 'that is what needs to happen. The people would be so pleased to see us. They would come to the meetings. Praise the Lord! I've been praying for something like this to happen,' Dora was like a dog with two tails.

So we announced at the next service what our plans were and where we would be visiting. How would we let the people know we were coming?

'Don't worry about that, I'll let my sister Annie and her husband Jack know Bro Bruce and Bro Frank are coming, and they will tell everybody,' Dora was confident that the news would spread. It did! We underestimated how news spreads through the Aboriginal community. It is almost by extrasensory perception, a thought one day and a hundred or so miles away the next day as a fact.

The setting up for the meetings was very labour intensive but we knew the Lord called us and it was exciting to enter each camp, set the musicians playing, light a bonfire and wait for the crowd. We always had a congregation in the tent or out in the scrub even around campfires but they listened eagerly. We never knew if we faced a riot or a revival, sometimes both or whether there would be one or one hundred.

Churches in general seemed glad that we were involved with the Aboriginal people. Their conscience pacified because they could pass the Aboriginal problem to us. The local doctors were glad to have somebody working amongst these fringe people, especially one doctor from Barmera. He treated most of the Aborigines in the area. He became the GP for our family and a close contact for many years.

Frank and I now knew many of the Aborigines intimately some of them becoming our best friends. Because of this, doctors, welfare agencies and church leaders approached us to be members of an Aboriginal Welfare Committee. It was a revelation for me to hear their view on the condition of the Aborigines, whom they never ventured amongst or were ever likely to.

The church backgrounds of the Aborigine people ranged from every denomination that had a name but they found no spiritual home that would accept them and they just drifted in name only, feeling unloved and unwanted.

Some of the older men were getting occasional work but the young men had no hope. They lived and died alcoholics no matter if it was by methylated spirits or alcohol. Methylated spirits on the human breath is one of the worst smells I have ever encountered.

If word got around that I sipped alcohol, I would never have been able work with these people. They believed Christians did not drink alcohol.

Alcohol has never passed my lips. I praise the Lord that he had strengthened me to keep that Band of Hope Pledge I made all those years ago. The Lord knew what was ahead of me back then and prepared me for what I would encounter as I took up my Call. I sure lived amongst the booze those years with the Aboriginal people and in my working life.

George Karpany was the angler, to beat all anglers. I had never seen anyone catch fish as he could.

'Bruce, come around Saturday morning and I will take you fishing,' George issued an invitation to me.

'I do not know, George, I'm not a fisherman.' I was very doubtful about the expedition although I knew I would enjoy George's company.

'Come on, we'll go out in my boat,' George was grinning as if he had a secret weapon.

'Ok. I'll come.'

George dropped an anchor just off willows growing along the riverbank at Berri. We threw in our lines.

George hauled in fish hand over fist. I hauled in zero hand over fist.

'Try my bait,' teased George. My line remained slack; there was no sign of a fish.

'Hey, you should have used black shoe polish before you came out,' George was enjoying himself at my discomfort. Zero fish!

'Tell you what,' said George grinning like the proverbial Cheshire, 'change places with me and use my line.'

We changed places and I took his line. Zero fish. His bag was full. He caught fish like there was no tomorrow. I came home with a bag of fish that I had not caught - they all had escaped. No, they never even nibbled my bait. George had caught enough for him and me both.

One Sunday morning when we arrived for church, George ducked out of the shack, (George was a beanpole of a man, and the shack door too low for tall people), 'Come with me,' he pointed with his thumb over his shoulder, 'got something to show you.'

I followed, mystified as to what George wanted to show me. He busily pulled in a heavy line on the end a sixty-pound Murray cod was tethered. The biggest fish I have ever seen. Wow! Did that fish have a mouth?

'Got this one tethered until the cod season opens on Monday,' he confided proudly. He dropped the line and the fish disappeared into the muddy water.

One Saturday afternoon Frank and I decided to take a few hours off from work and go fishing with our families. The worms had taken time off as well and we could not find any. Frog hunting under stones and bark did not find them at home either. Eventually, we found a log just below the Berri pumping station from which to fish. We threw in our lines and sat down to wait and wait and wait.

Coming up river in a rowboat, we recognised George.

THE MAVERICK'S ROUNDUP

'How you getting on, boys, getting any fish?' he called out.

'Nah! A few bites that's all,' Frank had to admit.

George shipped his oars, he rowed his boat facing frontward not backward, as white people do, and he grabbed a big callop out of the boat, hit it on the head with a shifting wrench and threw it to Frank.

'Here's one for dinner,' he chuckled.

'No, no,' Frank objected, 'we can't take your fish, you want to sell them.'

'Don't worry, I've got plenty,' and George pulled up what he calls a pond made of wire netting. It was full of fish. 'I've got another one of these down there by that log.'

My life of fishing ended there and then. It seemed more sense to do what I was good at, fishing for men. The fish and I now RIP together.

'Why don't you like to fish, Bruce?' I am often been asked.

'I don't believe it's Christian.' I smile wickedly.

'How can you say that?' They inquire in puzzlement.

'Easy! It's murder. We catch lovely little worms, cockles and frogs. Thread them onto a hook while they are still alive, tease the fish all day until they take the bait then chuck the fish in the boat. We shout and dance with delight at what we have caught. That is not talking about the agony of me sitting in the boat or on the bank all day hoping a fish will jump on my hook. Spare me! It bores me to tears. I would sooner swim, or lie on the bank and read a book.

I must divert here and tell my best fish story: Alan, the Boss's son, was a great angler. A day away from the fruit block fishing was his idea of a great day. When the men of the Berri Church of Christ arranged a fishing competition as a social outing for men, Alan kidded me to enter.

The Saturday before the competition, I thought I had

better get some practise in so I went fishing - I caught twenty from tiddlers to cod. This was unbelievable. It was a good year, though; there had been a high river.

When the day of the competition arrived, I stood on the bank of Katarapko Creek geared to fish, waiting for the starting whistle to blow at 10 am. I found a quiet spot away from the others to throw in my line. The fish jumped on my line and kept me busy, all day. They were not very big but numbers were important.

'Catching any fish, Bruce?' A couple of lads came by to see how I was doing.

'Yeah, I've got a bagful. How are the other blokes going?' I wanted to know if I was in the running for the prize.

'You've got it in the bag,' they said.

'The fish have dropped off,' I felt a bit bored and wondered if I would continue.

'Come on, let's go for a swim,' they suggested. It was quite warm and it seemed like a good idea so I stripped off and joined them swimming for a while.

'I'd better get back to the fishing,' I yelled to my mates. I found that the fish were on the rise again.

'How is it going, Bruce?' My Boss and the local pastor came along to see how many I had.

'Fancy seeing you fish, Bruce,' the pastor scoffed.

'How many have the other men got?' I showed them my bagful.

'You got the prize, for sure,' my Boss said, looking at his watch. 'It's four thirty, time to pull up your line.' The Competition closed at four thirty.

I pulled in my line and it was a double header. I carried my haul back to base to get it counted. I can identify with Peter on the shores of Galilee when the Lord said, 'Try the other side of the boat.'

I caught sixty and Alan caught 66. The prize was a

fancy cigarette ashtray. Alan did not smoke nor did I. The hardest job was getting rid of sixty fish.

It was George who underlined my failure as an angler and I realised I needed to concentrate on fishing for the souls of men.

Chapter Four
memories

I was sitting in a café, one day, reading a newspaper when I saw the death notice of Miss Mona Verco. It brought home to me just how much influence as a Sunday school teacher that woman had on my early life.

I was amazed and said to Gwen, 'Fancy, Mona Verco is dead. She was ninety.'

'Well, she lived to a ripe old age.' Gwen replied absently, gazing out of the window into the street below.

'She was the best Sunday school teacher I ever had.' I was remembering this dedicated Sunday school teacher. 'I wish I had told her how much she influenced my life.'

'That's the way of it,' Gwen commented. 'We never think about these things until it is too late.'

'The foundation teaching that she gave me has been priceless.' I mulled over this woman's passing, thinking about the kind of woman that she was.

First memories are vital just as are first reactions. First memories are threads woven into our life that produces wisdom they are part of God's dealing with us. Even the ones that are innocent day-to-day events but which for one reason or another remain cemented into our memories and affect our life. No one ever considers, especially at the time, that these could be the foundations for a Call of God. I cannot help asking, what is your first living memory.

Mine, regretfully, still makes me tremble. I hope you will empathise with me although don't waste time praying for me. I was number two child seventeen months behind Peter and was supposed to have been a girl.

Mum had two teenage girl friends that shared the name of Jessica. They might have shared the same name but they were very different, one was a dumpling and the other like a flagpole. They loved to come and visit with Mum and play with her babies.

'Oh, you're going to bath the baby, Grace?' Jessica, the flagpole, asked as they walked into the kitchen and saw the small bathtub on the table and towels, powder and nappies all laid out in readiness.

'Yes, you're just in time to help bath Bruce.' Mum said picking me up undressing me and sitting me in the bath.

'Look at him, isn't he cute,' Jessie, the dumpling, cooed, scooping up handfuls of water and splashing it over me.

'He loves his bath,' Mum smiled proudly at her offspring happily splashing.

Jessie Flagfole lifted me from the bath and dried me. Jessie Dumpling sprinkled the powder and dressed me. Jessie Flagpole picked up the hairbrush and brushed the hair on top of my head into a curl.

'Doesn't he look like a little girl,' she giggled.

'He does too. He is so adorable. Let's tie a ribbon in his hair' Jessie Dumpling suggested with a laugh.

'Here is a red ribbon,' Mum said, rummaging in a drawer.

The two girls brushed, curled and tied the red ribbon in my hair and then sat me on the floor.

'He's just gorgeous.' They admired their handiwork.
'He's so sweet.'

I started to bawl and bawl and crawled under the kitchen table to get away from the laughing trio. I was hurt Mum had betrayed me. She was laughing with the enemy. When they had all had their fun Mum repented, picked me up and gave me a cuddle.

I jokingly tell people the experience scarred me for life, psychologically. Of course, it did not affect me except the incident remained indelibly written on my memory for life it was my first memory. There are many memories stored away that have had an effect and which I have had to come to terms with. I learned over the years that Jesus took those memories with him to the cross. He bore them so I do not have to and am free from their effect.

I was born Feb 1st 1929 the year when the Wall Street market crashed in October of that same year, creating the Great Depression. It was the backdrop to my early life and affected my formative years and certainly, God used it to prepare me for his service.

The depression affected Australia because of its extreme dependence on exports from America. Australia was one of the hardest hit countries in the western world.

Scholars estimated that nearly 50% of children during the Great Depression did not have adequate food, shelter, or medical care.

Many suffered rickets. Some people who became homeless would jump on moving railroad cars because they did not have money to travel as they tried to find work.

Located fifty miles from Adelaide and not much more than a settlement, Mount Compass, where my family lived, became a centre for the newly formed communities of Yundi, Kuipto and Enterprise Colony in the 1930s. These communities, set up by the South Australian Government of the day, consisted of 20 to 30 acres giving people a home and an opportunity to make a living. Each settler received 400 pounds to provide a home, fowls and sheds. They received assistance for three years then expected to fend for themselves.

The dwellings were built of corrugated iron, covered with a skillion roof and lined with white washed hessian and divided into two rooms, hardly more than shanties. The people allocated to these holdings were very poor with large families and often looked down on because of their extreme poverty. The gap between the so-called rich and poor was a great gulf. Mum and Dad had dumb little but these people had even less and considered Mum and Dad rich. A bush track connected Yundi to the settlement of Mount Compass. Mount Moon separated the two settlements.

Dad had a few acres of swamp and grew vegetables for these people, teaching them to garden and manage animals. The soil was very poor much like the new owners and it was hard to wrest any sort of a living.

'I wish I could do more for these people,' I remember Mum saying in despair over the terrible circumstances that the settlers lived in. My parents had become involved because the church assumed some responsibility to help the colonists.

Mount Compass received its name when in the 1840s, Governor Gawler lost his compass while he was surveying the area. Mount Compass comprised of a number of dairies strung along the swamps. A Co-operative store, a bank, butcher and baker and post office sat cheek by jowl on the edge of the main road. The chapel was set below the road on a corner block and the institute was set back in the pines above the road.

In the mid 1930s when money was very tight, uppermost

in the minds of my friends and me was how to get some pocket money. Quite suddenly, we found a way.

'Hey, you boys, I found the door to the Institute is unlocked. Shall we take a look after school?' I suggested mostly out of curiosity to start with.

'Yeah,' the group chorused. Nobody needed a second invitation.

'We'll meet at the back of the Hall in the pines so no one can see us,' one of the boys added.

'Yeah,' the group chanted excitedly.

Our plans made, we could hardly wait for school to be over. One of the boys turned the latch and the door opened.

'Look here,' someone called and we clustered around to look at old pictures stashed in a corner.

'The stage curtains don't work,' someone else remarked when trying out the curtain ropes. We went through that hall with a fine toothcomb.

'Look at this, boys,' someone breathlessly exclaimed. The group rushed to see what he had found.

'Wow!' everyone exclaimed in one breath. Our eyes bulging at all the drink bottles packed in under the stage of the Mount Compass Hall.

'What are they kept here for?'

'They're used to sit prize cut flowers in when the Show is on.'

'Nobody would know if we took the Woodroofe drink bottles, would they?'

'Nah! We would only sell a couple at a time every now and again.'

'How much do you reckon we'll get for a bottle from Mrs Beaumont's store?'

'About a penny each,' another of the lads suggested.

'Phew! That's big money.' We could taste the globs of sweetness on our tongues.

'Next year when the Show is on they'll wonder where the bottles went but it'll be too late then.'

'We'll share the lollies, won't we?'

'Yeah! We'll share.'

'Who's goin' to be the first to take a couple in?'

'I will,' was an eager reply.

We made several trips to the store trembling like jellies.

It worked very well and we were getting away with it successfully until …

One day we were down weeding the vegetable patch with Dad, when he said,

'Listen boys, I would like your help, I've just been told that some bottles have been going missing from the local hall, which seems very strange. As you know, I am the Secretary of the Show Society. Now you know everybody at school, if you hear anything about bottles going missing would you please let me know. The bottles are not very valuable but we would like it stopped.'

'Yes Dad, OK, Dad, we'll listen around.' Pete and I chorused. Looking like the three monkeys: Hear no evil, think no evil and do no evil. We could not wait to catch up with the rest of the gang.

'Hey you blokes, we've been found out. Don't take in any more bottles. Dad is the Secretary of the Show and he'll raise a stink. We'll cop it from him.'

'I bet Mrs Beaumont potted on us, the old bag.'

'Yeah, that'd be right.'

We listened very well and funnily enough, no more bottles walked. I have never forgotten the incident. It was my Dad's love for his two sons, to teach us and then forget our crimes, not holding them against us.

'That's like you Lord?' I thought as I meditated in later life, on the incident.

'Yes,' the Father God seemed to say, 'my only son has taken your crimes and misbehaviour upon himself so that they are no longer held against you ever again. That's how great my love is for you.'

'Lord, what kind of love is that?' I asked. A love so vast and deep was hard to comprehend.

'It's called unearned favour,' the Father God replied.

How good is that?

Dad never, ever mentioned the incident again. Yet it was among one of the first experiences of a father's unconditional love that I remember and which revealed God's unconditional love. The incident shaped my life.

At this point in my life, I had no thought about the future. As I grew, I began to ask how I could ever have a future when asthma seemed to rule my life and the people around me thought I was a malingerer.

All of my school years – the whole seven of them – I was a chronic asthmatic and for many years after. Consequently, I missed a massive amount of schooling. Always Peter would have to take a note saying, 'Bruce is too ill to come today.'

About sixty kids attended the school at Mount Compass; one senior teacher and one junior teacher (never seemed junior to me); anyway, Miss Florence Woodgate was the kingpin. The very name makes me shake. She was a giant of a woman, to me anyway.

She used to pass comment that I was malingering, swinging the lead was the term used.

Word got back to Dad and one day, he came up from the vegetable garden at a trot aiming to reach school before closing time.

'Where are you going, Len?' Mum asked. She was worried. Dad was on one of his missions.

'I'm going to get Florrie,' he said as he tidied himself

up.

'Whatever for,' Mum rushed up to Dad to try to stop him.

'Because I'm sick of her telling everyone that Bruce is malingering; I want her to see how ill he is.'

'Now Len, I don't think it's good idea.' Mum stalled not wanting to create a row or embarrass everyone.

'No! I'm going to bring her home, Grace.'

A bit later, the front door slammed and Dad shouted, 'Miss Woodgate is here.'

Mum rushed about tidying up the bedroom.

'Hello, Mrs Leane, your husband tells me Bruce is not very well again' Miss Woodgate shouted so she could be heard in Victor Harbour. Suppose she thought, she was still talking to kids.

'Yes, he's very ill with asthma.' Dad said, 'Come through to the bedroom.'

'Ooh, you poor sweet boy,' Florrie cooed. 'You don't look very well, dear. You mustn't get up until you are quite well.'

I was feeling very ill, and could hardly breathe I wished they would all go away and leave me alone.

Turning to Mum and Dad, Florrie gushed, 'He is a lovely boy. I'm so sorry to see him like this.'

After what seemed an agonising time spent chatting to Mum and Dad in front of me, she said, 'Well, I must be going. Another kiss before I go.'

She must have been love starved, or guilt riddled, because I got about three more kisses.

'I will take you home now, Miss Woodgate. Thanks for coming to see Bruce.' Dad was as nice as pie to her.

Thanks Dad for sticking up for me when I could not do that for myself. That is my Lord also, sticking up for his loved ones when they cannot help themselves.

'Another kiss before I go,' has remained a family joke. I have certainly never forgotten the incident and Peter has NEVER let me forget.

When I look back on the experience of always being ill, of never feeling fit and well, I often wondered what the future held. God had my life in his hands though from the beginning and while constantly ill, he was teaching me patience, determination, and persistence needed for the time when the Call became reality.

I can see looking back; just how much of my childhood shaped the early foundations of my life. 'Bring up a child in the way he should go and he will never depart from it,' is an old Biblical adage but very much a true one because I was raised under a fundamental evangelistic influence that later became a solid launching pad for a great life. The Christian leadership of my parents and others, though it could not save me, it surely gave me direction.

Chapter Five
Decisions, Gas Producers and Stand-In Dad

Mum got a bright idea one day, by now I was about eight years of age.

'Len, wouldn't it be wonderful to have a day at the beach over New Year?'

'Yeah, where will we go?' Dad agreed.

'Let's go to Glenelg for the day,' Mum suggested. She had it all planned and only needed to convince Dad.

'Yippee,' we kids shouted agreement.

There was a flurry of activity.

'Peter, you pack your things and help Dad feed the animals before we go.' Mum ordered. 'Bruce, you pack your things and watch Clare while I pack up the food.'

When every thing was packed and stowed in the car off we went. The excitement of anticipation was making the air shiver.

It was wonderful to see the sea spread out before us, gulls screeching, people laying on the sand or swimming. I breathed as deeply as I could; looking around me, I noticed something different.

'What's going on over there?' I asked eyeing off several

people standing before a large crowd of kids. One adult was playing a musical instrument, another was holding up cards with words on. A third grown-up was sketching on a blackboard.

'It's a beach mission. Some church people are holding a meeting for kids.' Mum explained her mind on seeing that Clare did not wander off. She was pretty much a baby. Dad was busy watching yachts and swimmers between snoozing.

My curiosity was aroused and I wandered over thinking about what might be in it for me. I joined in and became interested, convinced and convicted.

'If anyone wants to give their life to Christ and follow him, please come and stand out here with me and we will pray with you.'

I got up from where I was sitting and moved up to where the leader was standing talking to each kid in turn. While I was waiting for him to reach me, Mum rushed up, 'What are you doing here?' she questioned, grabbing hold of my arm, 'Come on, we have to go home.'

'But Mum…' I hung back, looking at the leader. I wanted to tell him I had given my heart to the Lord.

'We can't hang around any longer. We'll be late getting the milking done as it is.' She yanked me along with her. I was still dragging my feet and looking back at the group on the beach.

It really made no difference in the end I had found the Lord. That mob never recorded me in their statistics but God did in his Book of Life. It was very real! I knew I was a child of God from that moment on. In over seventy years the assurance of my Salvation never waned. I do not believe in backsliding, that is, if you have really given your life to Christ. What is fair dinkum is that God gave his only son to save everyone who believes. God does not change his mind.

Three years later, at age eleven, Dad approached me 'It's about time you gave your heart to the Lord isn't it?'

'Yes, Dad,' I agreed, though I wondered, why? I had already accepted Christ but I did not like to argue with Dad. He could be very overbearing at times.

The next Sunday night at the Gospel service in the little stone chapel built on the corner of the main road to Victor Harbour and Nangkita, I went to the front of the church and stood before the preacher and about fifty other people. I repeated the sinner's prayer bit and later at another service, as a true believer I observed the teaching of baptized by immersion. Several of my mates were baptised at the same time.

Now I was truly 'done' and Dad was satisfied that his duty as a father to his son was complete, I have never told Dad otherwise. I knew though, I had found Jesus my Lord at the beach mission. Mum's bright idea might have seemed innocent enough but it was God's moment for me to accept his gift of salvation, but there were further steps to take.

During Nov 1947, a Christian Endeavour rally organised in the local church by the church elders to challenge the youth about their faith walk in Christ. I was about eighteen and Clare, my sister, would have been just sixteen. The atmosphere was tangible with the presence of God. I felt it and so did many others as the guest speaker, Stan Riches, addressed us at the evening meeting.

'Who will go?' Stan Riches posed the same question to us. The same question had been asked of a prophet of old by God thousands of year before.

'Here am I Lord, send me,' the old prophet replied.

Clare and I were hearing that same voice again, asking us the same question, 'Who will go?'

I felt God's hand on me though without goose bumps or pounding heart. We heard the voice within and calmly and unhesitatingly answered, 'Here am I send me.'

Clare and I with several others responded by going to the front of the church. It was a turning point in our lives. That night I gladly became the Lord's man, regardless of where he might lead me.

Clare's call took her to Ghana, Africa. Many of the others became leaders in various fields. I still suffered with asthma, still had to milk the cows and earn some pocket money working for other market gardeners. The outworking of my Call was not how I wanted it to be but it is how the Lord made it happen.

In those early formative years, I signed a Band of Hope pledge not to drink alcohol. As a teenager, alcohol was not a question but I never forgot my pledge. I have never made promises lightly to God or man. It was a precious foundation for later in life when I had to deal with drunkenness. 'Christ in me has always been stronger than alcohol in them.'

The greatest pressure to drink alcohol has always come from broadminded Christians; they get embarrassed if I am around and know of my stance on social drinking.

Many things fashioned my spiritual values. Many leaders from different areas of life imparted their ideals and their values to me when a young man. Youth leaders and parents have an awesome responsibility in how they lead.

My thoughts jumped from Mona to Ray Bishop, the leader of the Christian Endeavour group at the Chapel and the role he played in my life. Thinking of Ray brought me to the Second World War and continued hardship.

Declaring war with Germany in September 1939 and with Japan in December 1941, the war advanced toward

Australia. Japan marched relentlessly through the Pacific. By the middle of 1941, the war became a reality. Many factories moved from producing widgets to building warships, and many civilians were engaged in voluntary work.

In anticipation, blackout restrictions became an actuality and air raid warning instructions issued. Barbed wire snaked across many east coast beaches causing people to feel very vulnerable. The war came ever closer to Australia with the cities of Darwin, Broome, Townsville and Sydney being bombed.

Prime Minister John Curtin broadcast to Australia on the 14th March 1942 these stirring words: 'There will still be Australians fighting on Australian soil until the turning point be reached, and we will advance over blackened ruins, through blasted and fire-swept cities, across scorched plains, until we drive the enemy into the sea.'

I can recall Mum's reaction and the effect it had on Pete and I when Dad came home from market one day and said, 'I've joined the Air Force, Grace.'

'Oh Len, you haven't' cried Mum. She was distraught, wondering how she was going to manage to bring up three children bordering on becoming teenagers.

'Yes, I enlisted today. I start training in Port Pirie next week. Just enough time to get things organised home here before I go.' Dad was excited over the new challenge.

'But Len, how are we going to manage the dairy?' Mum was near to tears.

'Peter and Bruce can leave school. They are old enough to run the dairy. Pete's fourteen and Bruce's going on thirteen. It won't hurt them,' Dad brushed aside her tears and fears.

The War became my War that day I had to leave school and help run the dairy and grow vegetables to sell and keep the land clear of blackberries. My heart was at war because I wanted to go to high school. I believed, even then, education would open the doors so I could follow what I termed 'full time service' whatever that meant. I felt deprived, years later, I realised it was all part of the plan of God. I would achieve beyond all that I could ask or think regardless of lack of education.

'What about…' Mum pleaded with Dad but he was not listening to what would happen in his absence. He was already away at the Front fighting a war, winning glory with his daring do.

Mum was aware her two sons were at the age they needed a father.

Enter Ray Bishop as a stand-in Dad. Ray was a dumpling of a man, work like a draft horse and an innovative backyard engineer where machinery was concerned. His dedication to the Lord inspired me as a teenager and I looked upon him as a role model.

'Why do you take your Bible and Sunday School lesson book to work with you?' I asked as I looked at the dog-eared, blackened Bible and tatty lesson book one day. I thought it was sacrilege to treat the Bible in such a way.

'I have to work from dawn till dark to get this property cleared, lad.' He spoke quietly in a gravely voice. Tall stringy bark gums and thick undergrowth covered the rolling hills he was clearing. He was working a caterpillar tractor and chain. He would stop the tractor for a bite of lunch and study the lessons for Sunday. Even while driving the tractor with falling trees and branches crashing about him he would have the Bible open and be reading. He gradually cleared his property, singlehandedly.

'But you could prepare when you get home.' I suggested.

'When I get home the wife wants the wood cut and the cow milked. Then I'm too tired.' Ray smiled indulgently.

THE MAVERICK'S ROUNDUP

As the war escalated, 'Petrol is getting pretty scare now. Soon I won't be able to buy any. I think I'll put a gas producer on the truck and tractor.'

'Bishy' said to me one day. Everyone called him 'Bishy', young and old.

'How are you going to do that?' I asked wondering what sort of a contraption it would look like knowing 'Bishy's' method of engineering.

'I've got plenty of wood to burn so if I build a big iron tank out in the middle of the paddock and fill it with wood, I'll be able to bake the wood into charcoal. I'll have to make a fire drum that fits on the running board of the buckboard and filter drums to fit on the front that will clean the rubbish out of the gas before it goes into the engine. I'm sure the idea will work, it should be a piece of cake.'

'Well, you know what you are doing,' I said with plenty of scepticism and watched as he went about creating a gas producer. He made two gas producers, one he fitted to the tractor and one to the buckboard. If they were a bit basic did it really matter as long as they were effective. He burnt and bagged many tons of charcoal for sale.

"Bishy', a great film is being shown in the church in Victor Harbour on Friday night.' A young teenage spokesperson for the group approached Ray. He was silent a moment or two,

'What's it about?'

'It's about the Power of God.' The group chorused sure that 'Bishy' was now hooked.

'Oh well, I suppose I could take a group of you down. The wife might like to go as well.'

Friday night came, yippee; we were going to the pictures in Victor Harbour. Eight of us, chattering like a flock of starlings, piled into the back of his old Buick buckboard fitted with his own engineered gas producer.

'What did you think of the film?' I asked my mate Don later on the way home.

'Ah, bit weak,' he replied.

'Yeah, pity,' I agreed.

We continued to discuss the film and its failings when suddenly we found ourselves tumbling into the bushes and trees along the side of the road; I struggled to extricate myself and straighten my clothes, hoping my best clothes were not torn and fearful of what Mum would say. I looked for Don, he was emerging from a bush and the girls were both giggling and crying, and sorting themselves out. Above the racket, Mrs Bishop cried out, 'I'm stuck, I can't get out.'

I stumbled across to see if I could help. The buckboard had tipped over onto the fire drum mounted on the running board of the vehicle throwing eight of us off the back into the scrub as we went around a sharp corner.

Mrs Bishop was sitting on the downhill side of the seat against the big fire drum.

'Are you hurt, Mrs Bishop?' I asked.

'No, but I'm stuck. Get me out, before I catch alight.' Her voice trembled, I am not sure if it was pain, fear, or anger, maybe all three.

'We can't seem to find where you are stuck.' I replied.

'I'll crawl in under the gas producer and see what's wrong,' one of the smaller boys offered. It was a bit embarrassing fumbling around a woman's figure trying to find where she was stuck.

'Her coat's caught on a broken spring,' the rescuer grunted trying to unhook the coat.

'Is she hurt?' one of the girls asked.

'No. I'm all right.' Mrs Bishop replied. 'Steady boys, steady, I'm stuck I can't move at all.' She surely was. It took a while before Mrs Bishop was unhooked, she kept saying,

'Steady, boys, steady.' Finally, she was free.

'Come on you lads.' Bishy said, 'let's tip this old girl back on her wheels.'

'OK,' we chorused and got underneath the buckboard and heaved as only farm lads do, setting the Buick back on her wheels.

'She looks OK,' Bishy walked around the vehicle, kicked the tyres and said, 'Let's go home.'

One girl was irate claiming Peter or someone's elbow had given her a black eye.

We had experienced the power of God in a more practical way than the film ever did, a lesson I have never forgotten.

I would have liked to travel the 250 kilometres to say goodbye at his funeral, but the information came too late, but that is life. There is no question about his place in Paradise.

Regardless of World War 2, people became my mentors; Ray Bishop was among them.

Chapter Six
Apology

As soon as church was over my cousin said, 'Beat you home.'

As pre-arranged, we would have lunch at the home of Brian and Ivern Simons, cousins of mine.

'Beat ya,' Pete and I shouted to each other, jumped on our bikes with boyish vigour and took off after Brian and Ivern.

'Look out!' I yelled, jamming on the brakes, the bike skidded and I landed in a patch of blackberry bushes. I was scared stiff of what Mum would say when she saw the rips from the thorns in my best clothes, never mind my body. One of the girls had run in front of me, to miss her I swerved.

'Why don't you look where you are going,' I was angry that this girl ran in front of me. I was now late for lunch and would have to face Mum.

'Why don't you look where you are going,' the girl retorted, smirking at my discomfort.

'I should have run you down. You'd laugh the other side of your face, then,' I retaliated.

As I climbed out of the blackberry bushes, I was met by Elder Ern looking like he had eaten a lemon for breakfast.

THE MAVERICK'S ROUNDUP

He was one of the church elders and seemed so fierce and legalistic that he frightened me.

'Bruce, you are a very careless boy, tearing off like that on your bike and nearly knocking down a girl.'

'But sir...'

'Next time be more careful and look where you are going. You need to learn to respect people.' Elder Ern's voice was rising as he traced my ancestry.

'But sir, she got...'

'Don't make excuses for your carelessness,' he roared.

I was very subdued and it spoiled my entire lunch.

I was so looking forward to eating at my cousins place. I wished fervently that I could escape afternoon church service but I had no choice. I arrived back at the church only to face Elder Ern.

'Oh no, what does he want now?' I whispered to Pete.

'You're really in the doghouse,' he agreed.

'Look, boy, I'm sorry that I growled at you this morning. I realise it was not your fault. I see now that you really tried to miss running into that girl,' Elder Ern apologised.

'Th...that's all right,' I stuttered in surprise. Elder Earn never apologised especially to the Leane boys.

Elder Ern wore a glass eye. We often laughed that he was not only one-eyed physically but he was one-eyed in his opinions. Elder Ern was Superintendent of the Sunday school. He would sit in a strategic position and watch with his one eye the boys Bible class one end of the church and the girls Bible class the other end to curb any misbehaviour.

It is now seventy years later and I have not forgotten Elder Ern or his apology. It was a sweet victory but a hard lesson in facing up to a situation where I must forgive for being misunderstood, it reminded of how much Jesus has forgiven me and how he has totally overlooked my misunderstanding of him.

To quote a sentence from the ancient writings in Psalms, 'Removed as far as the east is from the west never to be remembered again.'

How many of us would gladly cut out our tongues to undo some of our mistaken judgements on people, their lives and attitudes? Ignorance can never be enough of an excuse.

One of my main character traits is to encourage and release people to reach the potential fulfilment of their abilities. When nobody else would consider them, I felt to give them a go. In countless areas, at different times, I gave people a reference for a job or promotion in some way. I have done so because it is my heart and my Call to give people an opportunity to rise. I have been let down and hurt at times but gloriously blessed by others.

I have to say, 'Thank you, Elder Ern, and all the other teachers in God's school of hard knocks. It has been an unforgettable experience and we will laugh together in Heaven. Thank you, Lord, for putting these people in my life to teach me and prepare me for your Call.'

Elder Ern was among the many human resources that God moved in and out of my life.

Chapter Seven

Becoming a Human Pincushion

It is not always what happens to us that matters but what we do with what happens is the point. We can be either an over-comer or an under-goer. It would have been easy to go under because of the hopelessness of the asthma and the hard work required to earn a living. Very early in life I developed chronic asthma there were virtually no answers for asthma suffers in those days.

Though I cursed the asthma at the time, it taught me self- discipline and total reliance on the Lord. It was part of the training for the Call even though I was still largely ignorant that there was a Call on my life. Asthma was not only my 'Achilles' heel', but also my mother's and the rest of the family.

'Let's go to the Mount Compass Show,' Mum was sick of staying home out on the farm and never seeing another woman from one week to the next. She missed her friends dropping in and chatting to her. The football field overlooking the Institute amid the pines was the venue for the Show.

'Yes, let's all go to the Show,' the whole family agreed.

While Mum prepared a picnic lunch, the rest of us

planned what rides we would take and sideshows that would test our skills. The unthinkable happened, and I did not understand why. An asthma attack began in the night leaving me gasping for breath. When morning came, I was too ill to go to the Mount Compass Agricultural Show.

'We can't go to the Show, Bruce is too ill.' Mum announced at breakfast. There was anger that Bruce was ill just when the family had planned a fun time together and the weather was kind.

'Why can't we go with the neighbours?' Clare suggested.

'Mum, why does Bruce have to get sick every time we want to go somewhere?' was a question on everyone's lips. The question hung on my lips all too often.

'I don't know,' Mum sighed in despair, hiding her disappointment as best she could, replanning her day around the chores that she had thought to escape for awhile, trying to nurse an ill son with limited resources available to her. Poor Mum! It must have been hell for her.

Another defining moment occurred when about eleven years of age. I awoke up one night to hear Mum crying,

Len, what can we do? It's costing us a fortune just to keep him alive.' Her voice was full of despair.

I lay very still in bed so Mum would not know I had overheard her crying.

I made up my mind there and then that I would not die but get better. I did not know how, but I would find a way.

'You'd better ring up the Asthma Foundation in Adelaide and get an appointment. Maybe they can find something to help him,' Dad suggested, trying to comfort Mum.

Dad's suggestion morphed into an appointment at the Asthma Foundation in Adelaide. I became a patient of Doctor Munro Ford. It was when my asthma was at its worst.

THE MAVERICK'S ROUNDUP

'We are going to inject your arms with the serums of different things to try and ascertain what you're allergic to.' The doctor explained. 'Then we might be able to treat you effectively.' I held out my arm and watched as they scratched it with numerous types of serums.

'Now we'll wait five minutes or so and see what you are allergic to,' the doctor advised.

'Good heavens! Just look at your arms. They are all swollen. We can't examine your arm like that.' The doctor sounded as if I had done it on purpose.

'You'll have to come back next week when your arm is better,' he said as if we lived next door instead of 50 miles away, so home we dragged bowed by fatigue and disappointment.

'Do we have to go back, Mum?' I groaned. 'Let's forget about it.' I knew what it cost Mum to get us up to town and did not want to put her through all that effort again. With no transport except a weekly bus and cows to milk and kids to get to school, Mum was hard pressed to get up to Adelaide so often.

'We will go back to Adelaide; you must have the tests and see if there is a treatment that will help you,' Mum was adamant.

The next week we dragged back all the way to Adelaide via the bus. The tests, this time, were double spaced up both arms and marked with indelible pen. Results - allergic to twenty-six out of thirty-two allergy tests, cats, dogs, horses, cows, poultry, house dust, grasses and many types of pollen.

Mum and Dad owned a few acres of swampland where they kept cows and grew vegetables for market. I worked and lived amongst the very things that made me ill.

During the years when Dad was away at the war and Mum was bringing up four children alone she had to inject me with serum to desensitise my allergies three times a week. We both hated it.

'Bruce, you have to have an injection today.' Mum would sigh.

'Aw Mum, do I have to?' I knew I had to if I wanted to have any semblance of health.

'It's going to be a big one this time.' Mum warned, 'They have to be increased every week, you know.'

'The needle is so blunt,' I groaned.

'I know. I can't get up to Adelaide to get a new one. What can we do? You have to have the injections.' Mum and I found ourselves between a rock and a hard place.

'Well forget about hurting me and just stick the needle in, then it won't hurt as much.'

'I don't know,' Mum sighed, uncertain what to do for the better, 'Bruce, I don't suppose you could sharpen this needle?' Mum held up the needle that looked like a mini crowbar, testing it with her finger. 'You can ride to London on it.'

'Give it here and I'll try and sharpen it on the oilstone.' I brought the oilstone from the shed and proceeded to sharpen the needle.

'How's that, better?' Mum asked after the injection was over.

'Yes a lot.'

It was indeed better and I sharpened that needle many times after that. It was a real hell for Mum, an impossible task using an old 200cc glass syringe, (I still have this syringe) and a crow bar of a needle. The injections proved to relieve the asthma and make life liveable.

Hindsight shows that I could have given myself the injections in my thigh but the doctors refused to allow it. Trying to give myself an injection in the upper arm was impossible. Giving the injection hurt Mum more than it did me. People think I am mad when I say I can poke a needle into my flesh any time. I did indeed become a human pincushion.

The use of puffers for asthma was totally unknown in those years and relief medicine unknown, except for one concoction. When I was almost unconscious, Mum would burn something that looked like sawdust and I would inhale the smoke. It seemed to be the last resort. It sure was for Mum!

Mount Compass in the Adelaide hills in winter was no picnic when the temperature dropped to zero or below. Our house was as cold as a morgue when the fires died out; there was no electric power or light, candles and matches had their special place so we could put our hands on them in the dark.

When Mum could not sleep because of my rasping breath and rattling chest any longer she would get up, 'It's no good,' she would groan through chattering teeth, 'I'm going to have to light that sawdust stuff and try and give you some relief.'

'OK,' I wheezed, half sitting up trying to breathe, watching her struggling to get the stuff to burn properly.

'There, I think it's going at last.' She would hurry back to bed only to hear me straining for breath again, and have to get up and again try to coax this damp sawdust to burn while she and I both shivered with the cold.

I felt like a piece of smoked fish inhaling the sawdust, though I have never smoked tobacco in my life and never will. Now in old age and with lungs just operating, the doctors always ask, 'Do you smoke?' My answer is an emphatic, 'No!'

I must pay homage to Mum's loving sacrifice and suffering to give me the best that was available to her. As I recall what my mother did for me, I remember the ancient

GWENNETH & BRUCE LEANE

Proverb concerning a good wife: 'Her children stand and bless her;' I bless my mother, Grace. It was a tough fight but I did win as I vowed, thanks to the Lord. I have also had a good life. God, the doctors, and mother and wife have kept me together for many years.

Chapter Eight
Without a Dad

I have been born twice by Grace. Grace was my mother's name and then I was born into the family of God by his Grace or unmerited favour. Being the son of Grace should have given me precedence in God's favour but his love does not rest on who a person is or does, being a son of God rests on his love and favour through Christ. Grace is an eternal position given me by God regardless of what life may throw at me or what I have done or not done, it is what my Call is about, clarifying to people their position in God. Is it any wonder my passion is to preach the message of God's grace, and total forgiveness by a loving Saviour? My natural birthday is the 1st February 1929.

Mum endured the war years stoically without Dad. They were long, lonely and never endingly hard. With four children, two teenage sons, a daughter ten or eleven years old and a baby son, it was no easy deal, but she never complained. Maybe it was because she was Grace by name and nature.

Frank, my youngest brother entered this world on the 8th September 1941. Soon after Frank was born, Dad went to Papua New Guinea with a Beaufort Bomber Squadron.

Looking back on those years I can see the funny side of many situations but to Mum living through them they were not always funny. One day when life was hard and Mum was alone and tired she asked Pete and I for help,

'Bruce and Peter, give me a hand and set the table for lunch,' weariness threaded through Mum's voice.

'OK, Mum,' we chorused, we'd come in from working down on the swamps hungry enough to eat a horse, Mum was running late, it was washday and so we were willing to do anything to get a feed.

'There is a tin of jam in the cupboard, you'll need to open it and tip some into a clean dish.' Mum directed while she was busy elsewhere.

'Look at that,' Pete laughed, pointing to the jam standing in the dish.

'Yeah, it's all wobbly like a jelly,' I gave it a poke and it drunkenly leaned over. It did look funny and we both laughed uproariously.

Mum had had enough; nothing had gone right during the morning. She turned from what she was doing to see us boys laughing over the jam and she lost it. She made a swipe to cuff Peter's ears, 'Can't you do what I ask you without making a mess?'

'But I didn't...' Peter tried to explain.

'All I asked was for you to set the table,' Mum snapped.

Peter looked crestfallen; Mum, usually very patient, had reached the end, even I thought she had gone too far. Pete threw down the can opener and stormed out of the kitchen banging the door for good effect, heading for the cow-yard.

I looked at Mum, startled, and got to work to finish setting the table without any further urging, the game was over.

Mum meanwhile watched Peter through the kitchen

window. She looked very guilty by now and was blaming herself for losing her temper.

Mum dished up the meal; we sat down and began to eat. The silence was so thick you could cut it with a knife.

'What have you boys been doing down the swamps?' she asked, trying to ignore the empty space where Peter usually sat.

'We were cleaning drains. They're overgrown with rushes and blackberries.' I reported, watching Mum pushing her food around her plate.

'It's no good! I've got to go and get him; I can't bear him to go without a meal.' She put down her knife and fork.

Serve him right, I thought even if I did think the jam funny. He won't die - let him suffer. I watched Mum cross the yard. Next thing, there was Mum coming back, looking so glum and sad, her shoulders hunched in tiredness and defeat. Peter was towering over her, a spring of triumph in his step, grinning like a Cheshire cat, eating a huge peeled potato raw as much as to say, 'I've got a mean mother, she banished me from the table and all I've got to eat is a raw, potato.' Poor Mum, poor Pete. Regardless of the upheaval, I had had a good meal and felt very pleased with myself.

Years later when we were at a picnic celebrating a family reunion in the Adelaide Botanic Gardens, I commented to Peter and Clare, 'Today people can't conceive the burden of every day living for Mum in that era.'

'No, there were no electric appliances, such as washing machines or vacuum cleaners, no electric lights, instead kerosene lamps.' Clare compared life then to now.

'Those Rubberoid coverings on the floors with hessian lined rooms and ceilings. No hot water other than a copper to boil water in.' I remembered the hessian ceilings threatening to fall on us.

'Mum, was always on our back to cut wood. The more we cut the more she seemed to burn,' Peter complained.

'The best part was getting to ride our bikes to the store for supplies,' I said. 'It's a pity Mum never learnt to drive. Any way there was no petrol during the War.'

'Remember how we used to bath every Saturday night in front of the kitchen stove, I used to get the clean water because I was the cleanest. You blokes had to bath in the dirty water.' Clare grinned at the memory.

'Yeah,' Peter growled, 'we should have made you cut the wood and light the copper for hot water and carry it inside in buckets.'

'That awful dunny way up the yard, it seemed like half a mile away when you were in a hurry or in the middle of the night,' Clare shuddered.

'I was the washday assistant. I hated carrying buckets of water out so I learnt how to siphon it by many different and elaborate methods. In fact, I could almost make water run uphill.'

Clare and Peter laughed at my water syphoning inventions. (It was a great training for water harvesting in later years.)

This is Mum's story and I cannot manage to cover all she was to the family and me. Mum was no whinging crybaby and I honour her for all she did for us, alone most of the time.

Mum never expressed her feelings about Clare becoming a missionary and sailing off to Ghana, West Africa. We were all aware that her heart was breaking but she let Clare go because she believed God was calling her daughter to serve him. Mum, in turn, felt it was her missionary effort even though she was still in Australia.

Clare trained as a fully certificated nurse and midwife and then studied at a Bible College in Tasmania covering

14 years and then spent another 15 years in Ghana. Clare met and married Ross Harbinson from Ireland while they were in Ghana. Ross was a Colporteur, selling Bibles and Christian literature.

During the time Clare was in Africa, Mum used her creative talents to make and sell crafts to help support her daughter financially. Treasured among her very big family and friends are her creations made from the seashells she spent hours picking up from beaches. Another craft that Mum became famous for was making kangaroos of all sizes from vinyl off cuts. She would hand cut the pieces out and hand-stitch them together. She must have made thousands, selling them through a shop in Hahndorf to tourists from all over the world.

Mum suffered much in order to try to relieve my asthma as much as possible. She was a great mum! I am reminded of an ancient Proverb 'My son, observe the commandment of your father; And do not forsake the teaching of your mother.'

Chapter Nine
Building A Foundation

Like a warrior, Mum fought Asthma by not allowing me to give in; by insisting I have a chance to do something with my life. She wanted the best where her children were concerned and was prepared to make sacrifices if needed. Little did she know that she was preparing a foundation for the Call that included my toolbox?

'Len, we should try and get Peter and Bruce some sort of training in a trade, don't you think?' Mum and Dad were sitting at the breakfast table during one of Dad's all too brief home leaves during the war, when she posed the question.

'I suppose you are right but what? Where will we send them to get training?' Dad had got by without learning a trade and thought his sons could do the same.

'Perhaps, we could send them to Victor Harbour to learn a trade?' Mum wanted more for her boys than what was on offer in Mount Compass as market gardeners and dairy farmers.

'Well what do you boys want to do?' Dad said, turning to us. We both stopped eating and looked at our parents in surprise. We had supposed we would work on the land all our lives. That we could be anything other than what our parents and neighbours were had not entered our minds.

'Yes, I would like to learn carpentry,' I piped up. Opportunity was knocking on my door and I wasn't going to let her get away.

I had often wished I could learn carpentering when odd jobbing for a local builder. I had made toys and given them away as presents at the community Christmas tree. I felt a great satisfaction in both giving and the creating, toys the kids loved the toys. I grew quite excited at the thought of learning a trade, my imagination took flight as Mum and Dad discussed the pros and cons.

'What would you like to do, Pete?' Mum turned to Pete.

'I would like to learn how to shoe horses and do blacksmithing.' Pete loved horses.

A few weeks later, we were again sitting over breakfast without Dad when Mum said, 'Bruce, I've enrolled you in the Adelaide School of Mines to do a carpentry course.'

'How am I going to get there?" I had visions of staying up in Adelaide. Hope flared then died. I could not leave home because someone had to help milk the cows and grow vegetables while Dad was at the war.

'Do you think you could ride your bike to Willunga and catch the train to Adelaide for the day?'

Hope flared again, 'Yes, I can ride to Willunga.'

My heart leapt, it was a nine-mile ride morning and night but I didn't care, it wouldn't have mattered if I'd had to walk to the moon, my dream was coming true.

'I've been talking to Mrs Jacobs and she's enrolled Don as well. You can both ride together,' Mum continued.

'Gee, thanks Mum,' I felt like doing cartwheels.

'You will do two lessons one day a week. Then catch the train back to Willunga and ride on home. It'll be a big day but I think you can manage it.'

Mum knew it was a big ask for a teenage boy but she also knew it was the only way for her son to get any extra training that might help him to better himself in adulthood.

It was a long hard day but I looked forward to it because I got away from the cows, garden, and saw lots of different things and people. I learnt how to use hand tools and do maintenance on them, which was part of the Carpentry Course in those years.

Willunga, including Mount Compass, are historic townships on the edge of McLaren Vale and located 47 km south of Adelaide. Mount Compass is a further 12 km south. Three years after the settlement of South Australia Willunga became a thriving township.

As far as can be determined the name Willunga comes from the Aboriginal word 'willangga' meaning, possibly, 'the locality of green trees' although some people insist it means 'black duck'. The town's first 'Bush Inn', the current structure is the third, was a slab hut when first erected in 1840.

The main road from Adelaide to Victor Harbour snaked up the side of the hill and was notorious for rollovers and load spills. For teenage boys to ride pushbikes up and down Willunga Hill to the railhead in Willunga, let alone spend the day doing woodwork lessons was a marathon ride. Don and I had the will to do it. Our incentives were a day away from drudgery and from parental control but also we were learning a skill.

After I had left home, I began to be involved in building and I used power tools in heavy machinery shops. A number of mentors' took Pete under their wings teaching him land and animal management enabling him to later take over and run the home dairy. Eventually motorbikes took the place of horses on the farm.

THE MAVERICK'S ROUNDUP

One does not have a great deal of foresight in youth. God though, sees the big picture and was, unbeknown to me, right on course with his plans for my life.

Chapter Ten
A Lot Of Bull

Life, as a young man was interesting and dangerous, and very funny. Laughter is always great medicine, especially when there is nothing to laugh about and you only want to cry.

Dad had bought some 250 hilly acres at Mount Jagged just off the main road to Victor Harbour after the war. It was virgin land and uncleared, meaning that there was no house, no dairy, and no fences, no anything. We moved to a small house on a nearby property until we had built our own house. Hardship still dogged our lives as Dad sought to build his dream at our expense but I suspect he wanted something for his sons as well.

Peter and I put a lot of time working for Linc Parkin, a cattle dealer, to earn pocket money. He was a comic and a larrikin. I do not think he will read this story having passed on but even if he did, he would laugh.

'What are you doing, today, Bruce?' Linc Parkin called up one day

'What do you want done?' I asked. I was in great need of some ready cash.

'Bruce, come and give me a hand to load up a bull. I've got to go down to a property at Nangkita and pick it up.'

When we got there the bull was in the yard snorting and pawing the ground and charging the rails. The trouble was the truck was 30 to 40 metres away backed up to a heap of dirt with the ramp on the truck lowered so we could load the bull.

'I'll have to lasso the bull,' Linc said. 'But I don't have a long enough rope.'

'Why don't you join all the ropes together? They might be long enough, then,' I suggested handing a bundle of ropes to Linc, which he proceeded to join.

'Blast!' He swore. 'They still won't reach from the yard to the truck.'

Linc looked at me with a gleam in his eye.

'Bruce, we'll hitch the rope to the bull and you run the ropes out as far as they will go and when I let the bull out, run like hell for the truck and put a hitch around the rail on the truck and get behind the truck wheel for safety.'

'That's not a very good idea.' I protested. 'What if-' but I never finished the sentence because Linc proceeded to undo the gate.

I've never found yet found out how fast 'run like hell' is but I certainly must have exceeded it because when the bull caught sight of me at the end of the rope he charged and I ran. I won!

The bull rammed the back wheel getting its horn caught in the truck chassis and tearing it off. It did not help the bull's temper one little bit. As for me - ¬¬I was shaken but safe.

'Bruce, shorten the damn rope,' cussed Linc, as I struggled to take up the slack rope.

'It's all right about you, standing out there yelling orders.' I shouted, struggling with the rope. With more puffing and cussing, the bull was in the truck and we returned to Linc's property.

'I'll unload him in the barn for tonight,' Linc said as he backed the truck up to the gate.

'Make sure you lock the gate,' was my parting shot. I thought that bull was a good candidate as an escapee.

'He'll be right. He can't get out the gate is 6 feet high.' Linc was confident that he had the bull securely yarded.

Next morning when Linc went to feed the bull it was gone, jumped the gate. I did not bother to ask Linc if he found it again.

I was not interested in being Linc's stooge and load that bull again.

Another incident involving Linc: One day I took a short cut through Linc's property on my pushbike on the way home from town. As I rode past his shed, I came across him struggling and puffing along carrying an old upholstered armchair. This looked interesting.

'Bruce, come and give me a hand,' he said between gasps.

'What's up, Linc?' I was intrigued by this time.

'I want to unload a bull.'

'What's wrong with backing up to an earth ramp?'

'No! The bull is stuck.'

'Stuck? How can a bull be stuck and where,' I questioned Linc as I followed him to where the truck was parked in the paddock. A big bull hung out of the side gate of the truck's hurdles by his ribs and stomach, his front feet dangled a foot off the ground.

'The chair won't be high enough, Linc, besides, it's not solid enough' I stood bug eyed and open mouthed ready to catch every fly in creation at what Linc had done and was considering doing.

'Help me get this chair under the bull's feet and get the

weight off his belly.' Linc ignored my logic and dropped the chair near the bull, still puffing from the effort.

'Go back to the shed and get a wooden plank, Bruce,' Linc ordered, 'We'll put it across the arms of the chair.' I ran for the plank, privately thinking he was barmy.

'Get his feet upon the plank, will you?' We struggled to get the bull's front feet on to the plank without much success and the poor animal was still hanging, even when we pushed and shoved trying to collapse its stomach.

'What now?' I asked. I had some ideas of my own.

'Well, its desperate measures now,' Linc jumped in the truck and drove up to the nearest strainer post, tied a rope around the post and the animal's horns and drove forward. Remember the bull was stuck in a side gate just behind the driver's door.

The animal flopped to the ground with an almighty Whump, staggering to its feet deflated, and gasping for air, but OK.

I bet some dairy cows had a lot of bull whispered in their ears, that is, if he did not make meat pies and you ate him. Linc was a man to whom interesting things happened.

One time, there was a mouse plague happening and mice are no respecter of people or places. Linc's front veranda was stacked with old bags of grain and junk and had become home to hundreds of mice.

'Come and give me a hand to clean up the mess on the front veranda and get rid of the mice, Bruce.' Linc asked.

'OK, I'll come over,' I reluctantly agreed. I knew the dust and smell of mice would play havoc with my asthma. I was not a happy chappie, but the small wage was precious to me in those days.

When I arrived Linc said, waving his arms towards the bags and then the Truck, 'Throw all these old bags onto the truck and I'll cart them down to the shed.'

I started on the job surrounded by fleeing, terrified mice and trying not to breath in too much dust.

'What's the matter, Linc?' I stopped work to watch Linc dancing around like a cat on hot bricks. The party had brightened up considerably, and I began to enjoy the scene, laughing at Linc's antics.

'A mouse has gone up my trouser leg. Oh, Oh, there it is' Linc was slapping at his body missing the mouse.

Linc was tall and skinny and without thinking, he whipped off his trousers, exposing his nether regions for all to see, prancing around flapping his trousers.

At that moment, the service bus from Adelaide slowly topped the hill catching Linc with his trousers down. The passengers on the bus had a good view of Linc. That made my day. I will admit morning coffee in Mrs Linc's kitchen was a great laugh. He offered me quite a bit of work at times. He played a role in the scheme of life, teaching me how to work.

Chapter Eleven
A Sense Of Fun

Dad and Mum were not able to marry until she turned twenty-one. Their marriage lasted beyond 60 years. My wife Gwen and I are nudging 60 years of marriage.

The example they set us kids was profound. For them it was not easy but together they created a marriage, a family and a living. Peter was born 15th September 1927; Clare celebrated her birthday 5th November 1931 when the Great Depression was at its worst. I do not know how my parents managed to rear us.

Dad worked like a draft horse, as for being a tool man - never. He was a stumpy 5'6". His lack of height looked a bit ridiculous among several brothers all 6 feet tall. Pete and I decided one day that Dad needed to be lengthened we carefully measured him against the wall then placed him on the table and one each end pulled for all we were worth. We quickly stood him up against the wall and measured him again. Dad had not grown an inch, but we had a lot of fun.

Mum never really had an easy life until Dad retired to Victor Harbour.

Victor Harbour, in the beginning of settlement, hosted a whaling station. Relics of the era emerge along the coastline. The settlement of Victor Harbor began with the arrival of Reverend Ridgeway Newland and 34 settlers at Yilki in July 1839, Yilki meaning Aboriginal for 'a place by the sea'.

The land between the Hindmarsh and Inman Rivers was virtually unoccupied until 1863 when the present town of Victor Harbor was established.

Seaside holidays were fashionable with Adelaide's upper crust by the 1870s, and the great scenery of Encounter Bay appealed to Adelaide's well-off citizens. In 1873 merchant and MP, Alexander Hay and his second wife Agnes made the long trip to Victor Harbour for a holiday. Mrs. Hay so fell in love with the place, that she persuaded her husband to build a house there. What a house! More like a baronial castle. Mount Breckan towers over the Hindmarsh River.

Victor Harbour is a resort for retirees and holidaymakers then as now.

Talking of great laughs and fun, the greatest gift Dad imparted to me was a sense of fun.

Life for Dad was very hard but he carried everyone along with him by his sense of fun. He and his young newly married mates all tended to be daredevils, hard working, hard playing, but never hard drinkers. I never saw Dad drunk ever, although he did smoke on and off, I suspect to make Mum mad.

As I grew up and acquired my own tools, I continually complained,

'Mum, Dad's been using my tools again,'

'Well, you'll just have to lock up your tools and hide the key.' Mum would try to be sympathetic, 'I know how much you prize your tools, but you know what your father is with tools.'

I would often hear Dad proudly say to Mum, 'The angels are looking after me.'

'Len, that's no reason to keep them on overtime,' Mum would come back at him. Dad would smile and continue to dare life to do its worst and keep the angels busy.

Thinking of Dad and his lack of respect for tools' turned my thoughts to Dad's early beginnings. He was a twin. His twin was a boy, Lawrie; they were the youngest in a big family living in Southwark, Adelaide. The Leane Family owned and operated a flourishing bakery in the area.

Lawrie and Len moved to Mount Compass in the 1920s and were conned into a doubtful land deal from which they tried to eke out a living. Lawrie and Len then married and started their families in Mount Compass.

The year I was born, 1929, Lawrie died in a plane crash in Victor Harbour. Dad was supposed to go up for a joy flight but for some reason he declined. Lawrie bargained with the pilot, 'I'll take Len's place if you loop the loop with me.'

'OK. I can do that,' the pilot agreed.

The crowd watched in horror as the plane plummeted to the ground. There were no survivors.

'Poor Doll, how is she going to cope with five kids to bring up on her own,' Mum said tearfully, thinking of the plight of her widowed sister-in-law.

'I should have been in that airplane not Lawrie. Maybe if I hadn't backed out of my flight he would be alive,' Dad blamed himself.

'I'm glad you didn't go up in the plane. I would have been the widow and struggling to bring up our four kids alone.' Mum could not bear to think about what she would have done.

'Well, I won't have Lawrie's name blackened with unpaid debts, Grace, and that's that.'

Dad then took over Lawrie's debts and managed the market garden belonging to his brother on the swamps at the base of Mount Moon.

Dad was a committed Christian with high ideals. He sought to reach those ideals though not always successfully, because sadly, he was very human.

That is the beauty of the Lord; he accepts humanity and its foibles and continues to love us having provided a covering for us by the willingness of his own son to die for us.

Chapter Twelve

Recovering The Lost Years

After the war, when Dad came home, he discovered two grown up sons. He had left us as mere kids who were now grown men, perhaps not in so many years but in experience. In his absence, we had had to grow up very quickly.

Dad now expected to tell us what to do, which we often did not agree with. We were inclined to do things the way we had done them in his three-year absence. The years lost between father and sons are hard to regain once the connection is broken. Over the years, Dad and I disagreed many times. Those times of difference only served to firm my character into what I am today.

Finding his sons now young men, Dad decided they could help build his dream of a larger dairy cheaply and so he informed the family.

'I'll be getting a payout from the Air Force, Grace.'

Mum began to dream of what would make life easier. Dad blew her dreams away when he outlined how he would spend the money.

'There's some virgin land up for sale out near Mount Jagged. What say we buy it and start a dairy?'

'What are we going to live in? There is no house or sheds on the property.' Mum despaired.

'We'll build a house, dairy, sheds, given time,' Dad outlined his dream.

'How are we going to clear the land?' Mum was clutching at straws her dreams killed off. She could see further years of hard struggle ahead and was already tired thinking about what it would cost the whole family.

'I'll get some free equipment such as a grubber, axe and horses,' Dad explained. 'It'll give the boys something to do.'

'We'll have to buy cows?' Mum felt Dad's payout was not going to stretch very far.

'We'll pick up some cheap cows at the sales along with a couple of horses.' Dad had it all worked out.

'There is no shed to milk in.' Mum objected.

'I'll make some bails and later we'll cut some posts and make a bough shed until we get the house built and a new dairy up.'

Dad had an answer for everything.

Dad bought the land and we worked at clearing the land with axe and grubber over the next few years.

To make a bit of personal pocket money Pete and I went grubbing out grasstrees or yacca, felling trees and splitting posts for fencing with doubtful success.

Everyday before starting work and last thing at night the cows had to be hand milked. Wherever we went or whatever we did we always had to come home to milk the # @ ! cows. Those early teen years showed no future or hope of money or marriage for Peter or me.

The new property was about 15-20 kilometres from Mount Compass. Transport for many years, was riding a pushbike for me, a horse for Peter. Sometimes I would get a horsetail pull up the hills. The land was eventually cleared and made productive, the house and dairy built by our blood sweat and tears without pay or hope of a future.

Building the house was a terrible time for Dad. The builder and Dad could not live in the same paddock for an hour without having a big argument.

'Len, the cement is too weak, the walls will crumble,' the builder complained

'I can't afford to buy more cement to make the mortar stronger,' Dad felt ashamed to admit he was building on a shoestring and so he would snap at the builder.

'Look at these window frames they are second hand junk,' the builder swore roundly, calling Dad all sorts of a cheap skate. 'You can't put up a new house with such rotten material.'

'There's nothing wrong with it,' Dad bit back, 'use it or I'll get another builder.'

'OK, get another builder. He will not work as I do with substandard material. You want me to build a house and you provide second-hand rubbish.' The builder was angry. Dad was livid!

Next day, 'Bruce you stay on the house from now on, I can't work with him. I'm going to go and grub out some stumps and get the ground ready for planting clover. I also want to dig some ditches to drain the water off the swamps.'

Dad may have solved his problems by going off to do other jobs but he only increased Pete's and mine. I operated the concrete mixer while Peter pushed the barrow of concrete to the builder along narrow planks as the walls of the house rose. Good job there were no Health and Safety rules in those days or Dad would have been in more trouble.

Peter ran all day with the barrow so the builder could do his job and that pushed me to the maximum of my lung capacity. In other words, I had a job to keep pace with the builder.

The builder and his son would square the walls; ram the cement between the pine board shutters. The walls were being raised one metre at each mixing over the whole house. There was a week between each pour to let the cement set and then the boards had to be moved up another metre ready for the next pour. I was glad for the respite, as I do not think I could have kept up the pace. Of course, we had to milk the #@!* cows, twice a day regardless of the weather as well as build the house. I do not ever want, now or in eternity, to milk#@!* cow.

The property, thickly covered in scrub, supplied uprights and rafters overlaid with skimpy boughs or ti-tree bushes for roofing and walls for our first dairy. The cow bales built out of thin branches to fit around the cows' necks. The yard paved with stones unevenly laid, at least kept us out of having to walk through mud. When it rained, the water came straight through and dripped down the back of the neck. Mount Compass has a thirty-six inch rainfall. Any wonder I hate cows.

Occasionally a cow with an attitude would walk through the bale and out the back wall of the brush shed.

We would just cut and lay more branches over the hole until next time. In the summer, we would sit the cans of milk in the creek water at night to stop the milk from turning sour.

After some years, Peter, Dad and I built another dairy of cement bricks. We poured cement into metal moulds on the ground then left the cement to set. We did this over many months until we had enough bricks made, and then up went the dairy. Eventually, we put in a milking machine driven by a petrol motor.

Peter changed to electricity long after I left home. I never saw the dairy operate by electricity.

He built the herd to three hundred cows along with a

third dairy installing a herringbone system, milking them twice a day on his own. He tells me he had a fiendish delight in pushing over the old dairy. I bet it did not take much pushing either. I should have cried because I laid those bricks. Very tough years, but they made me tough. Peter stayed with the dairying for many years.

Dairying is a cow of a way to make a living. You feed them one end, clean up after them at the other end and somewhere in between you squeeze out the milk. I was never a good milker. OK – I may be a man with an attitude where cows' are concerned but I am not changing my attitude. Dairying does not leave you with much of a social life.

Some animals I will never forget, Pam for instance. She was the sweetest, nicest Jersey cow ever. Eventually she became ill and wasted away to skin and bone. When she walked, she cracked and squeaked. Dad, tough man that he was, did not have the heart to get rid of her. He found it impossible to kill anything. That meant I became the farm executioner.

Any animal that needed to be destroyed it was 'Bruce see to that little matter we discussed.' Dad would then disappear.

'I've got to go to Victor Harbour on business today.' Dad announced over breakfast one morning. Did he have an ulterior motive in taking off for Victor Harbour for the day? I was very suspicious. Did he hope I would put old Pam down? Though Dad did not ask me to, I picked up the rifle and walked out to the paddock where Pam was trying to graze. She was standing near the road that led to our house. I shot her and then spent the rest of the day digging a whole deep enough to bury her.

Dad came home at the end of the day, driving right past the mound of freshly dug earth. He never remarked on why the dirt was there or asked what happened to Pam. He never mentioned it right up to the day he died at over 90 years of age.

Then there was Clover a big black and white Friesian. She became a test of faith in my growing Christian life, would you believe.

Peter always milked her and she always kicked him. So he decided to leg rope her, which upset her and she fought against the rope. Then Peter got mad which caused Dad to see red about the situation. All this cussing from my Christian family upset me and so we were all angry.

In the midst of an angry exchange of words I spoke up, 'From now on I will milk Clover, so shut up!'

Silence fell like lead over Dad and Peter. When it came time to milk the cows, I brought Clover in and bailed her without the leg rope, trembling with fear, praying like mad that Clover wouldn't kick me out of the shed along with the bucket of milk, I grabbed a bucket sat down on my stool, shoved my head into her flank and began to milk. Clover moved her weight ready to kick but I blocked her by shoving my arm between her legs and grabbing the off side hock. She was not able to kick me and did not try again. There was no comment from Dad or Peter then or since, a blanket of silence has fallen over that subject. I milked her for a long time, possibly until we put in the milking machine. It was a victory for the Lord, his wisdom, my trust in his keeping power grew. Many of my greatest victories in faith came out of those formative years. The presence of the Lord was a powerful experience in those days. Jersey cows are sweet, cuddly and placid mostly but Jersey bulls – never trust 'em.

It was Dad's practice on Sunday mornings when the milking was finished to take the milk 2 kilometres out to the collection point on the main road by horse and cart.

Then he would come home, wash himself, change his clothes, and prepare himself spiritually for church.

When the milking was finished, Mum would organise us four kids to pack up lunches, feed calves, dogs and cats and get dressed along with the thousand and one jobs to be done before a family goes out for the day.

Church services began at 11 am and 3 pm. The dairy farmers would attend the morning service have a picnic lunch and then stay for the afternoon service getting home in time for evening milking. It was quite a big trip in our old Studebaker buckboard (ex hearse).

On the morning in question, the bull escaped from its yard and rather upset Dad's sanctification and spoilt his holy hour.

Dad, Peter and I tried to herd the bull back into its yard. I ran myself to the point exhaustion and retired to what we called a cow-yard.

'Lord,' I said between gasps, 'show me a way to catch this bull.' An idea formed in my mind. I found a 10-metre steel cable, made one end into a noose and tied the other end to a big gum tree down by the creek.

Dad, on foot, puffing and cussing; Peter on horse back with stockwhip and me standing at the other side of the yard with a pickaxe handle raised and an open gate. When Dad saw the open gate, he saw red and yelled,

'Shut the gate, Bruce,' he yelled angrily, but I stood and waited for the bull to charge through, praying like mad the noose would catch.

The bull took one look at the open gate and freedom and made a headlong dash. One horn and the nose of the bull caught in the noose. The momentum of the animal took it down over the bank until it hit the end of the cable with a bang! Arm over tip went the bull. Peter jumped the fence and sat on the bull's head, 'Get a rope.'

'That was a good idea,' Dad was begrudging in his praise.

At that moment all I could think,

'Thank you, Lord, for the idea and that it worked.'

Away we went to worship as usual.

Every one of these experiences with my father, of life on the dairy, struggling with asthma, all served as a foundation for the Call. Dad might not have been a perfect father but he taught me to appreciate fatherhood and to understand the Fatherhood of God. Those who never know a father and his position in the family find it hard to establish a relationship with God. A good father portrays the fatherhood of God but an abusive father sadly depicts God as an ogre. It is no wonder many people turn away from entering the Family of God.

Chapter Thirteen
Just Practising

Really, the Christian Endeavour Society was the focal point for cementing the young people attending the Chapel into a mighty group. This group of young people were a fine body of youth and many great ministries came from that group; there are many unsung heroes among them. To mention just a few names: Brian, Don, Melva, Doreen, and Betty.

The group met every Tuesday night at the Chapel in Mount Compass. The meetings were presided over by 'Bishy' and Betty Jacobs. Words cannot express what these two people built into my life. Many incidents such as the one I am thinking off helped to cement the group together.

It was a bitterly cold night and after the meeting was over and every one was freezing with long miles to travel before getting home and a warm fire, one bright spark suggested, 'Why don't we make ourselves a hot drink?'

'Good idea!' You girls get the cups and we'll heat the water up.'

'Are there any biscuits around?' Cupboards doors banged in a search for biscuits.

'Hey, there isn't any milk? What are we going to do for milk?'

'Let's go and milk a cow?' Another capable dairy farmer suggested.

A couple of the young men dashed outside. Next door to the church was the property of farmer Giles. His herd was resting under the shelter of some pine trees nearby. Almost every one of the young people could milk a cow but Pete and another lad jumped the fence with a jug, roused a cow and milked her.

'Thanks, Mr Giles for giving us some milk,' we all laughed.

'I bet Farmer Giles will wonder why his cow hasn't got much milk in the morning,' another added.

'No, Mr Giles won't even know.'

Betty, an older member of the group often acted in a motherly fashion, was not too sure about the deal; she had a feeling it was next door to stealing. What did the loss two pints of milk matter we were warm for the trip home?

At these meetings, everyone had to give a talk. The Endeavour Society was really about training young people to speak in public, conduct public prayers and preside over meetings as well as arrange social outings.

'Listen you young 'uns what about we hold make-believe church services for several weeks on Tuesday nights to teach you how to lead the Services,' Mr Bishop suggested.

'Oh no.' There were groans from the girls.

'I'm not going to preach.'

'Church on Sunday is enough.'

'Yeah, let's try our hand at preaching. Surely we can do better than old so and so,' several young men were eager to flex their preaching skills.

Mr Bishop wrote out a roster. We would have to lead the services, conduct communion, pray public prayers, preach and give an invitation to accept Christ after the sermon. After the meeting, there would be a discussion over our efforts and suggestions on how we could improve our performance.

'Brian, you're first on the list to preach next week you have to prepare a sermon as well as conduct the service,' Mr Bishop pointed out.

Brian went home and swatted all week preparing his sermon.

'Very good,' Mr Bishop pronounced. Everyone agreed that Brian did a great job. He went on to pastor a church later in life.

'Next week, it's your turn, Bruce.'

The next Tuesday I arrived at the church for the meeting to find the meeting moved from the hall into the church. It was supposed to be more like the church service. I spent hours in preparation on my sermon was geared to go. I was determined to do it properly so I went into the vestry for a prayer before the service began or at least to stop my knees from knocking.

Right on the minute I marched out onto the raised platform to face, what I thought would be the young people and surprise, surprise, all the church Elders were there. Elders Ern, Mel and Dad and many others, as well, had come along to see and hear the next generation of budding preachers, elders and leaders.

The old organ, played by one of the musicians among the young members, wheezed its way through several hymns; then I stood to preach, right down to challenging Ern and Mel to give their lives to Christ. 'Bishy' did not allow any critique that night, thank goodness, as I had had enough by the end.

That was the very beginning of my preaching career. I was sixteen years old. The gift to preach began to bud.

As I practised my preaching skills, the cows and the trees became the congregation. They all heard the gospel. I have never seen a cow raise its leg to my invitation only flick its tail but that could be at the flies. It was great practise for me, I had to start somewhere and nature does not criticise or answer back.

Over a number of years, the Churches of Christ organised annual scripture exams. I participated in these exams and to obtained top marks was very important to me for I believed it was essential to the Call of God on my life. I have lost the records unfortunately, but I learnt entire chapters of the Gospels and Acts so that my quotations would not be wrong.

Learning Acts Chapter Two about the Holy Spirit quickened my heart at that time and I drove my teachers mad asking questions. They were careful to explain that the teaching in the scriptures I was learning about was not for this age such as the laying on of hands and praying for the sick. If Biblical text was not for this day and age, I reasoned, why include it in the Bible? The Bible was either true or false. Either it was the Word of God or it was just an ordinary book, was my reasoning.

I was sick! I wanted to know why I could not ask the elders to lay hands on me for healing. If the Bible was a true record as declared, then there had to be answers rather than contradictions. The platform of the church I attended was 'Where the Bible speaks we speak, where the Bible is silent we are silent.' The Bible was not silent about the laying on of hands for healing but the Elders were and I wanted to know why. When the church leaders fell silent, I went walking in the bush sending my many questions above.

In my quest for answers, I dropped a clanger at one Christian Endeavour meeting. The meeting, packed with young people, and I just had to ask, 'what is a Eunuch?' (Acts Chapter 8) A gasp went around the group.

'Well, we'll leave that question for now,' 'Bishy' spluttered.

'But I've learnt by heart all of Acts Chapter 8. I'm sure to be questioned on it during my scripture exams.'

You could cut the air with an axe.

'But I need to know what a eunuch is because it is in the Bible.' I persisted. I was frustrated and asked the question twice more.

'Please, Bruce, leave it! I will explain later when we have more time,' Mr Bishop said in a voice that I did not dare ask any more. Later Mr Bishop took me aside to explain the Eunuch; he rebuked me, 'Bruce, sometimes you just will not shut up.'

'Well, what is a Eunuch that is so hush-hush?' I was more than curious by now.

'A Eunuch is a man that has been gelded. Do you know what that means?'

'Ye-es, but why,' I was a farm boy and had helped geld horses, steers and wethers, but why a man?

'Eunuchs were made because they were slaves and chosen to serve the women in their harems. Now do you understand?' snapped Mr Bishop.

'Thank you, but how does one know unless one asks? I can now answer that question. I won't be an embarrassment to the girls in the group again.'

The Bible has always been a foundation textbook on which I have based my belief and so I continued to search for many years for answers to many questions. Eventually I found my answers. The same book said, 'Seek and you shall find, ask and it shall be given to you.'

I have always encouraged people to question God. He needs to hear from you and you need the practice of talking to him. My conversations with God have gone on all my life.

Since my first sermon, I have travelled thousands of miles, preaching in churches, shacks, camps, in the streets and the open air. I still preach at age 80+ years. The fire of the Call still burns in my belly as bright as it ever did.

Chapter Fourteen
The New Girl On The Block

My upper teen years were very lonely times; the asthma isolated me from the family and a social life; it enslaved me. I could not stay in the living room in the evenings when all the family came together because the movement of people always created a dust, which in turn, would set off an asthma attack, especially if the family was in a mad mood and started trying out tricks and stunts.

I would have to go to bed in an open sleep-out on the back of the house; the only light a kerosene lamp with a glass reflector behind the flame to increase the light. I would read books - Zane Grey was my favourite. (My older son, Philip has the collection now.)

Girls, well, I had a couple of mild crushes on girls in the Christian Endeavour group. They did not last long living miles out of town with only a pushbike for transport across a mountain range was obstacle enough to kill off any budding romance. Dad was directional in trying to pair me up with suitable local girls.

'Now, she is a pretty girl, Bruce,' he would say, trying to direct my eyes toward certain girls in the district that he considered were pretty and would make a suitable wife.

'She's OK, I suppose,' I would answer noncommittally.

'You could do worse with that girl, Bruce. She's smart and a hard worker.' Dad would try to organise a meeting,

'She doesn't appeal to me.' I would hedge, wishing Dad would let me choose my wife, myself.

The annual Sunday school picnic arrived and it was always a lot of fun. If Dad was involved, the competitions and skylarking seemed to go on all day. This picnic was to be different.

My lonely years were to end.

We young men grouped ourselves at the gate of the paddock used as a picnic ground on the pretext of directing picnic goers to the right spot under a big gum tree. We were fooling around telling tall stories as lads do, when along came a young chick. She was a new comer to the district, living down Nangkita.

'Wow! Wonder who she is?"

'Oh, I heard Hector Brown's sister-in-law's come to live with him and his wife.'

'What does she do?'

'I was told she works on the dairy.'

'Where'd she come from?'

'Hey! Hands off her, you guys, this one's mine,' I butted in on the conversation so emphatically that the other boys fell silent with surprise continuing to watch the girl on the bike as she rode over to where the rest of the picnickers were gathered under a huge gum tree in the middle of the paddock.

At this moment my world went into a tailspin, I had made the truest prophecy in my life. It took about six months before it became obvious that the new girl and I were destined to be a pair in the Master's service. Gwen, the new girl at the picnic, is the typist, advisor, terrific friend, wife and partner in this story.

Getting back to the picnic, I was smitten, but Gwen did not even see me that day and besides I was very girl shy and ignorant in how to court a girl.

Courting Gwen was from afar. We met at Christian Endeavour on Tuesday nights. Gwen would ride her bike several miles from Nangkita to Mount Compass, sometimes getting a ride with other members of the group that lived along the valley. I rode eight miles on a bike from the opposite direction, until Peter learnt to drive the family car.

Our meetings alone were a brief few minutes after the meeting was over in a secluded spot.

'Come on, it is time to go home,' Peter would yell, and we would part for another week. Peter saying goodnight to his beloved interrupted our journey home; Clare would get thoroughly bored sitting in the car waiting for her two brothers to say goodnight to their girlfriends.

The family, as usual, did not have a clue that some girl had stolen my heart until at a social gathering in the local hall. Mum was sitting beside a Mrs Brown, curious about the new girl on the block, she asked,

'Who is that girl asking my son to team up with her in a 'Women's Choice game?'

'Oh, that's my sister. She's living with me and working for my husband on the dairy.'

My cover was blown but I still did not 'tell all' to my family. I kept my romance close to my chest for as long as I could. My thinking was that it was my business and no one else's. Mum, though, did not agree and would not be put off.

'When are you going to bring Gwen home?'

'OK, OK, Mum, don't push me.'

GWENNETH & BRUCE LEANE

It was all right for Mum to invite Gwen to come home but the execution of the visit required some discussion with Gwen's brother-in-law and boss because she must be home to milk the cows. It was her job.

Distance was another problem, there was the mountain range between us to cross, a round trip of thirty or forty kilometres. My problem was how to transport Gwen across the dividing range of hills. She had no transport other than a pushbike

The day of the visit, arrived Gwen came home to meet the family.

She was a nervous Nellie and no mistake.

She presumed our family to be major dairy farmers; our Spartan life style was not my idea of big time though.

The visit was progressing well and the whole family including Gwen were standing out in front of the house looking over the property, trying to impress each other, except for Dad; he was mending a road along the hillside with a horse and cart.

Next minute there is an almighty shout, 'Shut the #@% gate,' Dad was coming down the hill, belting the horse into a gallop trying to race a herd of frisky calves to the gate. Dad lost the race, but undeterred, he raced across the rough ploughed six-hectare paddock trying to round up the calves. Spades and forks were flying out of the cart, Dad hanging on for dear life, stilling shouting #%$@.

Fear stricken, the family stood and watched, wondering who was going to get the blame and what would Gwen think. What would my girlfriend think, I was mortified and ashamed.

I looked at Gwen; the tears were starting to flow down her cheeks with suppressed laughter, that was it, the romance was over. She burst out laughing and we forgot our fears and saw the funny side. Dad, when later over afternoon tea and the calves had been re-yarded and the horse and dray put away saw the funny side.

'Lovely to meet you, Gwen, we've been wondering when Bruce would bring you home to meet us.' Dad smiled disarmingly. He could be a charmer when he wanted to. After that, we thoroughly enjoyed afternoon tea. My girl was accepted.

Over the next months, the romance developed nicely. Gwen had found out I existed and we soon became recognized as an item.

The hardships through those early formative years were very important for Gwen and me as we learnt the lessons of endurance and moving toward our calling in God. It imparted a powerful determination to disregard circumstances and taught us that the real values are not in things but in our walk with God. To use a phrase from the ancient text: 'Press forward toward the mark of the high calling in God.'

Gwen and I both knew we had a call of God upon our union from the very beginning, just where that call would lead we had no idea. For me there were great obstacles to get around, such as a job, health and housing. There was no hope of getting married, as the dairy could not provide for one family let alone two. I despaired for our future both physically and financially.

For the reasons I have just mentioned, Peter had left home and taken a job on a property elsewhere. He too wanted to get married.

Pete and I had worked a joint bank account during our bachelor years while working for a pittance with axes splitting posts, grubbing grass trees and bunching vegetables for a market gardener. When we both found girl friends financial cooperation was over.

Those first years on the dairy, we had tried to grow cash

crops such as potatoes but new soil, a lack of superphosphate and water always resulted in zero potatoes.

One day in desperation, I approached a neighbour, Murray Turner,

'Murray, how about you and I jointly plant a patch of potatoes?'

'Why not,' Murray agreed after some thought, 'On your property or mine?'

'You've got a paddock that has been cleared for some time and looks to have pretty good soil. Let's try there. If you'll let me have the use of your tractor and plough I'll rip up the ground ready for planting.' Hope was beginning to grow in me again and I envisaged a flourishing crop of spuds, their tops waving in the breeze, I already had dollar signs in my eyes.

'OK,' Murray too was beginning to think the idea might net a quick cash crop.

'I'll bring over the seed spuds tomorrow and we'll plant them.' I wanted to get the crop in as quick as possible.

The dream of a world beating spud crop still eluded me. The crop was only partially successful. However, it was amazing how that small cheque made big waves on which Gwen and I rode all the way to Easter Camp.

Every Easter one of the great highlights of the year for the Christian Endeavour group was to attend the Churches of Christ Young People's Camp on the trotting track at Gawler.

Peter, Clare and I took in turns to attend the camp because someone had to be home to milk the cows. This particular year it was my turn to go, I had attended about eight camps in all. My reward was a promotion to leader of quite a large group of younger teenagers.

These camps were reputed to be matrimonial agencies however, this year I took Gwen with me.

'When we get up to town we'll go and find a jeweller's shop.' The cheque was burning a hole on my pocket and I badly wanted to present Gwen with a ring.

'Yes,' Gwen sounded as excited as I did. It was a great moment to be able to buy an engagement ring. We were riding the crest of a wave of life-long love.

'Here's a jeweller's let's see what they have!' Gwen and I walked inside, gazing around at the glittering array of rings.

'Can I help you?' the male assistant asked so politely.

'Er - yes, we'd like to look at some engagement rings.' I stuttered.

'We have these rings.' A tray of the biggest and shiniest rocks I had ever seen was set before us; I could only see the price tags.

'No I don't like any of those,' Gwen ummed, aaahed, and another tray appeared before us. The price tags were not that much better. Finally, a tray with the right price tag sat before us and I nudged Gwen, 'What one would you like?'

'I'd like this one,' she pointed to a certain ring

'Would you like to try it on and see if it fits,' the assistant offered, 'so it can be altered.' The ring needed altering and later we returned to pick up the ring.

'Do you want to wear it now?' I looked at Gwen.

'No, let's keep it and put it on later when we are by ourselves.' I guess she wanted a more romantic moment.

How big was the diamond? The size of the potato cheque that's how big,

the waves it created were huge.

Off to camp the ring in its box and two very excited people waiting for that romantic moment to slip it on Gwen's finger.

Next day with the ring on Gwen's finger, one of the

girls grew suspicious, grabbed Gwen's hand, saw the ring, and gave a great shout. That put the cat among the pigeons and by the fuss it caused the ring should have been the Kohinoor diamond.

Now Sunday nights became the night when about 200 or so young people in the camp would attend the local church service. After the service, the camp leaders allowed us to make our own way back to camp by a set time in order to watch a film.

Just before we set out some of the lads in my group came up to me,

'Can we borrow your watch, we want to set our watches right.' Max sidled up to me.

'Yeah, OK.' I took off my watch and gave to him.

'Here, you can have it back, now.'

I put the watch back on and Gwen and I dawdled along the way, we had stardust in our eyes but tried to keep an eye on my watch. Horror of horror, the lights were out and the film was well under way when we arrived back at camp. Around to the back door to sneak into a back seat, but the seats were taken by the members in my study-group. They gave a rousing yell as we tried to squeeze in. The young monkeys had changed the time on my watch just so we would be late and get into trouble.

Our unobtrusive entry failed to our embarrassment. I have developed the habit of not lending my watch to anyone again. The ringleader, Max Jacquier, would have been a leader in whatever stream life took him.

Monday at Easter Camp was sports day and the country groups were determined to beat the daylights out of the city groups. Peter decided to bring Clare and Mum to the camp for the day and watch the fun and so he could enter the endurance races, which he usually managed to win.

I did not know they were coming and was in the middle

of a heavy theological discussion with my group when I saw the old Chevrolet come in through the gate. Then I saw Jean Young from the West Coast run across to the family and 'blab off' the news, 'Bruce and Gwen are engaged.'

I freed myself from the group, found Gwen, and went to meet the family.

'You might have told us first.' Mum glared.

'Why?' I was unrepentant. Anyway, the bush telegraph could not beat Jean. We cannot recollect anyone else announcing his or her engagement at camp but logistically, it was the only way and it was romantic.

The months following our engagement did not solve our problem about getting married.

'What is our next step?' Gwen queried.

'How can we get married? We don't have enough to get married on and nowhere to live!' I despaired.

Whenever we met, we talked about our future. We prayed together, 'Lord, where to from here? What will you have us do? I still feel the Lord has called me to serve him in ministry somewhere, somehow.' I was honest with Gwen.

She accepted that God had first call on my life.

When we made our marriage vows, vows we promised to love and live together 'until death do us part,' I was determined to keep those vows and I have. I have never made promises lightly to God or man.

The next drama in our lives was the Adelaide Show to which I had never been. It seemed that our planned outings always contained a drama of some sort.

'My wife and I are going to the Adelaide Show,' 'Bishy' said to me when we met at Christian Endeavour. 'Do you want to come?'

'Yeah, I do but only if Gwen can come as well?'

'No worries, nine o'clock sharp at my place, we'll pick Gwen up in Mount Compass. Don't be late.'

'Right O, I'll be there.'

I was up at the crack of dawn to get the cows milked. I got ready and walked the one-mile over the hills to Mr Bishop's place, hurrying as fast as I could. He was gone. Woe is I, what now! It was over four miles to the highway. I ran and walked and ran and walked, reaching the highway. The first vehicle to come along was a small 4WD, possibly a jeep.

'Want a lift, mate?'

'Yes, please, I want to go to the Show.' I puffed, 'I missed my ride.'

'Hop in. We're going to the Show ourselves.' What an answer to prayer.

The trip was good but I was worried; where would Gorgeous be? Would I be able to find her in the crowd?

I bought a ticket, which I do not remember doing, and mooched around on my own looking for Gwen and not seeing anything of the Show. Suddenly I spotted a familiar figure it was Sylvia, Mr Bishop's daughter.

'Is Gwen here?' I held my breath.

'Yes,' Sylvia said, grinning at my barely concealed eagerness, 'She's over there with Mum.' Sylvia waved her arm in a general direction. I looked but all I could see was wall-to-wall people. I dashed around some fixtures and there in front of the embroidery stall was poor dejected Gwen trying gallantly to make the best of a bad day. I said a quick 'Thank you, Lord.'

'Hello,' I puffed, touching Gwen on the arm.

'Where have you been?' She looked as if I was a ghost, 'I thought you must have had an asthma attack.'

We had a great day after that, one of our few dates. Since then I have made it a lifelong policy - do not be late. Impatient to be off and be on time makes me push those around me.

Chapter Fifteen
Changes In The Air

Not long after our engagement the family was sitting down to a meal when Mum surprised me by saying,

'Dad and I think you ought to go away for a holiday, Bruce. It might be good for your health.'

'Who's going to milk the cows?' I stated the obvious. Pete had obtained a job and left home. He planned to get married as soon as possible.

'Clare can give a hand at milking. You will won't you, Clare?' Mum looked at her daughter hoping she would agree. What could Clare say? She was doing housework for the neighbour.

'I suppose I can.' Clare was reluctant. She had other plans and was waiting for the moment to propose her intentions.

I had been very ill and a holiday might give my health and spirits a boost.

'Where will I go?' I had not a clue where to go. I had no money for a holiday and did not think Mum and Dad had either.

'I've been in touch with Uncle Alb and Auntie Chris in

Barmera. They are very happy to have you stay for a week.' Mum had done her homework and it was all cut and dried that I should go and stay with her brother and his wife and family.

It was great but lonely with out You Know Who.

Uncle Alb and my cousins were all at work. Auntie Chris was at one of her interminable CWA craft meetings so I decided to borrow a bike and ride toward Berri about seven miles to visit two girls, June Andrews and Roma McKinley, from the church youth group. The two girls found a job on a fruit block, picking grapes. I discovered where they worked and asked if I could pick grapes with them for a while. I enjoyed the work and the chat with the girls and their boss.

At afternoon smoke-o, I noticed Mr Chapple and his son Alan in a huddle outside of the shed, having a big debate. They signalled me to join them, 'Bruce, do you want a job for six months in the winter pruning? Uncle wants to retire and we need help on the fruit block.' Mr Chapple said.

'No, no, the family need me on the dairy, but thanks. I would love to accept but I wouldn't be able to get away,' I explained the way things were at home.

'Well, anyway,' Mr Chapple said, 'keep it in mind over the next month or so. You would be boarding with me and my wife.'

Alan was the only son and married. There were four daughters, all left home. That was that but it looked mighty tempting and I badly wanted to take the job, though I did wonder what Gorgeous might have to say when I told her about the job offer and leaving her.

I suffered one of my worst attacks of asthma ever when I returned from my holiday. I was in total despair, unable to cope, and I had to take another visit to the specialist.

'Bruce, have you ever been to stay somewhere where you felt better with less asthma and allergies?' The doctor had no help for me. He had done all he could.

'Yes, I sure have,' I wheezed, 'I've just spent a couple weeks in the Riverland and was very well.'

'Well, young man,' the specialist looked at Mum, as he spoke to me,' you had better pack up and get back there. You'll die if you stay here.'

That news put the fox among the chooks.

When Mum and I returned from the specialist, there was another family conference over the evening meal.

'What was the specialist report?' Dad wanted to know.

'He's got to leave home, or he will die,' Mum's shoulders slumped with anguish, a catch in her voice.

'It's funny but while I was up the River, I had a job offer for six months to work on a fruit block pruning.' I admitted to the family, 'I didn't say anything because I didn't think I could leave the dairy.'

'Well, you'd better take it.' Dad was practical.

'But who is going to help milk the cows? I asked.

'I could help out for awhile,' Clare offered. 'I'm not able to start my nursing training for another six months.'

Clare began work in the dairy; meanwhile, arrangements were in place for Peter to take over the dairy. Clare would be free then to do her nursing training. When Peter took over the dairy, Mum and Dad moved to Victor Harbour where Dad soon found a job as a grease monkey with a car firm until he retired. Dad fitted into the job like a glove and was better off financially than as a dairy farmer.

The changes were huge and involved a lot of heart searching, it meant the family would each one go their different ways. It proved to be an answer to prayer for everyone.

'Is that pruning job still open, Mr Chapple?' I asked

over the phone.

'Yes, it is. Have you been able to work out something for the dairy?

'I was very ill after I arrived back home and have been advised to leave the district. I was very well while here in the Riverland, so I want to come back.'

'Right, you can start when the pruning begins on three months' trial,' the Boss said. Somehow, he forgot to tell me when the three months was up; I was still working on the block eleven years later.

'Does it matter that I can't prune?'

'No, we can easily teach you.' Mr Chapple brushed aside my concerns.

There was a great deal of soul searching for Gwen and me.

'If I go to work in the Riverland,' I looked at her searchingly, 'I will have to leave you here.'

'I'll still be working for Hector, my brother-in-law, I won't be going anywhere, I'll really miss you, but if your health is going to be better then you must go.'

'It's the only way we are going to get any money together to get married,' I was wondering how I would manage without Gorgeous. It would be a difficult time for us both. Looking at the big picture, we agreed that God was in it and was making a way for us to be together and to serve him.

Moving was a 360 degree turn for me. It was my first time away from home. I would have to leave all that I knew and loved and start again. What could I take and what would I leave behind?

'What about my tools and my study books?' I did not particularly want to leave my tools behind – I had acquired them as birthday and Christmas presents and by any other method available to me. My Bible and study books were tremendously important to me, even if I was only going for six months.

'Yes, bring your tools,' the Boss said, 'They will come in handy along with your books.'

'Can I bring my dog with me?' I asked Mr Chapple.

'Er… sorry, no, you won't be able to bring your dog up here.' Mr Chapple, or as he later became known as the 'Boss', was adamant. That was the second sacrifice made in the new life ahead of me.

Flash, my big, black and white border collie, had been my best friend through the lonely teen years, had hardly ever left my side. How could I leave this, faithful creature behind? He had a wonderful disposition, except when I sent him to deal with wayward cattle then look out; the cattle soon acknowledged Flash as boss. Flash was intelligent and valuable, saving hours in time and effort when rounding up cows.

Wherever Pete and I were working Flash was there. When I left home, he became Pete's companion and shadow.

There are many stories about Flash but I must tell this one: Between the house and the dairy was a cleared ten-acre paddock. Good grazing land but still roughly ploughed. One morning after milking, I was walking across the paddock toward the house carrying a can of fresh milk for household use. Peter, at this time, was standing out in front of the house throwing sticks for Flash to retrieve, and then he started yelling at me.

What is the matter, I thought, I wish he'd shout louder. I noticed that Pete was very agitated and looked behind me. I saw our Jersey bull in top gear, charging for me. He definitely had an attitude. I raced as fast as my legs would go fearing the worst. Plan A was to reach the fence and scramble through, but I had no hope of making it to the fence. I could hear his breathing. Plan B was to throw the can of milk in the bull's face and perhaps buy me some time. As I raced, considering my options, all hell broke loose behind me.

The miracle equation came into play.

Flash, without any command from Peter had seen my danger and raced to my rescue. He tore the skin off the bull's hocks without mercy. The bull suddenly had a change of mind and forgot about me. I made the fence and safety. Peter was white as a ghost and immediately went and saddled the horse and with a stock whip dispatched the bull to the butcher for meat pies.

'What did you get rid of the bull for?' Dad was irate; he had lost a good sire for his dairy herd.

'He's too dangerous to have around,' Pete muttered. 'If it hadn't been for Flash, Bruce would have been gored.'

'Oh, well, I suppose you did the right thing,' Dad decided it was better to have a son than a bull with an attitude.

I do not know how the dog managed to cross the distance so quickly, my interpretation was, God's hand was on my life and I gave God the thanks.

On the rare times, I returned home to the dairy farm, I would reach the boundary fence and give a shrill whistle. Soon I would have a big black and white dog kissing me all over. If Flash missed me, it was nothing compared to how I missed him. It always brought tears to my eyes at our reunion. I missed that dog nearly as much as I missed Gwen.

Flash had a stage career. During the war I had trained him to do tricks and also harnessed him to a small cart and drove him across the stage at fundraising 'do's' to help the war effort. Just for fun, we used to sit Frank, when he was a little boy, in the cart and let Flash pull him along. Flash's career was very successful.

I learnt to count the sacrifices as nothing as Gwen and I both felt a new world opening up for us. We were excited at how God was working out his plan for us. Gwen was only eighteen and I was twenty-two when I put the diamond on her finger then almost immediately left for new and greener pastures in the Riverland, maybe not always greener pastures either.

For Gwen and me, our paths had miraculously converged from very different roads but we both felt the call to serve God. We really could not conceive the occupations and circumstances that we would find ourselves in because of that calling over the years ahead.

The worker- priest or tentmaker calling that Paul the Apostle spoke of as his calling was a challenge for us to take up as our lives opened up before us and challenge our faith to the highest degree. Everything we owned we laid down for God. We never became rich materially but we were rich in seeing the miracles God brought about in our lives.

Chapter Sixteen
Everything New

The mighty River Murray meandered through the semi-arid lands, harnessed by locks to irrigate the land turning the Riverland into a rich food bowl. After the First World War soldier settlements were created and again after the Second World War to resettle men returning from the war.

I remembered the history lessons at school that depicted Sturt's voyage along the Murray in 1830, and the overland journey of Hawden and Bonny with stock from Sydney to Adelaide. The pastoralists and squatters were quick to move into the region and establish large stations.

After pioneering voyages from Goolwa to the upper reaches of the Murray in the early 1850s, steam navigation serviced the isolated settlements that sprang up along the river. Following the advent of the steam vessels, the gold rush brought an influx of people to the goldfields of Victoria increasing the demand for agricultural produce from the Riverland.

The River Murray Waters Act, an agreement between the SA, Victoria, NSW and the Commonwealth Government, came into operation in 1915. Work on the construction of six locks, to control the flow of the river, took shape. Two of these barriers are obvious from the Sturt Highway - Lock 1 at Blanchetown and Lock 5 at Paringa.

By harnessing the river flow to assist with irrigation of the land, paddle steamers then had ample draught to ply the river throughout the whole year. This was to be my world for the next twenty years though I did not know it at the time.

I understood something of what Abraham, that patriarch of old, must have felt when he left the land of Ur and journeyed to Canaan. To use a quote from Abraham's story, 'Leave your own country behind you, and your own people, and go to the land I will guide you to…' I was leaving my land, my people, moving out on my own, reliant only on my wits, my strength and with the Lord as my guide.

The first shock; the world was flat, I could see for kilometres in all directions.

It was very strange to see the horizon after hemmed in by high mountainous country, unable to see beyond. The land had to be flat for successful irrigation from the Murray.

The boss, Mr Len Chapple, was a senior elder in the Church of Christ in Berri. Despite the hard work, his figure had become rotund. Of average height, in his youth he would have been a dark, handsome man. His fruit block was about seven kilometres from Berri on the Winkie road. The fruit block was 22 acres of mixed plantings brilliantly planned first by the Boss and later by Alan to provide consistent work and income throughout the year.

The Boss had pioneered his block in the early days, as a young single man, cleared it using horse drawn implements, developing it into a very profitable block - today his grandson owns it.

There was no real change in my church life; I very

quickly became swallowed up in church activity, teaching a class of senior youth, preaching regularly.

Shortly after arriving, I established a Boys Brigade Corp. I was appointed the Captain soon after.

There were Church of Christ Centres in Berri, Loxton, Moorook and Barmera. Soon I was rostered to preach in all of these centres. It refined my public speaking skills and left no time for activity beyond the church, this was familiar territory to me.

My work place was where the changes were. My first job was learning to prune. I had never used a pair of secateurs in my life but the Boss and Alan were champion pruners, having won numerous awards over many years in the annual Agricultural Pruning Competitions. The credentials of the Boss and Alan were impeccable. They both mentored me in pruning and I soon held my own with them. Another winter job was orange picking for the export market.

I soon realised what a remarkable horticultural teacher I had in the Boss. I loved the challenge of the work and the church but I felt it was only a mentoring situation for the future.

The Boss and I would debate spiritual issues by the hour; he was an amazingly open-minded man with great insights. Alan became like an elder brother and was argumentative just as an older brother. When the Boss was not working with us, Alan would air his ideas on what he would preach as we worked down the rows of vines pruning or picking grapes.

'What would be a good way to present our walk with God?' Alan would inquire.

'Well, you could look at it from this point of view,' and I would outline several options.

'Yes, but…' he would raise several questions and away

we would go, lost in the sermon that Alan would preach the next Sunday. This was what made the work interesting - never boring.

Rivalry is like a sharp knife and the rivalry between Alan and I was sharp. Our relationship grew to be more than boss and employee to that of brothers. As between brothers, there was certain rivalry that kept us at our best. Alan had a strong work ethic that rubbed off on me. Alan was a tall, red haired, blue-eyed man with broad shoulders. Wherever he went, he generated noise. He would shout, the dogs barked and kids ran amok; chaos would reign. His wife would stand on the side and sigh, 'Oh Alan!'

Hardly had I learned to prune when one day while working down the block,

the Boss came to me and said, 'Bruce, I want you to enter the Pruning Competition.'

'What! But I've only just learned to prune.' I stuttered in surprise.

'You can enter the beginner's section. You might do very well. You've picked up the principles of pruning very quickly,' the Boss pointed out.'

'It's a waste of time, I've only just learnt. But I suppose if you think I should...' I gave into the Boss's suggestion and put my name down. I won more money that year than at any other time in my life.

The Boss and Alan took all the credit for my success. Their pride in training a winner nearly burst the buttons off their shirts. For many years after that, I competed but against the Boss and Alan, I was always second, third or fourth, consistently. I could never beat them. I finished with over thirty certificates.

Letter writing was not one of my better skills but it was a very important task, because it was the only way I had of communicating with my beloved. I missed her so much.

I ate with the Boss and his wife and slept in a small single room situated between Alan's house and the Boss's house. Mrs Boss was of German descent and could she cook, she would have won any bake off competition she entered. Her food was delicious. I have never known before or since anybody who could use so many pots and pans. At night, the Boss and I would do the washing up. She also washed my clothes that first year.

Neither the Boss nor Alan drank alcohol. Every year though, the fruit processing cooperatives would give their members bottles of wine. The Boss would lay them down in the cellar at the back of the shelf out of sight. Every now and again, the Boss would send me to the cellar for something, just to tease him I would stand the bottles up at the front of the shelf. It became a bit of a game in the end.

'Somebody has been down the cellar,' the Boss would say when he next met me, 'Know anything about it, Bruce?'

'Not me, Boss.' I would say, trying to look innocent. He would chuckle, knowing I was the culprit and lay them all down again at the back.

Every morning he would be up early to sweep the cement paths around the back door where vine leaves had fallen, for Mrs Boss, whistling cheerily as he did so, then he would come down the block and do a day's work.

The first six months was interesting, so much to learn: so many new people to adjust to, such a very different manner of life without the cows.

When the Boss discovered my ability as a tool man, my toolbox came in for a work out. Alan did not have many handy-man skills, but he was a fast learner.

The Boss had only just changed over from using horses to work the property, he had bought his first tractor just before I arrived. I did not get to drive the tractor very often and when I did, Alan picked at me unmercifully. One day

THE MAVERICK'S ROUNDUP

I stopped the tractor, and jumped off,

'Alan, I've had it. You can do it yourself.'

After that, he always drove and I worked the implements on the tractor. I did not mind the harmony was sweeter.

Wanting to show Gwen the Riverland I organised for her to come and stay with Auntie Chris and Uncle Alby at Barmera. The idea was to see what I was up to and get a feel for the area.

I will never forget cycling over toward Barmera. Gwen had elected to walk along the highway to meet me. I still remember the dress she wore that night. We had a great week and it gave her an idea of what her future would be.

These days, I can hardly tell you what she wore last week. That is years and years of marriage for you.

'Fruit picking time is coming up, how about you get a job fruit picking?'

I suggest to Gwen during that week.

'I don't know I've never worked anywhere but on the dairy. That's all I know to do.' Gwen, strangely enough, was uncertain about change and a new job.

'It's not hard cutting fruit or picking grapes,' I pointed out. I wanted our long separation to end.

'The wages would be better than I'm getting now. It would help towards getting married.'

'Yes, you would work piece work and get paid according to how much you did.' I could see Gwen was warming to the idea of a higher wage and pressed my point. 'We could work on Saturday's picking grapes and pick up a bit extra that way.'

I approached the Boss, 'you will need a picker in the harvest? What about Gwen coming up, we want to get married and need some extra cash.'

'Sure, she can have a job. My wife needs help in the house so Gwen can help her out as well as pick grapes. She can live in the room next to yours and eat with us,' the Boss agreed. To be honest though, I do not think we earned our wages gazing into each other's eyes. The Boss overlooked our poor bucket tally.

The Boss had planted up his block with apricots, peaches, nectarines, pears and grapes. He dried all his fruit and that was very labour intensive at that period in the Riverland. That year worked out to be a good drying season.

'Taking the water,' was the phrase on every block owner's lips because every few weeks the blocks received a quota of water. Three furrows between the vines and trees fed the water onto the blocks. It was hard and very responsible work and not much rest. I still dream about 'taking the water.' All my life, it seems I have been involved in some way of conserving water or draining it.

The block work was a good life and I loved it and even dreamed of the day when I might have a block of my own and be the 'blocker' not the 'block hand'. I never became a 'blocker', which was very disappointing. Being a landowner was not part of the Call and I had to realise that my disappointment was His appointment. Life has many twists and turns especially under the hand of God.

Of course, with Gwen's stint fruit picking and my job, the wheels of hope in getting married started to turn faster and real plans were on the drawing board. Some people thought I was a cradle snatcher, but Gwen's father had passed away and she did not really have a home even though she was living with her sister. I too had left my home and family. Marriage and setting up our own home looked a very good option. Did we have any money? Well, not really. We were in love and it did not make sense to stay apart.

'I think I should spend the time to our wedding with

THE MAVERICK'S ROUNDUP

Mum at Moonta. I'll give notice to Hector that I'm leaving the dairy,' Gwen said when the fruit picking was over.

'I'll borrow a car and trailer and come over and pick up the bits and pieces that mum gave you and what you have stored with her, in a couple of weeks time,' I said. I could see that the next three months was going to be very busy

America gained her independence on the Fourth of July I lost mine on the 5th of July. I cannot remember why we chose that date to be married. However, we believed our marriage divinely planned as an unbreakable union. We have been tried and tested in the crucible of life but only death can separate us and I do not believe that will or I shall have something to say to the man at the Pearly Gates.

Chapter Seventeen
The Wedding

'Where will you get married?' Mum wanted to know. She would be doing the flower arrangements for the bridal party and the church, floral art was her thing.

'In the Chapel at Mount Compass,' I replied. 'All our friends are at Mount Compass, Gwen's family live in Adelaide, we want to be among our friends when we make our vows.'

Gwen and I had made our plans,

'Where shall we go for our honeymoon?' Gwen had asked.

'How about we stay in a caravan in Adelaide? I suggested.

'Sounds a good idea, we cannot afford anything too posh.'

'I saw a caravan advertised the other day at West Beach, it sounded to just what we were looking for and at the right price.'

'That would be good.' Excitement filled Gwen's voice.

'I'll ride my Bantam from the Riverland and leave it at my Auntie's. We'll pick it up after the wedding and we can explore Adelaide then,'

'That sounds fun,' Gwen agreed.

Pete was my best man and Barbara Williams was Gwen's bridesmaid. Barbara was a teenage girl friend. They were closer than sisters were.

What do people do on their wedding eve? Get drunk; undertake a prayer vigil; go to bed early and dream of their bride?

I was too ill to do any of those things, asthma had returned to bedevil me after months of health in the Riverland.

'I think I'll stay here at Mum and Dad's for tonight. It's too wet to go home to the dairy and milk the cows.' Pete was glumly staring out the window looking at the grey sky from which sheets of water were pouring. A great start to a wedding.

'That's all right by us,' Mum was happy to have her boys together under her roof for perhaps one last time.

'My engagement's broken off; we should have been married before you,' Pete confided when we went to bed.

'Why has your engagement broken up?' I wanted only to go to sleep and be fit for the next day.

'I don't know. Wish I did,' Pete was broken hearted.

'Haven't you talked with your girlfriend?' I thought that was what should have happened.

'She's gone off somewhere or other and won't talk.' Pete groaned.

'Can't you go and find her.' I thought I would jolly well go and find my girl.

'No. I know she is the one for me. I can't live without her,' Pete reasoned long into the night. How I longed for the relief of sleep. The situation had the hallmarks of a stressful wedding day. The whole show went off brilliantly.

It was a justifiably white wedding. We both believed

in virginity. Since becoming a pastor, I have conducted weddings and been led to understand the participants were virgins but it was an empty statement. God is a forgiving God. I must be likewise.

Pastor Harry Manning conducted the service, do not ask me what he said, it was hard to concentrate and absorb his remarks. Three weeks later, he had passed away.

The gracious members of the home church provided the wedding feast with a lot of organising by Mum, Clare and Doris, Gwen's sister.

I remember the bride getting cheeky with several of the young lads who wanted to take a rise out of me. She threw some peanuts at them.

Much later, after the usual photo shoot in a studio in Adelaide, we arrived by taxi, at our supposedly romantic honeymoon rendezvous. Even arriving at the caravan was bedevilled, as the taxi driver got lost. The caravan was eventually located in someone's back yard.

'The van is not a bit like the depiction in the ad.' I was bitterly disappointed.

'Where's the key? It would be good to get inside and get warm.' Gwen's teeth were chattering with cold and fatigue.

'It's only an old plywood van,' I was still trying to get my head around that this van did not live up to the description of the advertisement.

'Come on, open up, its cold out here. It might be better inside.' Gwen's optimism was in vain. 'Why it's not even clean and there is no heater.'

'Can we make a hot drink?' I fumbled around for an electric jug in the semi dark and could only find a saucepan. 'What a dismal start to our romantic honeymoon first night.'

'We don't have to stay here in the van,' Gwen was trying to put a good spin on the situation; 'we can make the van a base and go exploring around Adelaide. We've got the Bantam BSA.'

A few months before our wedding I had bought a Bantam BSA motorbike, it was not brand new but it was mine, my very first vehicle.

I felt six feet high at the time.

'Yeah, guess you're right.' I conceded, glad we now had the Bantam.

In our wanderings, we came across a Baptist church at Semaphore with big, red neon cross on the front, a billboard beside the neon advertised meetings every night during that week. The speaker was a Welshman, Ivor Powell.

'Shall we go and stick our nose in?' I suggested.

'Why not,' Gwen eagerly replied. 'There isn't anything to keep us in this miserable excuse for a caravan.'

We went every night to hear him. Today I can tell the theme of his sermons. He could sure tell a story with power and conviction. We felt abundantly blessed. We forgave the caravan owner for cheating on us.

It has always stayed in my mind the night when he invited people to the front to accept Christ into their hearts. Two teenage girls wandered down the aisle giggling together as though they were going to a party.

'What are you girls doing?' Ivor stopped them in their tracks.

'We want to become Christians,' one said, batting her eyes at him.

'Yeah, we want to be better people,' the other chimed in smiling at Ivor, charmingly.

'No you don't. Neither of you intend to become Christians. If you did, you wouldn't be walking down here giggling. You'd be on your knees asking God to forgive you your sins.

Go back to your seats and think about what you want

to do,' the girls slunk back to their seats.

They had fallen in love with the good-looking Welsh preacher instead of the Lord Jesus Christ, their Saviour.

Many times in similar circumstances in my own ministry, I was encouraged to offer a similar challenge.

Our honeymoon was full of incidents, one was life threatening. We were

about to cross the Birkenhead Bridge in Port Adelaide on our Bantam and were following a huge petrol tanker. Our little bike would have fitted beneath the monster. As he was going so slowly I thought I should try to get ahead of him assuming he was crossing the bridge, I sped up to pulled out to pass him when he decided to turn in front of me.

Because of our smallness and his height, he had not seen us in his rear mirror. We found ourselves under his tray top; we could touch the tanker with our hands. All I could do was follow him around the corner and when it was safe, pull out from under him. We went back to our 'opulent' caravan to recover from the experience.

'Whew! Thank you Lord, for getting us out of that one,' I looked heavenward.

'Amen, we were nearly squashed,' Gwen's voice was very shaky.

'It wasn't our time for Heaven. The Lord didn't want us yet,' I can joke about it now even though I was shaking like a jelly at the time.

Chapter Eighteen
Double Harness

Working horses in double harness was a large part of my life, as a teenager. We would couple two horses together with a swing tackle that meant horses not necessarily the same height or size, could be worked together by adjusting the swing loading with the tackle.

Gwen and I soon learnt to adjust the loading in wedded bliss, sharing in the weight of responsibility in marriage, each according to our abilities or natural gifting and responsibilities. This proved priceless in later years as we sought to pioneer and mentor new church groups across South Australia.

After a few months of wedded bliss, renting a house from a church member, the harsh reality set in.

'We have decided to sell the house and property, you will need to find elsewhere to live.' our proprietor said when I paid our rent for the week.

That threw us into a spin. Where would we live? We looked about but nothing was offering.

'We've been thinking, seeing as you have to vacate the house so quickly we have three front rooms that you could use until you can find elsewhere,' the landlord offered.

'Ok. Thanks, very much we will accept your offer. We haven't been able to find anything as yet.' I said, still trying come to terms with the speed at which events happened. To be homeless was unexpected.

'It's pretty primitive,' Gwen looked around at the dismal sleep-out that was going to be the kitchen. No cupboards, kitchen sink, or floor covering.

'We can make this room the dining and lounge room. It's not too bad. The room across the passage can be our bedroom. That's not a bad sort of room.' I was pointing out the good things trying to hide my concern. Gwen was expecting our first child, Diane.

'It will get pretty hot during the summer,' Gwen commented despondently.

'We'll get something better as quickly as we can. Meantime we'll get a fan.'

'Mum, can you come up a week before my baby is born and stay until after it is born?' Gwen had asked her mother a month prior to the birth.

'I suppose I can. I don't know Bruce very well. Is he easy to cook for and look after?' Mum was a bit hesitant not knowing what was ahead of her.

When Mum was due to arrive, Gwen was on tenterhooks.

'Bruce, to give Mum some privacy let us move the piano so it will be like a partition. We'll put Mum's bed behind it. She can hang her clothes in my wardrobe.' Gwen worried that our living quarters would not be very comfortable for her mother. Next day was Saturday and I was to meet the bus at the winery and bring her home.

Morning came and I figured I had time to get a load of firewood before I had to meet Mum. While I was busy getting ready to go out Gwen informed me, 'I think the baby is coming. I have all the signs.'

'What?' my stomach churned. All my plans were out the window. 'Are you sure?'

'Yes, my case is packed, ready.' Gwen too was panicky. The big day had arrived. She had been expecting it a few weeks later, having misunderstood the doctor's prediction.

I went to start the old Morris Cowley that replaced the Bantam.

I cranked, pushed and pulled the choke, did everything I could to start the old bomb but it would not go.

I finally rang Alan, 'Can you come and take Gwen and me to the Barmera hospital, the baby's on the way and the old bomb won't start.' I hated to have to ask, my pride was hurting because I could not take my wife to hospital like a good husband.

We arrived at the hospital and the Sister met us at the door, reached out, took Gwen's case, and drew her into the hospital admission centre. 'I'll take her case and you can go. I'll let you know when you can come and see your wife and child.'

I faced the hospital door alone, wondering what would happen to Gwen. It was scary! The labour ward was out of bounds, in those days to husbands. Childbirth was women's business and husbands only got in the way.

At noon, I met the passenger bus from Morgan at the Berri Winery, on which Mum was travelling. In those days, she had to catch the train from Adelaide to Morgan and change to a bus at Morgan. It was an all day trip.

'Did you have a good trip up, Mum?' I helped her off the bus and gathered up her luggage.

'Yes, not too bad a bit tiring. How is Gwen?'

'She's great, Mum and so is Diane.'

'What! You mean the baby has arrived?'

'Yes. Gwen seemed to have got the dates mixed up and

Diane has arrived.'

Poor Mum, she nearly had a heart attack. Because of the mistake, Gwen had missed out the drag of those last weeks of pregnancy but Mum had landed in at the deep end feet first trying to find where every thing was kept and settling into a less than comfortable situation and a son-in-law she hardly knew.

When I visited Gwen for the first time, I feared at what I might find. Newborn babies always scared me. They seemed so fragile. Gwen, however, did not look too bad to me and I soon found that new babies were tougher than they looked. Diane's arrival was in June 1953. Parenthood was a steep learning curve, but we managed to rear Diane somehow.

The Boss took me aside one day soon after Diane was born,

'Bruce, I would like to do something to help you get a place of your own.'

'That's pretty good of you but we'll get something soon.'

'It would be good to get a place of your own wouldn't it?' Boss queried. He really did take an interest in us.

'I don't know what to say, Boss. I wouldn't be able to pay you back for a long time.'

'There is a block of land going cheap in Glossop. Supposing I stood you enough to buy the land and put a two roomed house on it. You would be on your own then instead of in a couple of rooms with no conveniences as you are now and you could pay me back a bit at a time.'

I was speechless. Why the Boss would do something like that for me, I could not understand.

Because it was a way to perhaps, get ahead and get something together for ourselves, I said,

'Yes.' I was so grateful to the Boss. I think if the Boss had said 'jump', I would have jumped as high as he wanted.

THE MAVERICK'S ROUNDUP

'We'll go to the saw-mill and get some sawn timber and Alan and I will help you build the house.' The kind of man I worked for was generous to the nth degree.

Red gum wood is hard and driving nails into it was like nailing cement. The wood twisted and would do so for the next ten years. The two rooms went up with a veranda across the back. Part of the back veranda became the laundry; the toilet was separate from the house. The neighbour on one side of us protested about a substandard house built next door. It would lower the resale value of his house. The neighbour on the other side was a motherly woman with a large family and took us under her wing.

We moved in to our own home.

It was not Buckingham Palace, more like a beach shack but we felt like the king and queen and had big dreams of how we would extend the house but again the dreams died as we struggled to make ends meet. Strangely, to this day, the house has not suffered any exterior renovations. It is as we left it.

Glossop was a small town of two hundred people straddling the old Sturt Highway halfway between Barmera and Berri. A General store, a garage and a Primary and High School and was next door to the Berri Winery, and several other businesses made up the town.

The town of Glossop commemorates the victory of the sinking of the German raider Emden during World War I by Vice Admiral J.C Glossop, Commander of HMAS Sydney. Today an anchor stands in front of the motel as a memorial to the commander.

To give my mother some free time, my younger brother Frank often came to stay with us during the school holidays. He had just reached his teens and I wanted to get to know him after being away from the family for several years. As we only had two rooms, he had to sleep in the main room, his bed across the front door.

One afternoon after being down to Lake Bonnie for a swim, we chugged home in my tired old Morris Cowly. We had met some friends while swimming and they followed us home for supper and chat. I asked Frank to go to the corner store and get a newspaper. He was very happy to do so; his pocket money was burning a hole in his pocket.

We were chatting and laughing as only the young can when a knock came on the front door, thinking that it was Frank returning from his errand, I yelled, 'Get around the back and don't be so stupid.' We all continued with our chatter, until seconds later an emphatic knock came on the back door. Silence - I went to the door and a very big man loomed up before me. I quaked as I recognised Sergeant Brock, Berri Police Force.

'Did you just come back from Barmera?'

'Yes,' I stuttered.

'Did you know that you only had one head light?'

'No, sir, I wasn't aware I only had one light.'

'Get it fixed!' he ordered abruptly and disappeared.

I returned inside. Feeling as though a bulldozer had run over me, after all, I had called the Sergeant of Police 'stupid.'

Frank walked in a few minutes later not realising what had just happened.

Well, we all managed to get over that little drama with Sergeant Brock and waited for the next one that might be just around the corner.

Learning to be in double harness together as parents proved a steep learning curve yet it was all part the plan of God. In our ignorance and zest for life we did not always think about any calling - it was enough to live and get by at this stage of our life.

Chapter Nineteen

At The Crossroads

To cross the river from Berri to Loxton meant a punt or ferry crossing. The fare to cross on the punt might have been a few cents but it meant that change had to be on hand. The punt always seemed to be on the other side when one needed to cross. In the 1950s, there were several high rivers, when the flats between Berri and Loxton were impassable.

'Bruce can you come and preach for us on Sunday?' The pastor of the Loxton Church of Christ was inviting me to preach for him in a couple weeks time.

'Yes, I can do that. That is if the river hasn't cut the road.' I said, wondering what to do if the high river coming down happened to cut the road across the Berri flats.

The appointed Sunday arrived; I pulled up at the punt at Berri, 'Is the road cut across the flats to Bookpurnong Hill?' I asked the punt operator.

'Yes, you won't be able to drive. Why, what's up?' he asked.

'I have to preach over there.' I explained, wondering what to do.

'You'd better forget the preaching bit. They'll have to do their own preaching today,' the punt operator grinned. I hurriedly found a phone box and rang the elder of the church explaining the situation.

'OK Bruce I'll come and meet you at Bookpurnong.'

I did not back out of the Lord's appointments. I collected my Bible, caught the punt across the river, rolled up my trousers with shoes tied around my neck, I paddled through a couple of kilometres of flooded river flats. As arranged, the elder met me and we arrived just in time for me to preach the sermon.

It was very tiring walking through water that was knee deep. The road was bituminised that was a plus. The incident provided me with my five minutes of fame in the local and church papers. Such admirable dedication caused comment; though I had not looked at it in that light – it was a principle of mine to keep appointments made in the Lord's service.

The year 1956 brought the 'big flood' and recognised as a one in a 200-year flood.

The flood became a battle between the force of nature versus the will of man and woman.

Floodwaters rose 30 feet above normal.

All block work ceased and all hands, tractors, scoops and mechanical shovels built banks trying to save the properties. Men and machines worked around the clock. 'Crash crews' were formed and stood by on red alert. Women worked around the clock to provide food and drink for the men. Acts heroism performed every day became part of the fight to save the towns and properties.

When the banks threatened to burst, the crash crews and equipment rushed to the scene to save the banks. Sometimes the workers just had to stand helplessly by and see the banks they had worked so hard to build collapse and their fruit blocks and houses disappear under water. At Renmark if the banks had broken, the town would have flooded to the ceilings. The water in Lake Bonny at Barmera rose 5 metres. All the locks were so far under water as to be invisible.

Such a big flood occurred because the rivers Murray and Darling flooded at the same time. Some contractors made a lot of money but the general community bore the cost gallantly.

The flood seemed to herald a time of change and development of God's Call in our life.

Frank Graetz, a fruit blocker and his wife, Sylvia, from Renmark became our very close friends. Frank was a quiet, steady man with an enquiring mind and passion for the Lord. He reminded me of Martin Luther an early reformer; once he latched on to a line of thought he was like a terrier, he never let it go until satisfied he had the truth. We would have many debates over Sunday lunches together after church, such as evangelism, does God heal and the Second Coming of Christ. Frank would pass on Christian literature for us to read. At first, we were cautious but gradually we began to adopt the new concepts confronting our minds.

Amongst Frank's literature was a catalogue of books from a bookshop in Sydney listed as the Evidence Bookshop.

'I wish we could buy some of these books, they look interesting,' Gwen commented browsing through the catalogue with longing eyes.

'Well why don't we spend that money we were given? I would especially like to get that book titled the 'Blood Covenant' by E W Kenyon. It's not very expensive and it might give me some good ideas for leading Communion.' I had already browsed through the list of books and had my eye on several titles.

'Yes, why not spend that money on books. It's not as

if we are wasting the money.' She was aware we had many other needs and felt a little guilty spending money on books. Gwen also planned to sell off some of the books and in turn buy more books and sell. In the end, she had a thriving book business.

'Let's make a list and then order them up,' because I was heavily involved in lay preaching and teaching I wanted some helps.

A few weeks later after I had preached an especially disappointing sermon we came home from church. I was tired and yes, feeling God had somehow let me down. All I wanted to do was to relax and have a read. We had picked up the mail in which was the box of books. The Blood Covenant was on top and I grabbed it eagerly,

'That's the one I wanted. Wonder what it's all about?' Sitting down I opened up the book while Gwen continued to look through the box.

An explosion took place in my mind. I glanced across at Gwen but she was still calmly sorting through the books.

I was sure the burst of enlightenment that flooded my mind should have affected her as well.

At that moment, I saw the entire work of Christ's sacrifice and my involvement in it and the place it held in my life. I saw positively that I had died when Christ had died and rose with Christ when he arose. Christ had given to me his righteousness. I was righteous now in God's sight, not because of what I had done or had not done but because of what Christ had done.

I needed to stop trying to be somebody I was not, stop trying to get it right every week or every day, and stop trying to pray or even preach my way to Heaven. The words, 'You are righteous now – it is done. Not by what you have or haven't done,' lit up my mind like neon lights. I could not understand why Gwen was ignorant of this momentous enlightenment.

I never finished reading that book - I did not have to. From that day forward, my preaching was with power not just words. Up to this time I would often become dejected and feel a certain sense of failure and I would remark to Gwen, 'I'm goin' to quit.'

'Why? You are doing OK!' She would encourage.

'No, I believe people should receive something from my preaching and they aren't.

'People like what you say,' she observed.

'What I say seems just a lot of words.' I complained. I knew there was something missing.

No more did I feel the sense of just speaking many empty words. Revelation of scripture opened up to me like a can of peaches. From now on, I would come home physically exhausted but spiritually knowing I had delivered a message and that it carried weight.

Using the words of an early Bible writer really explains what I felt, 'My preaching was very plain, not with a lot of oratory and human wisdom, but the Holy Spirit's power was in my words, proving to those who heard them that the message was from God.'

More revelations have occurred since that day but this one changed my preaching forever. Many books in the New Testament clearly explain the truth I received that day as a revelation. All the learning of scripture and study of the Bible throughout my life, were like seeds now bursting into life within my heart. I was bursting to preach.

One Sunday when I met Frank Graetz, he was so excited he could hardly wait for the service to be over.

'There's going to be an evangelist, Billy Adams, an American, visiting Adelaide,' Frank thrust a flyer into my hand.

'Ok. He sounds interesting,' I said glancing at the flyer

and thinking, 'Fat chance I have of hearing a preacher like him.'

'What say we both go down and check out what he's got to say?'

'I suppose we could,' at first, I was doubtful. I did not know if I wanted to hear somebody from what I termed 'a radically different faith'. In the end I agreed, 'Yes, why not.'

I had been supportive of evangelistic type preaching to this point. Three very outstanding preachers come to mind, men with very powerful messages of salvation: Mr Heinrickson and Mr Newman and Billy Graham with his message of a personal Saviour that rocked the world. People discovered they needed a saviour regardless of whether they belonged to a family of churchgoers or not.

To Frank and I, Billy Adams sounded to be inspirational. We discovered another aspect of worship and teaching we had never seen or heard before. The meetings were organised over eleven days by a group of people under the title of Christian Revival Crusade in Fullarton, Adelaide.

We found ourselves sitting in a big tent bursting with wall-to-wall people.

The worship, singing and praise of which I had never heard the like. They were quoting miracles of healing all the time. The final night saw 1300 people crammed into the tent. There were eighty-one decisions on the last night, 61 people were baptised by immersion in a canvas baptistery on the Saturday afternoon with a large group of people in attendance. These events startled Frank and me; we came home with more questions than answers.

'Well, what were the meetings like?' Gwen was excited she wanted to know
what happened?

'Honey, I've never seen the like. All types of healing

took place.

I've never heard preaching like that before and it was quite Biblical too.'

'I didn't think healing was for today.' Gwen remembered her earlier Bible training.

'That is what we've been led to believe but I tell you, God seemed to be at work in these meetings.' I was remembering the experience of the recent revelation I'd had when I read The Blood Covenant.

'Do you think God is trying to tell us something?' Gwen queried.

'I don't know but I'm not going to close my mind, because I don't want to miss what God has for us.' I felt that we were at a crossroads.

While the day-to-day labour on the fruit block went on, God on the other hand, seemed to be leading us away from the normal humdrum life of the traditional church into unknown areas. Gwen has always been a great prayer and she too was in uncharted waters in her prayer life.

At this time, we were living in three rooms built on the end of a block owner's shed consisting of a small kitchen and two small bedrooms. Because of many circumstances we had moved from our cottage at Glossop to a house on another property and then to these pickers quarters owned by Syd Moyle. The rooms were small, inconvenient and hard work for Gwen. We were now a family of three.

There had been a big highways camp a couple of miles away toward the little settlement of Winkie. The camp had closed down and the sleeping quarters and sheds were up for sale. I became curious and paid a visit to the site. My eyes popped: baths, stoves, chip bath heaters and whole rooms all abandoned. I rushed back to the Boss,

'Boss, there are buildings up for sale at the old highways camp. They would be good for building the pickers' quarters and the sheds you are planning.'

'Sounds like a good idea.' He saw the opportunity to acquire material cheap and gave me the go ahead to buy. This was an era when fruit blockers did not provide accommodation for their pickers and block hands.

With the acquisition of these buildings, the Boss saw the desirability of having permanent quarters for his pickers and building became a sideline for me. Alan and I had a lot of fun building pickers' quarters and sheds. Since arriving on the fruit block my tools had come out of the box and stayed out.

I approached Syd with a proposition, 'If I buy two of the rooms and a bath heater and bath can I put them up to make a bathroom for us and a lounge room beside your pickers' quarters for a bit extra room?' The rooms would not be exactly luxurious but certainly an improvement. Syd was agreeable; he saw the acquisition of building materials as an asset.

Syd was a stumpy man, a better mechanical inventor than a fruit blocker. He was extremely generous to Gwen and me. He had allowed us free rent of the three small rooms on the end of his shed plus the extensions. Often I would do odd jobs for him on weekends to repay his generosity.

If something went wrong, he became very vocal and the air turned blue with his remarks. If the tractor would not start he would cuss until the birds took to the air and the stray dogs ran home, and kick the hapless machine, but he was generous to a fault.

Syd's workshop was on the other side of our rooms with only a thin partition between.

We had two sweet little daughters by now, Diane and Robyn. Syd would have cut his tongue out rather than swear in front of them.

THE MAVERICK'S ROUNDUP

Because of poor drying seasons, Syd decided to build a dehydrator in his shed for drying his grapes. He produced grapes dried on the stem known as London Layers. The London Layers graced the tables on the luxury ocean liners and hotels for the guests and the wealthy.

Syd was a bush engineer and mounted a huge fan to push the hot air through a steel tunnel. A smaller fan blew air into an oil-fed furnace.

When the dehydrator was running, there was a constant roar for 24 hours a day for several weeks. Gwen and the kids had to live with it during that time.

Living in this situation, we came face to face with danger. One night we came home from a meeting. It was a hot, stormy night and thunder rolled across the sky. One loud clap sounded very close.

'You get the girls settled into bed, Gwen and I'll make a cuppa.' I suggested.

'Ok. I hope the storm doesn't wake them up - it sounds very near.' Gwen worried, after tucking the girls into bed, adding, 'we had better wait and see if they settle down properly, before we go to bed.'

We each picked up a book to read while we drank our coffee and waited,

'That clap sounded like a lightening strike,' I observed, looking up at the ceiling.

'Yeah,' Gwen looked up from her book.

The lights flickered and went out and in seconds were back; the dehydrator stopped momentarily then started again.

'Did both fans cut in?' I commented after bit, I was sure one of the fans had not started up because the sound was different.

'Yes I think so.' Gwen was vague. She was used to the roar.

'I think I'll go and have a look.' I felt concerned.

'It'll start in a minute, it always does.'

'I want to make sure before I go to bed.' I got up and went around to the shed.

What I saw sent shivers down my spine. The fan that blew oil onto the fire had not restarted and burning oil was running across the floor toward our flimsy rooms. I rushed across the yard to report to Syd. He too, was white faced when he entered the shed and saw the burning oil. Because we could not use water to put out the flames, we had to bring in shovelfuls of sand to put out the flames. Had we gone to sleep… well the idea of what might have been is horrendous.

Syd closed down the dehydrator until he could fit a solenoid switch that would automatically switch off the machine when the power failed. Another thing, asbestos had been used to build the sheds where our quarters were located. God certainly had his hand on our family and us. The guardian angels were doing overtime caring for us that night.

The question arose, 'Did you put your family under the covering of Christ's blood at the beginning of every day?'

'Well no, I didn't because I believe I'm under the covering of God all the time. Living in Christ and Christ living in me does not mean I have to call on God continually to keep me and mine from danger. God has promised never to leave us at any time and that is enough, I do not have to keep on asking.'

'How can you be so confident of what God will do?' The question arises.

'Because I know Christ is living in me I am confident of his covering. That frees me from having to strive all the time to do what I think God wants. It gives me the freedom to just be,' I reply with boldness.

Chapter Twenty
Society's Underbelly

Talk about knocks on my door – the surprise this time on opening the door was finding a good-looking young Aboriginal man facing me and wearing a great big army overcoat.

'Can I talk to you, Brother Bruce?'

'Sure, come in. What's the problem, Harry?'

With no further conversation, he began to empty his pockets onto the kitchen table, a big block of chocolate, a large slab of sultana cake, two packets of biscuits, and a large paper bag of sweets.

'I just pinched these from the Glossop store. I feel very bad. I think I should own up but if I do the shop keeper will report me and I'll get picked up by the police and gaoled.'

'Ok. Put them back in your pocket, we are going back to the store.' I wondered why Harry chose me as his confessor. It occurred to me that making him face the shop owner might just cause him not to repeat the exercise again.

'Harry's got something to show you,' I said the shop owner.

'Why, what's he got?' The owner wondered what an

Aboriginal man had to show him. Surprise, anger, flitted across that man's face as Harry began to empty his pockets onto the counter.

'How did you manage to steal all those things without my knowing?' he growled.

'Easy, I asked for something that you had to go out the back to get.' Harry had the grace to look ashamed. The storekeeper gave Harry a big lecture and let him off.

It is great to see people convicted - it means they do have a conscience. It means God is not finished with them.

I have heard the Holy Spirit described as the Hound of Heaven.

A good name because the Holy Spirit seeks out the human strays, not letting up until conviction sets in and the lost ones return to God.

Harry was one of those people whom I sensed the Holy Spirit pursuing and was just one of many who emerged onto our radar screen from society's underbelly as we pursued the Call among the indigenous.

I poured out my heartache to Gwen as we sat over a meal,

'I will never be able to express the despair and sense of rejection felt by this branch of society. These people were, and in many cases still are, the saddest and most broken people I have ever met. To be able to pick them up and rehabilitate them is one of the biggest challenges we face in our call.'

'One of our hurdles is overcoming the belief that Jesus is a white man's God that he is not for the Aboriginal people. They believe in the Law with its signs and wonders. Why believe in Christianity that, in their eyes, has no power.' Gwen pointed out, adding 'The second hurdle is alcohol and the third hurdle is immorality.'

'My greatest regret in life is the many young men who

we can't seem to help and despite all our attempts are dying in total despair,' I felt frustrated and heartsick.

'It's true. Virtually, a whole generation, some of whom are really wonderful young men of the 20 – 35 age groups, are dead,' Gwen agreed.

'They have died through a multiple of doubtful actions or rather non-action by Governments and the community. Drunken brawls are just so common and the result of loss of status and nothing to do,' I said. There was no place or standing in the community for Aboriginal people. They were never employed or educated, just given handouts for a subsistence living.

Only the missionaries worried about educating Aboriginal kids. The Aboriginal people were certainly society's underbelly in that era.

Sometimes the phone would ring and Auntie Dora would ask me to mediate between brawlers. One day I arrived at Dora's camp after she had phoned me for help. I found a man sitting on a bed in a fighting mood, cursing his wife. He held a piece of board three feet long by four inches wide with three three-inch nails driven through it.

'What are you doing with that piece of board, Keith?' I quietly questioned him, taking the board away. 'Now sit down,' I spoke to him kindly.

Dora and I prayed for him, he wept buckets of tears and things simmered down. As I turned to leave, I brushed against the door that was hanging by a leather strap nailed to the shack with one nail. Thinking that the door was dangerous in that state, I ripped it off and stood it back out of the way.

Keith erupted like a volcano, 'you are a %&*% so and so and don't touch my #@%! door.'

I was taken aback at his abrupt change of mood, he hadn't turned a hair when I took the board away and told him to sit down, yet here he was tracing my ancestry over making the door safe. Dora took Keith's wife back to her camp until he could sleep it off.

I would like to point out just for the fun of it that I am the second son and nothing like Keith intimated. I am also born again as a child of the King of Kings who does not have any illegitimate children or even grandchildren.

Living several hundred miles down river from Berri, an Aboriginal couple existed. They were alcoholics and practically always drunk. They certainly did not believe in Christianity.

'We heard that there was a revival at Berri and God told us to come,' Annie giggled.

'Yeah, it was weird. We didn't have any money but anyway we set out and when night came we camped in an isolated tin shed.' Jack interrupted Annie.

Annie took up the story again, 'It was in the middle of the night, something fell on the roof, and it woke us up. We were really frightened because there was nobody or nothing around us and we couldn't understand why something fell on our roof.'

Jack butted in again, 'When we got up and walked outside to have a look and see what happened, we found a small gold religious medallion lying on the ground by the hut.'

'Yeah,' Annie agreed taking up the story, 'we knew we had to get up to Berri because God was speaking to us and was going to do something in our lives,'

When they arrived at Dora's shack, I went over to meet them. I was sitting on the running board of Jack's old buckboard talking to Annie. Jack, already drunk, had heard somebody was talking to his woman and he was roaring around the camps with an axe threatening to kill whoever it was.

Being white, I was unable to hide in the dark.

However, when he did catch up with me he dropped the axe and behaved like a lamb.

Later this couple accepted Christ and became a great support to our ministry. We saw God work among the Aboriginal people with many signs and miracles like this couple about whom I have just written.

It soon became obvious that our ministry would be much more than spiritual, what these people needed was honest direction in living in every way and friends to help them accomplish it. This period of Aboriginal Welfare was very weak to almost non-existent. Frank Graetz and I were always at war with Aboriginal Welfare Officers.

The influence of the Christian Missions Australia wide, foundered when governments intervened and took over, installing the reserves, and mission stations installing managers. With extra money the means buy old cars made it easier for Aboriginal people to travel. They were not semi-isolated any more. Alcohol became more prevalent carried on to the missions hidden in taxis and hollowed out loaves of bread, or by other means. The government protection of Aborigines was a joke.

I began to understand what Christ must have felt as he cried over Jerusalem saying, 'How many times I would have liked to gather you as a hen gathers her chickens under her wings, but you would not.'

Our hearts cried out in the same way, 'Where is the political punch to do something?' I met Mr Robin Millhouse many times in an effort to change legislation and make changes that would treat these people as human beings. Alas, for one entire generation any sort of help was too late.

Through the Welfare Committee established in the Riverland by local doctors and clergymen, Frank Graetz and I approached Premier Don Dunstan requesting a change to policies concerning Aboriginal people.

The local Welfare Committee agreed to a partial lifting of the ban on alcohol, instead the government lifted the ban over the whole state, even in the tribal areas. This was a drastic mistake because the people in the remote areas were not ready for it. I wonder how many mothers and grandmothers lost everything by that decision and had to care for the extended family. The senior elders became alcoholics and gave no leadership. The women assumed the responsibility for family and community to try to maintain the culture and the Law, and still do in many remote areas.

One tough male elder commented on my efforts to win these people and lift them up; 'Bruce is always trying to round us into heaven.'

'Yes, if I could round up you people, my friend, with a shotgun to get you into heaven and give you all hope in a new life I would do so.' I replied.

Inside of two weeks, I was holding him up beside the grave of his son who had taken his own life with a shotgun. I still hurt with a deep hurt at the waste of life. Though I willingly followed my call amongst these people, yet I seemed helpless to help against such terrible problems.

Despite the problems we faced we did not flinch from the Call. I remembered Paul, one of the founders of the early church, his story is recorded in the biblical records, received a call to, 'Come over into Macedonia and help us.'

The people of Macedonia were anxious to hear about Jesus Christ. We received the same call, 'Come down to Meningie. We want to have meetings down here.' Meningie was 400 kms away.

'Come up to Robinvale, we need you up here.' That town was over 300 kms away.

'We live in Dareton. There are no meetings here.' That

community was 200 kilometres away.

'Wish you could hold meetings in Balranald.' That town was 400 kilometres away. I had to work five days a week and sometimes six on the fruit block to make ends meet. Frank had to manage his own fruit block at Renmark. Dora was keen to answer the call and so was her brother Gerry Mason from Gerard Mission, the mission was 30 kilometres away.

In an effort to answer the Macedonian calls - through the cooler months we would do at least one trip a month to of the above-mentioned places over a weekend. That meant leaving wives and kids behind most times. The logistics were enormous. We had to carry bedding, food, and music. Frank, in the end, bought a big International Van. It was a glorified bus fitted out with seats in the back. How he paid for the petrol to run it is a miracle of provision by the Lord. We never received any monetary help from the Aboriginal people or anyone else for that matter. They could not give what they did not have. It was by God and guts that we pushed ahead to follow our Calling to preach Christ and him crucified.

Robinvale was a new fruit block settlement. When you first entered town it appeared to be very prosperous. However, there was a sub-culture of Aboriginal people. The local Council had moved them three times, the latest site was in and around the refuse dump and local sawmill. It was hard to find them, nobody knew where they were, and we eventually located them.

Our policy was to set up a meeting place in a suitable spot, collect firewood and start a bonfire. The nearby sawmill allowed us to use off cuts for our fire here at Balranald. Our musicians would bring out the accordions and guitars and begin to sing once the fire was burning. The marquee went up next and then the seating was arranged; just on dark the crowd would begin to gather and the meeting would be under way, finishing with the preaching.

Advertising was unique. Jack, who had chased me with an axe, was now the forerunner. He and Annie would set out several days ahead of the planned trip, pick up bottles on the way and pay for their trip from the proceeds. As they went, they told everyone, 'Bro Bruce and Frank are coming.' Theirs was a very special ministry and they were faithful for many years.

'Enlarge your tents, strengthen your stakes,' Isaiah. Chapter, 54: a Biblical text kept burning in our hearts like a fire. We would cry to the Lord, 'How big can we get? How far can we go?' There did not seem to be an an asking of, 'You've gone far enough.'

One long weekend Frank and I set out for Balranald to find out how interested the Aboriginal people living there might be. We had not yet visited Balranald. We found a little old galvanised iron church on the edge of the Aboriginal camp. The missionary woman living in the town and travelling out to the settlement regularly, was very elderly and after twenty-five years, she had called it quits. We trod a path to her door as directed by a local. This brave, intrepid woman was packed, ready to leave, her bed was the last item unpacked. When Frank and I knocked on her door, she burst into tears, 'My prayers have been answered.'

'How come?' I asked.

'I've been praying that someone would come and take my place.'

'We can't exactly take your place. We live three hundred and fifty kilometres away,' Frank explained our situation. 'It would be impossible to come here very often.'

We also found a lovely senior woman in the community with a family of eight. Stone deaf and living in the midst of a drunken community, this woman had kept her faith and raised a voice for the Lord in a wilderness of hopelessness by teaching Sunday school. She was so thrilled to find that somebody cared and wanted to help.

We then organised a team to return to Balranald. There were several teenagers included in the party as well. We were sleeping on the floor of the little tin church and eating there as well. Sometime after midnight, a riot started up outside the church. It sounded like all the demons of hell were loose.

'Lock the doors and windows,' I ordered, 'and no one go outside.'

The drunks banged on the tin walls, yelling and cursing at us to let them in but we remained silent. Eventually peace reigned, by now the night was almost over.

Our young people faced initiation into what life without Christ really meant and the memory of that night would surely last them a lifetime, yet good people live in these circumstances and rear their children; they live with abusive husbands and wives. Sometimes it is necessary to see the work of evil to make an informed decision for life. Next morning all was quiet and we had no more trouble and made many new friends. 'Come back again,' the people clambered. We did, many times after that.

One trip to Robinvale a delegation of Aborigines met us with a strange request. 'In three days a big mob of government officials are coming to interview us about housing, would you two guys be able to come back and represent us and put our case for us.'

Wow! Go home, ask for time off, and then come back on Wednesday, still camping all the way, an impossibility.

'Yes, we'd love to,' we tried to sound like we did but it was the second long trip in a week. We returned and were successful in our representation.

The first major housing projects in VIC came from that meeting. People received plots of land and new houses made of cement slabs for roof, walls and floors surrounded by fences. The houses may not have been the Ritz but they were a tad above the shacks built from material from the dump. Later, the people could move into the town into regular housing.

'Why don't we hold a street meeting?' I suggested during one trip to this town.

'Yeah, what a good idea,' some firebrand enthused.

'We'll need to square it with the Police first,' I did not want the team to fall foul of the powers that be. We received permission. We had a great musician in the team that day. Harry was self-taught and brilliant on the piano, accordion, banjo and guitar, drunk or sober. Just listen for the music and you will find Harry.

This trip he was playing Gwen's accordion and was playing up a storm, in between short talks by some of the team and me.

A milkman's delivery Ute drove down the street and the driver leaned out of the window and threw two shillings at us. The coin rolled into the gutter. Quick smart I yelled at him, 'you can't buy salvation. Jesus has already paid for it.'

The 'milky' heard me and pulled into the curb and came back and joined the crowd. When the meeting broke up he asked, 'What happened to the two bob?'

'I haven't a clue.' I shrugged. Nobody owned up to picking it up.

I was glad to be able to say I didn't know. What I do know was two Aboriginal men surrendered their life to Christ in the main street at that meeting.

We were not able to go back again for several months and I was curious to know what had happened to Syd and his mate.

THE MAVERICK'S ROUNDUP

When we did return I found that Syd miraculously became a non-drinker, he had obtained a job and rented a flat in town.

He then persuaded his mother to leave the alcohol-riddled camp and live with him in his flat. That was until he succumbed to a tumour and died. Syd is on my list for a high five when I meet him in glory. My God is able to keep you if you trust in him.

Among our many friends in Balranald, lived Sam and one thing he could do besides drink was carve emu eggs. I bought one each for my Dad and my sister-in-law. They both have passed on, the eggs are mine and very valuable today. Sam's hands so misshapen and crippled with arthritis yet he could hold an egg and a pocketknife and carve scenes like there was no tomorrow.

On one visit, he gave me a young joey kangaroo. I brought it home and made a yard for it. Joey escaped one day, we traced him to the main Winkie road. 'Robyn, come and help me catch Joey,' I said and we jumped into the car and chased him up the road. When the roo sat up, Robyn hopped out and put her arms around his neck to hold him until I could catch hold of his collar. We bundled him into the car somehow, his legs and tail were hard to contain. Robyn held onto him as best she could until he was safely in his yard. Joey seemed to sense that Rob was an animal lover and allowed her to handle him.

'Dad, there is a Pet Show being held in Berri,' Robyn was excited. 'Can we take Joey along?'

'No, I don't think so. How are we going to get him there?' I did not think much of the idea.

'Aw, come on Dad,' the other children chorused. 'We could put him in the boot.'

'He's too big.' I still was not very happy.

'Come on, Dad. He'll be all right in the boot.'

'Ok,' I relented. The kids were over the moon. Saturday dawned, Joey was stowed in the boot of the car somehow and we drove the few miles to the Pet Show. Joey was a hit.

The judge stood up to announce the winner and every one gathered around wondering and hoping that it would be their pet to win the prize.

'First prize goes to Joey the kangaroo.' The judge announced with a cheesy grin.

Our kids jumped up and down with joy. We had to get Joey home again. I decided to nurse him and Gwen could drive, the three older children sat in the back with Diane nursing baby Raymond. Folding Joey's tail and back legs into the car was like trying to stow away a blown-up balloon - just when you thought you had control of his legs his tail would escape or if his tail was controlled his back legs would break loose. I think first prize should have been award to me, all the trouble I had to get Joey to the Pet Show and home again.

I digress, my thoughts return from the vagaries of kangaroos to motorcars. About the time when we answered what we think of as the Macedonian Call and started to visit Aboriginal camps along the river, I owned a Fiat car. It was a great car in many ways, but it had one weakness, the bolts on the clutch housing kept coming loose from the block. I longed for a reliable car. Alan, at that time owned a Morris Minor 8 HP that was very reliable. It made me commit the sin of envy.

Somebody had told me that I must be specific when I ask the Lord for something.

It sounded a bit ho-hum to me. She Who Did the Praying around our house pinned me down, 'What do we believe for?'

'I'd like a light blue Morris 1000.' I said dreamily, envisaging myself behind the wheel of such luxury.

THE MAVERICK'S ROUNDUP

'Red upholstery would look nice,' You Know Who was also dreaming of doing the weekly shopping in style.

'Bit flash for us, isn't it?' It all seemed out of our reach, but I dreamed on.

'Let's take the family for a ride,' I suggested, 'after I tighten the bolts on the clutch housing once more.'

'Where are we going, Dad?' the kids shouted and Gwen started organising everyone into clean clothes.

'Renmark, we haven't been up there for a while.' I had an ulterior motive in mind. Wandering around the street, I steered the family to the Morris car yard. In the window of the salesroom was a pale blue Morris 1000 with red upholstery! I entered the showroom and walked around our dream. A salesperson, all business and bustle came along, 'Can I help you, sir?'

'Yes, you can. I'll buy the Morris 1000 if you will give me enough for the Fiat out front.'

The salesperson gulped, he was not used to a customer being so up front. Then came a lot of chatter - chatter, like,

'Sir, how much a week do you earn?'

'Well, so much.'

'Does your wife work?'

'Er- no, she doesn't.'

'Well, sir, I don't think we can let you have the car. You wouldn't be able to keep up the payments.'

'Of course, I do lots of weekend work.' I did not tell him it did not pay very well.

'I don't know,' the salesperson was very doubtful. He reached for the forms and we signed up for the Morris 1000 with the pale blue duco and the red upholstery. We drove home feeling a million dollars and left the Fiat behind, my first new car.

When I went to work on Monday morning, Alan informed me that the school where our children attended needed a cleaner. The school was in a Soldier Settlement area and only people with connections to return soldiers could apply. Both Gwen and I had returned service people in our families and though we were newcomers to the area Gwen decided to apply for the job and she got it. The wage from the cleaner's job just covered the car payment exactly. Gwen was able to keep the job until the car was ours.

So pray specifically! God wants to bless you according to your heart's desire; he is much bigger than we are. God had an agenda in giving us our desire. The new car became a packhorse to tow a trailer with gear for a weekend travelling to the indigenous camps up and down the river. Society's blot that most people were ignorant of - never reported on or barely given much thought to by Governments unless pushed.

Chapter Twenty-One
The Testings

Gwen is pregnant again. Number three. We were still living in the pickers' quarters on the end of Syd's shed. How did it happen I wondered.

She became very ill with the German measles or Rubella. It was not until the doctor was called on a home visit was there any suspicion of pregnancy, which was confirmed later when she was well enough to visit the surgery.

Then came the awful diagnosis, the child could be seriously affected. The pregnancy was at the very crucial stage of seven weeks. Termination of the pregnancy was suggested. A second opinion was sought a pastor was confided in, and everyone unanimously agreed a termination of the pregnancy was best. A tough decision to make, for who wanted to bring into the world a child with serious disabilities?

When our emotions settled and we could weigh faith against logic, Gwen felt strongly that she should not terminate the pregnancy believing that God had given his word and that she was to take the situation by faith. We confided in my sister Clare, training then as a nurse. She was not in favour of termination, believing that God was sovereign and had a plan. She was the only one to stand with us.

The pregnancy went well and in some ways was easier than the previous two. Diane was four and Robyn two years old.

When the baby arrived, the doctor very quickly checked him out to see if there were any of the feared disabilities. Yes, the baby was a son, Philip, a very healthy child. He is now a happily married man with four grown children of his own.

A new GP took over the surgery in Barmera where we attended. When Gwen was visiting him concerning some health issue he asked,

'I see you terminated a pregnancy, Mrs Leane, why is that?'

'I contracted rubella in the early stages of pregnancy and was advised to have a termination. But in the end we decided not to terminate the pregnancy but continue and have the child.'

'How is he? He has not been to the surgery; I have attended your other three children but not Philip.'

'Yes, he is Ok and healthy,' Gwen replied.

Our God did not let us down. He kept faith with us and kept his promise.

When Philip was two years old, Sylvia Graetz became pregnant with twins. Concern for the pregnancy meant Sylvia was not such an active member of our team amongst the Aboriginals. We were one musician short and so Gwen felt even with only a limited amount of musical training maybe she could learn to play the accordion. She acquired a small, black, shiny accordion. The squawking and squealing nearly drove me mad. She finally retired to the shed to practice. One night when I came home from work, she met me at the door,

'I've cracked the code. I know how to play the accordion.' She was jubilant. So was I. The caterwauling coming from the shed sounded like a tune at last. From then on Gwen started to play along with the other musicians, becoming more accomplished as time went by.

Identical twin sons were born to Frank and Sylvia. They rejoiced together over their baby boys but only hours after the birth a cerebral haemorrhage occurred and Sylvia lapsed into a coma for three weeks from which she never recovered.

Brenton and David were beautiful bonny red headed boys. Frank was now alone to bring up two girls and three boys. It does not get much tougher than that. He was a man adrift, with only his faith in a faithful God. However, Frank did his grieving quietly pushing on with his block work to support his family. He had one prayer and that was to keep the family together.

Gwen offered to take the twins and care for them along with our three. May, Frank's twin sister gave support with clothes and extras. Frank himself did what he could to support, which meant that most weekends Gwen had two men and eight children to care for. She continued to clean the school requiring Diane and Robyn to care for the twins wheeling them around in their pusher.

During the holidays when extra cleaning was required at the school, Frank would come and give a hand. He wanted to keep contact with his little boys because he hoped to take them back into his family circle at some future stage. So bringing up the twins became a team effort.

With extended families, transporting our families became a problem.

'I'll have to get a bigger car, my family has grown too big for the Morris,' I mentioned to Frank as we sat over a meal while the kids were out playing.

'Well the other day I saw a Volkswagen Ambulance van for sale. It'd be just the thing for you. What say I buy it and we swap cars,' Frank suggested.

'I don't know,' I was hesitant for Frank to spend the money.

'I think it's only fair. You are caring for the twins and must have extra room. My family can fit into your car,' Frank pointed out. The ambulance came complete with sirens and fittings. The van stripped later was adapted as a family vehicle.

Through all the difficulties of our personal lives, we managed to continue to follow the Call amongst the Aboriginal people. Sylvia's illness and later death caused us all to ask many question over whether God heals today or whether healing is for another era.

I do not agree with the idea that sickness is the result of sin and that Sylvia's death was the result of sin in her life. There was no lack of prayer offered for her healing, the entire Christian community in South Australia was praying. God took her home for reasons of his own. It is one of God's best-kept secrets as to why He took her home. One day it will become clear.

Human nature always wants to lay the blame on something or somebody when God does not answer prayer according to our dictates. We are not here to manipulate God for our own gain.

'I have prayed for people and they have been healed. But then I have prayed and they have not been healed.' I pondered the question many times using Gwen as a sounding board.

'I believe God heals but why everyone isn't healed is more than I can answer,' Gwen agreed.

'If as some believe, it is part of Calvary's redemptive

work then why aren't people healed when they are born again? I believe it is part of redemption and only completely fulfilled when we reach Heaven.' I pondered aloud.

God heals today, yes! I believe in a supreme God who does great miracles in response to our faith and trust regardless of who we are or what we are.

We are all living to die sometime and God holds that time in his hands.

Sylvia was one of the most generous, quiet, talented people I ever knew - her passing was a great loss.

Frank did not quit; he pushed on with his life. His aging mother came and lived with the family for a long time to help with the older children. When Rita, Sylvia's sister returned from teaching at a girl's school in Africa, romance blossomed and flowered into wedding bells for Frank and Rita. Rita became an instant mother to five children because Frank's dream of his little boys residing under his roof had come true when he took the twins home. A son Adrian was born to Rita and Frank later. Top marks to Rita for having a heart big enough to pick up a large readymade family.

Though none of us realised it at the time, changes were afoot. Frank and Rita would settle back into fruit blocking, Frank would lead a prayer group while we would move on to other pastures and our two families would grow apart.

Sylvia's death brought into focus prayer and fasting and its relevance and power; Gwen at one time put in much time fasting but for me my workload was very intense and I was unable to take part. We both agree today, fasting is not a means to blackmail God into action but a way of setting one's self apart, to hear more clearly what God has to say. Many may disagree with this but this is our story.

Though Sylvia had passed away, the work amongst Aboriginal people went on in the local area. The Call had gripped us and no matter how we were hurting; we could not forsake the Call.

During the fruit-picking season, many Aboriginal people would leave the Gerard Mission and come into the settlement of Winkie and surrounding settlements to earn a bit extra money.

The blockers were glad of the people to harvest their fruit but they almost never, in those days, provided accommodation for Aboriginal people. The people had to live in sheds with no amenities and where there was no shed, the people built humpies in the scrub. The blockers would then grumble that the people were polluting the water channels and littering the scrub with rubbish.

As well as Sunday morning services across the river at Dora and George's place, we established Sunday night services in our tent in a central area of scrub in Winkie during harvest time. The services could end either in a riot or revival or both.

We would never know the size of our congregation; people would be hiding in the mallee scrub listening.

Harry, whom I have mentioned before, would wait until I began to preach and then he would imitate the caller at the horse races in top voice. We would then sing choruses until he grew tired and quit or else, overcome by the grog, went to sleep.

During our visitation rounds, one day, Dora and I came upon a bitter inter tribal fight. We jumped out of the car and weighed in with our tongues.

'What's the matter with you blokes?' Auntie Dora, shrieked above the yells and thuds

'Hey!' I too entered in, 'what's got under your saddles, that you are half killing each other?'

'Those #$%* blackfellas from the West Coast have come over here to work and have taken our women,' a

THE MAVERICK'S ROUNDUP

voice croaked from beneath a battered face.

'We don't like the blackfellas from around here,' the West coast men swore.

'You're a mob of idiots,' I rebuked them. 'I could get the police to come and lock the lot of you up before you kill each other.'

'Yes, you could kill somebody. Then you'd be in real trouble. Brother Bruce and I will pray for you.' Auntie Dora was at her queenly best, so we prayed, the fighters wilted.

'OK, Auntie Dora,' the men shuffled from one foot to another and looked anywhere but at us.

'Promise me you'll quit now and go home?' Dora glared at them

'Yes, Auntie Dora.' They muttered reluctantly one at a time.

Dora and I drove off around the scrub,

'I bet if we go back now, they'll be fighting again,' Dora predicted.

'I'll swing past them and see what they're up to.' I swung the car around and returned to the arena of war. Sure enough, they were trading punches, bottles and sticks, amid dust, barking dogs, and screaming women.

'Let the silly fools kill themselves, come on Bruce, we'll pay a visit elsewhere,' Dora shrugged in resignation and we continued on our way.

About on dusk, I said to Dora, let's go and see how the war's going?'

'Yes, see who's dead.'

We found men under bushes nursing sore heads; some were under tarpaulins mopping up blood. Black eyes abounded - it looked a casualty zone. The doctor at Barmera would be up all night and the next day, stitching up the wounded combatants. For his efforts and sleepless night there would be no pay. The people had nothing to pay him, and the Government refused saying he must bill the people and they must submit the bill to the Government. The people would toss the bill into the fire not knowing what to do with it and the Doc would write off the consultation as a bad debt. Frustrated, he told the Government to stick their policy he was not going to waste money sending another bill.

On one occasion I was alone and facing a tough situation.

The Winkie General Store was isolated from other businesses, and closed being after hours. Fortunately, the phone box was outside of the store. I needed to reach the police but discovered I had no coins. I went inside the box anyway, wondering how I could get a message through. When I got inside, there were enough coins on the bench to make the call. I then noticed just outside the door a half flagon of wine.

I made the call and spoke to Sergeant Brock from Berri. I stated my business and then said, 'There's a half flagon of wine just outside the phone box shall I tip it out?'

'No, don't be seen tipping it out. You don't know whose watching or what they'll do. Put it in front of the door so that when you leave the door will knock it over and it'll look like an accident,' the Sergeant advised. The police were always supportive of our work and ready to come if we needed help.

We were all under pressure and tested in many ways. Dora and George came face to face with tragedy.

'A phone call for you Bruce,' June, Alan's wife called. I was picking oranges near the house. Alan did not like me getting phone calls and I did not like receiving them either while at work. Such calls almost never brought good news. I have never like phone calls full stop. To a pastor they can

THE MAVERICK'S ROUNDUP

be very invasive.

'Bruce, could you please come over the river?' Dora's distraught voice came down the line.

'What's wrong?' I wondered who had been murdered or gaoled this time.

'Charlie, (not his real name) and Bill (not his real name) had a fight and Charlie hit Bill with a piece of wood. Bill has died and Charlie is up for murder. They were drinking together.'

'Ok, I'll come over and talk to Charlie.' Two more families shattered. I could not do anything but just be there and try to pick up the pieces.

'Brother Bruce, I'm so sorry. I never meant to kill him.' Charlie sobbed. He was distraught.

'If you hadn't been drinking it wouldn't have happened,' I suggested.

'Yeah I was only going to have one glass, but I couldn't stop after that. I don't know what got into me.'

'I do. The booze sent you off your head.' I stated.

'He was my best mate.' The tears flowed down his cheeks. Charlie went to prison and our paths never crossed again.

There is yet another incident, involving a very tall, broad shouldered Aboriginal, Fred, very placid by nature until riled then look out! Fred drove onto the Berri punt in his old V8 utility. He and his wife were nearly sitting on the floor the springs worn out with the two heavy weights sitting on them daily.

Some local louts leaning on the gates, decided to have some fun at Fred's expense,

'I wish these $#% boongs would clear out and stop clogging up the punt,' Mr Fancy Pants sneered.

'Come over here and repeat that statement,' Fred, straight faced, beckoned to them.

'What do you want, boong,' Mr Fancy Pants mocked sidling up to the utility.

Fred opened the door unfolding himself to his full height. With one hit, Fancy Pants was on the deck. Fred dusted his hands looked at the microbe at his feet, jumped in his utility and drove off the punt by which time had crossed the river. Funny, the story never made the local newspaper but it made news over the Aboriginal grapevine and fast.

Sitting on the punt on another occasion, I was listening to two young men discussing in front of a Police Constable where the 'goom' and 'munthum' were hidden, meaning wine and methylated spirits. The constable was blissfully ignorant but I caught on. I drove off the punt and pulled up alongside of them, 'Boys, I know where your grog is. You'd better be careful what you say in front of people.'

'Aw, Brother Bruce, we didn't see you. We'll be careful next time.' they laughed, but worried all the same if I would report them.

'Boys, don't you think it would be a good idea not to have that booze-up. It will get you into trouble.' I suggested. I did not want to destroy the bridges that I had built up by reporting them. I needed to challenge them though, let them know where I stood. I also wanted to get to know them better and be able to influence them for good.

It was another instance when I nearly got myself into trouble. One Saturday afternoon I believed I should pay a visit to a very big, loud voiced and colourfully dressed woman. Her shanty was a place of ill repute. As I lifted my hand to knock on the door I, thought I would have some fun and called out in Aboriginal language, 'Policeman coming.' The house shook from roof to foundations with the frenetic movement inside. People jumped out the back window, burst though the back door, then silence reigned and the front door opened.

'You!' The woman of the house could hardly contain her anger when she saw me standing at the door.

'What's the matter,' I gave a strained laugh.

'Don't you ever do that again, Bruce, or I'll get you.' the woman threatened. I knew I had done a very dangerous thing just thinking to take a rise out of that particular person.

I did not repeat the exercise but I also did not regret what I had done and the woman knew it.

What I disturbed in that house was something illegal and I never found out what, I did not want to know.

Establishing confidence and bridging society's huge gap was so important and very hard work especially when dealing with such immorality, drunkenness and total abandonment to evil as I did continually. My attitude to ministry and life was changed. I was coming to understand what God had prepared Gwen and me for and what the calling stood for.

Amongst Aboriginal people, there is a dimension beyond the ordinary that we whites are not aware of. Some might call it evil others might say it is the sixth sense well developed. For me, I saw it as a sixth sense developed from generations past.

One evening after a meeting, we were sitting on drums in Dora's shack and drinking George's tea, eating our biscuits, and just yarning. Suddenly, George and Dora fell silent and looked at each other in alarm.

'Did you hear that, George?' Dora said.

'Yes, I wonder what it means. I'll go and see Fred and Janet and see if they heard it.' George hurriedly left the shack. Fred, George's brother, and Janet, his wife, lived a few metres down river.

'What's the matter? 'I asked, but Dora didn't reply. A

few minutes later George returned.

'Yes, they heard it too.' He looked very worried.

'What's the matter? Tell us, please. We didn't hear a thing.' I felt that here was a mystery.

'We heard a certain bird call. When we hear that bird call we know there's been death in the family.' George explained.

'But we only heard the ducks and water hens on the river,' I was puzzled. Dora is a Christian and always declared she was not superstitious so I didn't know what to believe. They remained very sober and thoughtful and shortly after, we left and went home. Next day while working on the fruit block, I received a phone call,

'Could you please contact Dora and George so they can contact their relatives. A car drove through the Wellington punt gates. George's brother, several cousins and other relatives were drowned.'

The accident occurred at the same time as Dora and George heard the birdcall. I crossed the river to deliver the message then stayed to comfort George and Dora. They left as quickly as possible for Wellington. I was silent though, I had no answer except to wonder if these people had access to a hidden sense that I as a white person and trained to think logically, had either lost in Adam's fall or just never had.

One of the great tragedies of human wastage was 'Sooty'. Her real name was Gwen. When young she showed promise as a great singer. Gwen possessed so much talent that Elsie Gribble and her husband, famous singers of their time, took her under their wing and gave her tuition. They must have had their hearts broken because when I met her she was a hopeless alcoholic and her voice ruined by the life style she lived. When she sang 'The Old Rugged Cross' it was enough to make one weep, the remnants of

THE MAVERICK'S ROUNDUP

a beautiful voice could be detected. What kind of a future could she have had, if only…

I was driving home one day to have a quick lunch with Gwen when I met Sooty struggling along the road. I picked her up and invited her home,

'Come and have some lunch with us.'

'No, I couldn't do that to Gwen on such short notice,' she wheezed.

'Don't worry, the Lord will provide,' I replied in that blasé manner that Christians use to impress others of their piety.

Our rented cottage was just across the road from the Winkie lagoon, a backwater of the river. A pipeline emptying tomato seeds and fruit refuse from the canning factory drained into the lagoon. This day as I drove into our driveway the outlet of the pipeline was black with ducks, teal and water hen.

I jumped out of the car, rushed inside and grabbed the shotgun, leaving Gwen to deal with Sooty. I pulled on an old pair of sandshoes and crawled down the slimy black ooze in the little creek, trying to keep the gun dry.

I hid behind a clump of rushes my eyes bulging in unbelief.

There were birds, birds and more birds. With trembling fingers, I aimed and fired one barrel. Whoopee! There were dead and dying bodies everywhere. I started to gather the birds on land then I realised that I needed to get the ones in the water before they swam out into the lagoon to die. I yelled to Gwen for help. She came running thinking that I was hurt. We picked up all we could before one or two swam off. We carried home 21 birds from one shot. I was too excited to pull the second barrel.

No lunch that day, we spent the time plucking birds. Gwen took the ducks and Sooty went home with the rest.

'I think the Lord provided,' Sooty gave a wheezy cackle.

I remembered a quote from the earliest Biblical text 'My God shall supply all your needs according to his riches in glory.'

When I returned to work, I told Alan; he took some convincing that it was true.

Sooty died in dreadful circumstances. One day crossing the river on the punt drunk, she sat on the edge of the apron of the punt and was crushed when it landed. I do not know if I shall see her in heaven but one is not condemned for drinking but for rejecting Jesus Christ and his death. Had she rejected Jesus? Was she a victim of the clash of two cultures?

To cite another quote from ancient Biblical text:

'God loved the world so much that he gave his only son so that anyone who believes in him shall not perish but have Eternal life. God did not send his son to condemn the world but to save it.'

Many people often never beat the problems of the flesh but salvation is not to save the body but the spirit of man, I want to add yet another quote: 'Take care to live in me, and let me live in you.'

Recapping my thoughts on testings, I remembered the words from that book, the Bible, that neither fire, war, or destruction of it has been able to annihilate: 'When we have trouble or calamity...is it because he doesn't love us? No!...we must be ready to face death at every moment... despite all this... overwhelming victory is ours...'

Chapter Twenty-Two
Gerard Mission

The life that the Call led us to live amongst the Aboriginal people was like walking through a maze. We had to be jacks-of-all-trades. Years later, Philip, our son, after obtaining his degree in Electrical Engineering, said,

'I would give anything to know what you know.' Life has taken him along many paths and maybe he has acquired the expertise he desired. He has outstripped me for knowledge, but I digress.

Amongst our many activities was conducting Sunday Schools. We ran meetings for kids on the Berri flats behind the pumping station. The poorer people lived down here in the shacks that they built. It was an area that churches viewed from afar and yes, these people viewed the churches from afar, feeling they could not attain the standard required.

Every Sunday rain or shine, summer and winter we would put up the marquee for kids' meeting in the afternoon and leaving it standing for a night service. These meetings attracted a number of both black and white kids and were the forerunners of a ministry amongst children in later years.

We contacted many adults who were trying to help these kids and gave them food and clothes from their own meagre incomes because the parents spent the money on grog or dissolute living. Among them was a very elderly woman who was caring for a mentally disadvantaged girl. Half the time she had extra children living with her because their parents were unable to look after them. She would cut herself short if she thought there were kids going hungry.

Into this area, the Government shifted a disused church from Winkie to become a place of worship for Aboriginal people.

The church hadn't long been resited when an Aboriginal couple and their two young sons arrived in the Berri area from Queensland. Bert and Charmaine Hollingsworth came from Cairns where Bert worked as a cane cutter during the season. When Bert and I met, we clicked immediately. He had a great work ethic and was very progressive, living in a nice caravan towed by a good car.

At the same time, Uncle Dick Piety returned with a team of musicians and singers. The visit of these people gave our ministry further impetus. However, the reaction to these Queenslanders by the local Aboriginal fraternity was very antagonistic. The local Aboriginal people were not going to have anything to do the blackfellas from Queensland.

***

Though we were not missionaries at Gerard Mission, we became very good friends with the South Australian United Aborigine Mission missionaries there and ministered on a regular basis.

The riverbank dwellers refused to live on the Mission station, preferring to live independently and free to some extent, from the alcohol, fights and immorality that was undermining the Mission in those days.

Gerard Mission was a tract of land along the riverbank bought by Mr Gerard of Gerard & Goodman, an electrical firm in Adelaide. This was a prime piece of real estate on the outskirts of the Winkie settlement twelve to fifteen miles from Berri. The Mission, administered by the UAM, was very poor and operated on a shoestring.

Pastor Samuels, President of the UAM, had been blind from a young age. He was a very remarkable man in that he had never let his disability hamper him in any way. It was hard to make him understand the condition of the mission. He would not listen when I tried to explain the state of the homes and how the people lived.

I saw him line out the inside of homes on the Mission by himself. Amazing when you think he has to measure the size of the sheets and then cut them and fit them without great gaps. The state of Gerard was not his fault entirely there were many other factors at play, but the determination that led him to overcome his disability was also a drawback in not allowing him to visually assess the conditions of the Mission. He refused to believe what he heard, 'blindly' rejecting change.

Once we became caretakers for a weekend. What a weekend! Everything went wrong that could go wrong. It was a baptism of fire. To start the weekend off I had to take a group of people to Renmark to a meeting, people did not arrive on time and then the cow escaped and had to be rounded up. Someone tracked her down and tied her to a tree until we returned hours later. We hitched her to the van and she came home a lot faster than she left. As substitute missionaries, all weekend drunks and people wanting this and that visited us.

The people who lived along the riverbank were relatives

of the people who lived on the Mission-stations so we could not help but become involved on the Mission stations. Frank and I continued as members of the Aboriginal Welfare Committee. Initially, the Welfare Committee endeavoured to assist in the goverment's development of Gerard Mission by planting up vineyards, orchards and market gardens. Workshops were fitted out so that peoples' skill levels grew and they could get work and the Mission become self-supporting.

The UAM could never ever finance the development of orchards, gardens, housing, employment and education that the people so desperately needed and eventually the Mission came under Government control.

It was a good thing when the Government took over all the Missions in one sense but it was also a bad thing because the influence of the Christian faith was taken away and the people were left without any principle or moral law in their lives. The spiritual welfare of the people became the responsibility various religious groups.

I had contended hard for change and improvement on Gerard but wondered if it had brought the benefits to the people that I envisaged.

The Chairman of the Aboriginal Welfare Committee, Mr Jack Foote, a fruit blocker himself, with a big heart as well as a big stature and a fine Christian, gave direction in the initial organization of the orchards.

When I first set foot on the Mission, the conditions, to me, were totally appalling. The homes of the missionaries and workers were very basic and the homes for the Aboriginals only a few sheets of iron removed from shanties.

When Gwen and I moved to Barmera at a later stage, we found ourselves more and more trying to help the missionaries whose health had broken down because of overwork and no support. Most of the missionaries had young children and in times of sickness, the isolation from medical help was worrying. A nurse and schoolteacher resided on the Mission they were very brave and innovative in their efforts to provide education and health care to the people. They lived in fear of being raped, and murdered by drunks, in fact, one female missionary was attack.

Having a school at Gerard meant the Aboriginal children never mixed with their white counterparts in the wider community. The Missionaries felt that this was detrimental to the development of the children and after negotiation with Government officials the school closed on Gerard and the children bussed into the Winkie Primary School.

Many of the Missionary couples had served in the UAM in the remote north at Maree, Nepabunna and Finnis Springs.

Gwen and I were looking back over the past while sipping a coffee one day, about the time when Gerard was a Christian Mission and when several missionary couples from Gerard moved into Barmera obtaining employment - settling for a time to get their health and finances together before moving on.

'Gerard was the final straw that broke the camel's back for most of the missionaries,' Gwen mused.

'The Missionaries were really pioneers in their own right,' I continued to dredge up the memories.

'There were Mr and Mrs Bateman, John and Norma Stevenson, Frank and Anne Doley, Harry and Barbara Villa, Ruth Bulpitt.'

'Don't forget Mr and Mrs Hartwig, Frank and Sylvia and you and I - we did all we could to support these courageous people even though we didn't live on the Mission,' Gwen added to the list.

The Welfare Committee with Government finance gradually broke through in the development of orchards and gardens. Jack Foote became the Superintendent of Gerard. It still has been hard to introduce the people to a progressive life style. The hurts and tragedies of the past run deep and handed down from generation to generation, they are never forgotten or forgiven. Various religious groups took responsibility for the spiritual welfare of the people.

'Another thing, I detest popular statements made calling missionaries 'child stealers' of the stolen generations,' I was on my hobbyhorse.

'That is right,' Gwen agreed, adding, 'in South Australia, in many cases, the children were given to the missionaries to care for in the children's' homes and provide a basic education because there was no one to care for them or want them. The missionaries were longsighted enough to realize that the future of the kids was taking their place in the wider community by going to local schools and fought tooth and nail for this to happen. Much doubt has been cast unfairly on the work of the missionaries and the sacrifice of their personal lives in trying to bridge a terrible gap between two cultures.' Gwen too became vocal over the way the sacrifice of the missionaries was brushed aside in the emotional wave in the emotional wave of the 'stolen generation.'

Missionaries have aged and even passed on carrying a great load of condemnation when they should be acclaimed as heroes, even nation builders.

Gerard will ever be in my memory, especially at Easter. Frank and his family, Gwen and I and our family and Auntie Dora, celebrated the Resurrection on Sunday morning at a service on Gerard. After the service, a group of us went down to Red Banks on a big bend in the river for

THE MAVERICK'S ROUNDUP

a picnic lunch under a big gum tree.

We were sitting on the bank while the kids paddled on a sand-spit on the edge of the riverbank. We were all being very careful and watchful but not careful enough, perhaps, because suddenly a cry went up,

'Robyn's fallen in the river.'

Without thinking I rushed into the river, it was very muddy and hard to see anything. All I could see was a faint colour of red; I dived for it and grabbed it. Up came Robyn, spluttering and coughing, but Ok.

As a little girl, Robyn loved the colour red. Being dark, it suited her and Gwen had made a red coat for her, the red coat saved her that day. I loved to tease Robyn by singing to her that song, 'When the red, red robin comes bob, bob, bobbin' along,' It could be that she loved to get mad at me for singing that song and embarrassing her.

It was a severe lesson to us never to take the river for granted. Be careful of the River Murray sand banks. The current will cut away the sand causing it to collapse.

Yet another experience comes to mind involving Gerard.

A group of young people including our own teenagers, wanted to go to a youth camp over Easter so I lent them my car. In turn, one of the young men, Ian Hooper, lent me his car while he was at camp.

I had accepted an invitation to preach at Gerard over Easter so Gwen and I braved the awful corrugated road to Gerard in Ian's old car. All went well until we were nearly home – turning into our street - suddenly there was a loud noise and the car skidded to a halt. I jumped out to see what had happened and stepped onto the front wheel of the car. People popped out of their front doors, 'What's the matter?' Someone yelled.

'It's Ok, the wheel's fallen off,' I laughed. I put the

wheel back on and drove home. I believe the Lord travels every mile with us. He promised, 'I will never leave you or forsake you.' He lived up to his promise that day. If we had broken down somewhere between Gerard and Winkie, there would have been a long walk in the dark to get help. The breakdown occurred almost on our doorstep. We experienced some funny moments as we followed the Call.

Chapter Twenty-Three
Time To Move On

I had now been eleven years working on the fruit block and been well trained in horticulture by the best. What the Boss and his son, Alan, had imparted to me was invaluable in my training.

Gwen and I were facing the fact that we would never be able to possess a fruit block of our own. I felt it was time to move on and leave the and leave the block work.

I had heard that there was a vacancy in a maintenance gang on the irrigation pipelines at a settlement called Loveday with a house and almost next-door to the school so I applied.

The Aboriginal work appeared to be phasing out. The Government was providing housing in towns and had taken over the missions. The riverbank dwellers were moving into the towns and onto the missions. The years of hard work was paying off. The changes were huge. No, the Call had not been phased out it was merely taking us in another direction. At Loveday, we found ourselves in limbo for a short time; it was a time for rest and recuperation for what was to be around the next corner.

I won the job in the maintenance crew and had the best working holiday I had ever had. The crew was formed for emergencies when the pipelines burst. We received wet money, depth money and any other money that could be a worthy excuse for payment, and when anyone received even an extra fifty cents in their pay packet the rest of the men wanted to know why. Whether it was a downpour or just a light shower, the crew would head back to the depot where they would sit and talk for hours and hours. Other times we would spend half the day walking the old telegraph lines looking for copper wire or piping to sell to pay for the Christmas keg.

During wet days, I would spend the time sharpening everything from knives to saws. I rehandled all the implements that needed a handle. I built new shelving for the work shed.

One day I became so bored that I walked home across the oval and measured up the kids' bed heads. The joints had come loose and threatened to collapse. I returned and threaded some rods to hold the bed heads together. Just when I had finished the supervisor suddenly thought to ask, 'what are you doing, Bruce?'

'I'm just turning up some rods to hold the kids beds together.'

'Aw, that's a great idea Bruce.' The other workers had not missed me. It was six months of extreme leisure.

The irrigation settlement of Loveday on the outskirts of the main irrigation area was crisscrossed with roads. One very long road went by the name of Hunt Road. It was unsealed and serviced market gardens and fruit blocks and led to the centre of the settlement. Every week trucks loaded to the maximum with fruit and vegetables would set off for the markets in Adelaide. Hunt Road crossed many by-roads and at every junction, there were spoon drains with large humps. Consequently, every time the trucks crossed these humps invariably vegetables not tied down or loosely loaded fell off.

Hunt Road became our bargain basement. Pumpkins, potatoes, turnips, swedes and fruit strewn along the side of the road had fallen from trucks on their way to market in Adelaide. There was nothing the matter with this produce, it would have just lain and rotted. We saw it as God's provision at that time.

'What did you find today, Dad?' The family would ask when I arrived home from work.

'Here are some oranges.' I would unload the citrus into a box.

'Ooh, I love oranges,' Robyn exclaimed and pounced on a large orange.

In July and August, the growers of Navel oranges started picking for the export market, a highly competitive market. Huge areas pushed out by bulldozers contained the marked or too large fruit. When the hole was full, a bulldozer covered over the fruit. Such wastage of resources in a starving world always seemed wrong to me and still does. People sometimes found these dumps and salvaged as much fruit as they could. We were among the recyclers. The fruit dumps later had kerosene poured over them and set alight so nobody could benefit from the waste. There is a saying: 'waste not, want not.'

One day after eating the last of our recycled oranges, Robyn said, 'We need some more oranges, Dad.'

'Ok, pray about it,' I answered rather glibly.

About two miles along the road from Barmera to Berri the tailgate of a semitrailer accidently came open and the whole load of oranges poured out along the road for miles. We stopped and filled our boot with oranges our prayer was answered. The fruit just lay along the road until it rotted the Insurance Company would have covered it.

We lived at Loveday at the time. I was on my way home after work one night, a big black official looking car pulled up along side of me.

'Can you tell me where I can find Bruce Leane?'

'Yes, I can. You're talking to him. Who are you and where are you from?' I racked my brains trying to think what he meant.

'I'm from the South Australian Housing Trust. Why didn't you notify us of your change of address? A house in Barmera is allotted to you, do you still want it?'

'Yes! And why don't you reply to my letter?' I shot right back at him. It was the first I had heard concerning our application for a house.

'You've got until next Monday to fill out these forms telling us what colour you want the house painted inside and out.' He thrust a sheaf of papers at me, through the car window and drove away.

After deciding to leave the fruit block and applying for a job at Loveday, we heard the Housing Trust were accepting applications for housing. The mine at Radium Hill had closed down and a number of houses moved to Barmera at Lake Bonny on the Murray River. We thought we would apply on the off chance that it was not too late. Because we had not heard anything about our application, we had given up thinking about the house.

I watched the car drive away then I ran home to tell Gwen the good news. The bad news it was Wednesday night and our letter had to be in Adelaide office by Monday. We poured over colour schemes, filled out questions late into the night, and posted that very important letter next morning.

We held our breath waiting to hear if the house was ours. The dream to own our own home had replaced that of the block. We had had enough of drifting from pillar to post.

Monday morning I went to work and informed the supervisor of the gang that I possibly might get a house in Barmera and be shifting. The news fell like a lead balloon. Before the day was over though, the Water Master dropped into the workshop and dropped another bomb.

'The big boss in Barmera wants to see you at 10am in the morning.'

'What have I done or not done?' I was alarmed I thought I was being hauled over the coals.

'I don't know, but you better get in there and find out,' the Water Master said.

At 10 am, I reported to the big boss in Barmera.

'Bruce, I was informed that you are looking to relocate in here, is that right?' he sat back in his chair looking at me.

'That's right.' I explained what had happened.

'That's what I wanted to see you about. We are looking to establish a new depot and spare parts store here in Barmera and we want you to develop and rebuild the depot.'

'Yes, sir, that sounds very good.' I stuttered in surprise at the unexpected promotion.

I was pleased to be out of the crash gang and get my teeth into something worthwhile amongst tools.

It was a great job and with a pay rise to carpenters' rates, it meant a few extras for the new house when we shifted. The new house may have been transported and refitted but to You Know Who and me it was a mansion, because we could call it our own. We had a back yard for our kids to play in at last.

It all had to be of God because it was not due to the efficiency of our organisational skills. To use another quote from the good Book, 'The steps of a good man are ordered by the Lord.'

The house was exciting but a lot of work. Transported from Radium Hill, the houses in the street stood on a reclaimed quarry site. We had to bring in truckloads of dirt so we could grow a garden. I bought a second hand shed and erected trellises on three sides of the house and trained vines up them for shade.

We were only one street away from beautiful Lake Bonney. The wealthy may have faced the lake but from our back door, we could enjoy a great view of the lake. In the early 1960s my three elder children and I watched Donald Campbell do test runs in his Bluebird on Lake Bonney from the roof of our house. There were eight great years picnicking and swimming in Lake Bonney after work, on hot nights and on weekends. All of our children learnt to swim in the lake.

There was no great fanfare or earth-shattering events to tell us that our Call was taking another direction, there was just a gradual change of circumstances.

Although we were no longer personally involved with Aboriginal people, I was still a member of the Welfare Committee particularly with the gardening projects sponsored by the Government on Gerard Mission.

On settling in Barmera, we adopted the Barmera Church of Christ as our spiritual home. Gwen and I became Sunday Schoolteachers. Doors unlocked, I became a leader of a teenage Bible study group, next step a church elder and regularly preached.

Before leaving Winkie, Gwen had endeavoured to brush up on her dressmaking skills by doing a course at the TAFE College at Glossop. She now hung out her shingle and became dressmaker to quite a few Greek women as well as other clients.

The Greek community was quite large in those years

and it led Gwen and me to begin to learn how to speak Greek. Gwen was hoping to be able to communicate with her clients instead of using their children as translators.

This period was like a holiday because we seemed to live in a backwater away from the Hurley-burley of life. Then the phone rang, and life took another turn,

'Auntie Gwen, can I come and stay with you?' a teary voice came over the phone.

'What's the matter?' Gwen inquired.

'My Auntie is making my life miserable. My Uncle is paying me so much attention, it's making Auntie jealous, and they are fighting. It's horrible.' The sobs grew.

'Well, you better come up and stay for a while, and see if we can sort it out.' Gwen invited eager to open our home to her once more.

Carol was one of the kids we had contacted while running the Sunday school on the Berri flats in the marquee; she was now eighteen and a very beautiful girl. Her father dead, her mother had moved on, her seven brothers and sisters placed in foster homes, there was nowhere to go. She turned to us for help and Gwen was quick to open our home to her once more. Carol lived with us for two years. She found a job in the drapery section of a large store in Barmera. Then she met the love of her life, Tim Marsh, moved to Adelaide, and married him.

It was not easy to bring another personality into our home. There was a lot of adjustment. Our house had three bedrooms and stretched to capacity with our own four children. We found space for Carol. Gwen always says that mercy is not one of her attributes but when it comes down the bottom line, she is the first to respond to a need.

There were changes in our circumstances, Government policy changed toward indigenous people allowing Auntie Dora to apply for a house. A house became available to her on the eastern side of Barmera; we lived on the western edge of town. When life became too much for her, she would catch a taxi and spend the day with us.

'You are the son and daughter I never had,' she often would say.

The move to Barmera didn't separated us entirely from our Aboriginal friends, because at 2am in the morning the phone rang,

'Bruce, can you come around immediately?' Auntie Dora sounded scared and she did not scare easily.

'What's happened? I was trying to get my sleep-clogged mind functioning.

'It's Donny, my nephew; he's been drinking and is threatening to kill us all and himself.'

'Have you called the police?'

'No! I didn't want to call them, because they will come in here and stir him up, he's got a shot gun and someone will be killed.' Dora worried.

'Ok. I'll be there.' I dressed myself and drove across the town to Dora's house. How do you prepare to calm a drunken, suicidal man? I had no idea and hoped for inspiration when I arrived. Meantime, Gwen was awake wondering and praying for my safekeeping.

Bold as brass but quaking inside, I walked into the house and up to the bedroom, 'Give me the gun, Donny,' I grabbed the gun from him, broke the breach, and extracted the cartridges putting them in my pocket and throwing the shotgun on the bed.

'Now what's the matter, Donny?' I said kindly, sitting down beside him.

Between blubbering and cursing, I heard a sorry tale.

'What will we do with him?' Dora was relieved but still worried. 'I don't want him here. He'll only get into more trouble.'

'There isn't much we can do at this hour. He needs help.' There was not much I could do full stop, Donny needed help that I was not able give.

'There is a relative in Adelaide, if we could get him to Adelaide.' Dora suggested.

I had an idea, 'I'll take him to the Kingston Ferry and find a semi driver who will take him to Adelaide. By that time he will be sober and able to find his way to his relative.'

I took him to the Kingston Ferry and found him a ride to Adelaide. I never saw him again later I heard he had taken his own life in the Gladstone gaol.

I may have lost sleep over Donny but our family could create events of our own. We were one of those families. I bought a Lambretta scooter to ride to work on. I thought it would be a good idea if Gwen learnt to ride it and so did she.

I was trying to teach her in the street where we lived, Chanel Crescent was the name of the street. I was running up and down shouting instructions, the neighbourhood dogs were joining in the circus, all the kids in the street were watching. A visitor arrived and took my attention way from Gwen. She went on riding the scooter until she wanted to turn it around and found herself heading for a stobie pole.

'Bruce, how do I stop this thing,' she screamed. I yelled advice, but she could not hear. She mounted the footpath, the engine covers fell off and a terrible racket ensued. I did not want to watch.

Somehow, she missed the pole, ending up in a vacant block between houses. The scooter had stalled. By this time the entire street, attracted by the noise had appeared at their front doors to watch the spectacle of Gwen learning to ride the scooter. She eventually did and took Raymond to Kindergarten. He stood in front of her on the platform between her legs and away they went. One could do things like that in those days. All the kids were very envious of Ray briven to Kindergarten on a scooter.

All went well until Carol and Gwen decided to go for a ride on it together. To enter our street they had to negotiate quite a steep hill. Gwen stalled the scooter and they fell off. Not being hurt they managed to push the bike home. The following morning when I jumped on it to go to work and rode over the rolled up newspaper lying in the driveway, the front wheel came off. The top of the fork had snapped. I was not hurt.

'If your face wants to smile, let it. If it doesn't, make it,' was a quote hung on the Boss's kitchen wall, quotes always fascinated me and stayed in my mind over the years. As a family, we put many a smile on our neighbours' faces where ever we lived.

Chapter Twenty-Four
Gathering Momentum

The changes gathered momentum when Cliff Beard, photographer, knocked on our door.

'What a pair of pretty girls, I'd love to take a photo of them.' Cliff commented when he saw our girls. It sounded a bit of a salesperson's gimmick to me and that was our first contact with Cliff. He would prove to be another person of significance in our lives.

Cliff was working as a photographer going from house to house seeking to take portraits of families, children and weddings. He was a good photographer; we have some lovely shots of the kids. At the same time as he worked for a photographic studio in Adelaide he was also looking to encourage people to accept Christ into their lives when and where the opportunity arose.

Gwen and I immediately clicked with Cliff and discovered that he was a member of the Christian Revival Crusade. My earlier experiences when visiting the Billy Adam's Crusade and with being struck dumb in my lounge room and meeting with the Aboriginal Brethren from Queensland, all pointed to the fact that God was leading us to become involved with the Christian Revival Crusade.

Because of the nature of Cliff's work throughout the Riverland, he drew together a group of likeminded people. We met together midweek, on weekends in our homes to talk, pray, and discuss the Bible.

As these times of fellowship became widely known and more and more people became involved it was not long before the pastor of the Barmera Church of Christ paid me a visit.

'Bruce, I'm over a barrel,' he was very upset.

'What's the matter, Pastor?' I wondered what I had done. I felt I had tried to be ethical in every way by not trying to shove my new beliefs down anyone's throat.

'The Home Mission Department have insisted I either ask you to leave the church or leave myself. I'm very sorry. I don't want to do this to you because you have been a faithful member and we have been such good friends.' The pastor was clearly uncomfortable.

'That is easily fixed,' I said, I felt sorry for him. This was his first church and had an unenviable task to perform. 'I'll resign. You are a young man and have your calling before you. You will make a good pastor; you must not drop out now.'

'Bruce isn't there some other way that we can get around this so you don't have to leave?' he did not want one of his right hand men to drop out in this manner.

'I can't see how I can remain, because I believe that God is directing me. I also have adopted teaching that our denomination does not.' I went on to explain, 'I hope you realise that the young people whom I'm teaching in Sunday School will probably follow me into this Pentecostal move, even though I have been ethical in trying not to influence them. Also, I'd like to talk to your team of leaders and explain to them why I'm leaving.'

'Yes, come along to the Elders meeting on Tuesday night.'

I shared my experiences with the Elders, and that I thought God was leading me into the Pentecostal movement and particularly the Christian Revival Crusade, and I wanted to move in that direction. We discussed the policies placed on the local church and young pastor by the Home Mission Department and everyone was unanimous that leaving the fellowship was the ethical thing to do for everyone involved - they gave me their blessing.

It was a cruel blow then but one I had to accept.

***

There had been a time when I had sought training in the Church of Christ Bible College but my level of education was too low to gain entry and there was no other way to enter the ministry in the traditional stream. It was a cruel blow then but one I had to accept at that point. I now faced the Right Boot of Fellowship. However, the Lord was in control and directing me in his Call.

Gwen and I again made a decision to follow the Call that would isolate us even more from family and friends. Fellowshipping among the Aborigines was one thing but changing denominations was beyond the pail.

The new direction saw a group of likeminded people come together as a team to do street witnessing visiting all the Riverland towns where young people gathered to drink, do wheelies and be sexually active. Cliff was a compelling preacher, and God was with him and with us.

I felt the need to try for a higher paid job as our activities took a toll on our finances. At the same time as we moved to do street witnessing, browsing through the local paper I saw an advertisement, 'Truck driver wanted to deliver sheds to agricultural areas across South Australia. Please apply Grant Engineering, Glossop.'

It would be different, I thought and the money would be good. It was close to home, about seven kilometres away. I applied. Grantly Telfer the owner/ boss of the engineering works interviewed me. The factory newly established was still developing.

'Well, Bruce I would like to give you the job, but my uncle who drives the truck for me isn't retiring for 6 months yet, you can work in the factory until he leaves. Will that be OK?'

'Yes,' I said, awed, as I looked at the overhead cranes, sparking welders, grinding machines, drills and lathes, 'but I haven't had any experience in welding or with steel work.'

'That's OK, you'll learn.' Grantly shrugged aside my feeble protest.

It was not the shed building section I went to work in but the machine manufacturing section. The wage was certainly better than I had ever received before.

The work became routine but my eye was still watching the truck, how much longer would I be in the factory? At least I can drive, that I do not have to learn.

'Bruce, Grantly wants to see you in his office,' the supervisor came by one day.

'What have I done now?' I asked him, thinking that it was crunch time. I was out of here one way or another.

'Don't know, I'm just the messenger boy,' and he went on his way.

'How are you getting on, Bruce?' Grantly was sitting with his feet resting on an apology for a desk.

'Ok, I think. How do you think I'm doing? I replied, steeling myself for the worst.

'That's a good point seeing as you raised it. You're not going to drive the truck. You are a natural with tools and machinery. I want you to stay in the manufacturing area. Somebody else can drive the truck.'

I was about to receive a crash course in engineering that was to take me into areas undreamed of. I was confident that God was in this change of plans because the training I'd had over the years with tools had stood me in good stead however, I faced a steep learning curve to gain new skills and quickly.

The one thing I would need would be a good mentor.

I had Cliff on one side mentoring me in the ministry of the Christian Revival Crusade, street ministry and church planting providing new challenges. Now it seemed I needed another mentor in the engineering world and that mentor was Grantly Telfer. God had never left me without excellent mentors for my PhD in the University of Hard Knocks and he had not let me down now.

The factory soon became home and the camaraderie was great. Grantly insisted that every person employed purchase his own toolbox and set of tools. I was very proud of my new toolbox and gear. My welding helmet I had not tried because I had not even begun to weld. I carefully engraved my name on everything and over the forty years, I have only lost one spanner from the original set.

'Let's move out of all the noise, Bruce,' Grantly called me aside, causing my work mates to glare at me and wonder why I was his favourite and not them.

'What's the matter, boss?' I was thinking that my work was not up to his standard.

'Bruce, I want you to work for me, entirely.' Grantly was very innovative and was developing ideas all the time. 'I want to make diagrams and plans for machine parts and every day I will give you sketches with sizes and dimensions and I want you to make up the part exactly as I have drawn it and then fit it to the machine that I am developing.'

'Ok, boss.' Was this going to be a piece of cake or a lemon? I wondered.

Sometimes the job would not last all day so I would go and ask the supervisor for work.

All was well until one day I made and welded on a bracket to the machine. Next morning Grantly came along to check, he picked up a hammer and knocked it off.

'I never want to see another weld like that again. Clean it up and re-weld it,' he said and walked off with out any further instruction. He never did, because every dinner hour I welded every piece of scrap steel in as many ways as I could dream up, after work and on late shifts. Among the workers was an English immigrant, he was a brilliant welder and took me under his wing and taught me so much. He knew and I now know welding is 90% practise until it becomes automatic. My tool chest had grown to include a welder in it. God was equipping me to reach men for Christ in all occupations in life with empathy, meeting them in their own work place.

'What do you do?' I ask men when trying to get to know them.

'I'm an elder in the church,' is the answer.

'I lead the Children's' Church,' is another comment.

These people expected me to want to know their church status and responsibility. I believe our Christian responsibility is also our workplace responsibility. Many people believe their work place and their church place are two different spheres. I do not.

It does not matter if we are welders, chippies, farmers white collar workers, blue collar workers; the trades and career places are ministries to which we have been called to minister in as well as work in. God does not have two separate compartments in our lives. My toolbox was also part of my calling. The tools may have changed over the years but I always kept them near my hand.

Taking the streets for Christ has always interested me. It is a special ministry and not everyone's cup of tea. During a visit to Adelaide, an invitation to participate in a street meeting came my way. What I found disconcerting was that when we arrived at our prescribed position the crowds were streaming by. Our leader called for a prayer time in the van. By the time our prayer meeting was over the people had gone and we were preaching and talking to ourselves.

'It is my very strong conviction that in this type of ministry we should do our praying and seeking God's blessing and covering at home, not when we reach the street,' I later complained to Gwen at home.

'Surely you don't mean that we shouldn't pray before the team begins to minister?' she asked, surprised.

'I believe strongly that I am a child of God all the time. The Holy Spirit doesn't leave me despite my fits and moods. This message of constantly getting ready means we never arrive at the position of rest or attainment.' I was still feeling frustrated.

'What you are saying, Bruce is we have already arrived, we have attained our position in Christ by faith?' Was Gwen trying to trap me? Did she not understand what I meant, I wondered.

'Yes, that's what I mean. As a new creature in Christ, I live in his covering of righteousness all the time. I am in Christ, he in me means the presence, and power of God is within me all the time. We should be prayed up at all times and at all times ready to do battle with the enemy to win people from his kingdom of darkness and sin,' I fell silent and Gwen looked at me and clapped her hands in encouragement.

When we started our street ministry with Cliff, we

worked from the belief that Christ was in us, we were ready for whatever might happen, and it often did. Taking the streets for Christ is exciting and exhilarating. The younger members went home full of excitement and inspired by their experiences that they had not encountered in any other ministry.

Very early in my ministry, God made me aware, do not send people out by themselves - go with them.

It was my policy when out on the streets that if a person was too shy or fearful to speak, I would encourage them to stand across the street and interject. A crowd would soon form and a great deal of personal ministry would then open up.

'All things to all people that I might win some,' is a Biblical quote that I adopted because it directed me to be among people. Taking the street for Christ was one avenue of service but we needed a base from which to operate.

Two couples, Gay and Ray from Renmark, Don and Judy from Loxton became close workers with Gwen and I. With some advice from Cliff urging us to take the step and leave our comfort zones and set up regular services under the umbrella of the Christian Revival Crusade, we hired the meeting room of the local Country Women's Association, Berri right across the street from the Police Station and under the eagle eye of Sergeant Brock.

Quite a few rallies were organised with Cliff as guest speaker. He has always had a positive message and a fearless manner. Many young people responded to the message and the type of meetings conducted. They never envisaged church could be so free, so joyous.

Gwen and Gay stormed the gates of Heaven with much prayer - the answers seen and experienced in the meetings. On one occasion, a number of young larrikin lads decided to attend our meeting. They sat up the back and tried to be as disruptive as possible.

When Cliff stood to preach, he dared them to interject. They looked at each other, smirking, Cliff then called them to, 'Come down here and I will pray for you.' They could not resist the challenge and like Brown's cows, they swaggered down the front, trying to be big and bold to impress everyone.

Cliff prayed for them and a dramatic change came over them. Then he told them that counsellors would explain to them what had happened. The counsellors made sure they spoke on a one to one basis with these young people in separate rooms. The team moved in and each member took one of the young lads, found a quiet corner and talked with them. They were different lads once separated from their mates and the need to prove their manliness. Each one wanted to know if the Lord was real, some lads did give a verbal acknowledgement of Christ, others gave a verbal commitment.

When the disruptions subsided, the rally continued. There was a great hush over the meeting. The spoken word was powerful. The Bible talks about preaching being foolishness, well it is to the ordinary way of thinking but to a renewed mind in Christ, it is powerful to the saving of the soul.

Preaching the word of God with authority and under the power of the Holy Spirit was now the very essence of my Call. Pity Party sermons were no longer my forte nor were they Cliff's. God was launching both of us on a journey under his authority. All we wanted to do was follow this way because we saw God at work as never before. Gwen and I knew God was with us, we never doubted even though things were often against us.

The CWA hall was our base for a long time. The members were very gracious to us but we became very conscious that with the type of young people we were attracting, and the large numbers, a great deal of property damage could occur.

Praying for the sick, counselling and follow up, was impossible with the workload that each of the team members carried. We all knew we were moving under the power of God and none of us wanted to retreat.

Word reached the Christian Revival Crusade Centre in Adelaide and the young people there began to come and visit and help where possible; all the time the police were being supportive and remained so in all our activities.

Ian Chamberlain and Tim Marsh were two young men who became members of the team. Ian was a tall, dark and handsome New Zealander and Tim was a tall, fair and handsome guitar player who charmed the girls with his singing. They loved him.

Tim wanted to flex his muscles as a preacher and leader. The Centre was in need of more workers so Tim was a welcome assistant. Carol, to whom we gave a home, had caught his eye and he spent a lot of time at our place.

Tim worked as a photographer, following Cliff's example as a door-to-door photographer. Tim loved big flash cars and was more American than Aussie.

Carol had settled into the family obtaining a job as a shop assistant in Barmera. Gwen and I had our first experience with a love struck young couple. Our children looked on with great interest.

'Pastor Bruce, I would like to take Carol for a drive around Lake Bonney?'

'You did that last night. She has to work, you know.'

'I realise she works. I won't keep her late.' Tim promised with a charming smile.

'Ok. Make sure you get her home early.' I was practising my fatherly skills.

THE MAVERICK'S ROUNDUP

An hour later and Carol is not home.

'I wonder where they are, it's getting late!' Gwen worries.

'They'll be home soon.' I tried to quiet my fears.

'We'd better go to bed we have to get up early.' Gwen sighed.

We went to bed but not to sleep and lay there listening to the activities in the street and the town. Born on our ears is the sound of a car engine revving its heart out?

'It would be funny if that was Tim and Carol stuck in the sand down at the Lake.' Gwen suggests.

'Yeah! Surely Tim would know better than to drive off the grass onto the sand,' I reply.

The engine stopped; we lay listening for Tim to bring Carol home. Footsteps marched across the veranda and a voice at the window, 'Brother, can you bring your car down to the lake and tow us out. We are stuck in the sand.' Tim sounded crest-fallen. He had had to come with his cap in hand and ask for help.

Funny, people always call me 'Brother,' when something is needed, any other time it is just plain Bruce.

The course of true love never ran smoothly for these two. Carol was a sparky person and Tim's charm did not always work on her. They later married and moved to America. Tim was able to become the American he tried to imitate.

Ian, the Kiwi, whom I mentioned earlier, was a great mate of Tim's. These two young men had great ministries in our church Centre. From their ministry two young men found the Lord, Bobby and Johnny. These four young men flatted together for quite sometime. Personality and attitude conflicts arose between the young men, plenty of testosterone flowed. They had great fun times together. It certainly helped them to mature.

There were two other young men, Ian and Vince, who worked under me in the engineering factory and were students of mine in the Barmera church; they were part of the team. God developed in these young men ministries that would take them across the world. Their call had roots in this particular move of God.

For me another part of my Call was beginning - that of mentoring. I now mentored others.

It is my privilege to see many people I have mentored called out of our fellowships to serve the Lord across Australia and overseas.

At the same time as I was busy taking the streets for Christ and setting up services in the CWA, things had developed well at Grant Engineering, perhaps too well.

The supervisor had resigned for some reason, which I cannot remember now.

'Bruce, I'm offering you the job of foreman,' the manager, not Grantly, approached me the week following the supervisor's resignation.

'Look, I don't think I can do the job. I don't have the knowledge of an engineering background to do the job properly.' I felt very inadequate.

'I don't think that will matter because you are able to manage the men well.'

'I maybe able to get on with the men but there are better men here that can do the job better than I.'

'Won't you give it a go?'

'No, but why don't you make Lou the foreman - he knows engineering better than I do and I'll take the leading hand position and handle the workmen.'

'Ok, if that is how you want it. You're turning down higher pay, you know.'

'Too bad,' I replied, 'this is the way to go.'

Lou was away at the time. While playing cricket he

had broken a leg. When he returned to work, he received the news of his promotion – and all the paperwork. He was now on the staff. I was in charge of organising all the overtime and was paid accordingly. In the end, I earned more than Lou did. He and I stayed together as a team for many years and later with another engineering firm on several very big projects.

My job in the factory was the development and assembling of huge guillotines used for cutting flat steel plate and bars. Some guillotines were compressed air machines and the very big ones were electric hydraulic machines.

The biggest machines were twelve feet long and cold cut one half-inch plate or anything from galvanised flat iron up to half-inch plate. The factory built several types of guillotines that would cut 5/8th of an inch plate 8 feet long, other machines to cut ten-foot lengths by ¼-inch steel plate as well as machines to cut steel for angles and bars. The responsibility of setting the blades on these machines fell to me. Extraordinary concentration over a day was required to set one blade. The blades had to be set at not more than half of a thousandth of an inch variation over ten feet of blade.

It was intense work and required living on one's nerves.

The price of a Tungsten steel blade would have broken my bank balance many times over. Setting the blades on these machines, hydraulic test cuttings and overseeing the general assembly of the machines was part of my job description.

The camaraderie between the men was excellent. Everyone got on well together and with the job. If there was discontent or a problem, it landed in my lap. I would negotiate on behalf of the men and always with a successful outcome.

On the shed-making arm of the factory, the leading hand had been a strong union man.

'It's time we brought the Union into this shed. We'd get a much better deal from the bosses.' Fred (not his real name) would spend hours telling us about the benefits of unionism. He wanted the whole factory to join a union, the men voted and those against unionism won. Fred was a bit upset but accepted the decision of the men. A week or so later he called me aside and said, 'I've just received a bill for ten years back dues for union fees. I never gave a written resignation when I left the union. I received a letter last year to remind me but I ignored it. The Court has received the letter and I have to pay. I've got a wife and eight kids to keep.'

'Looks like you'll being paying union fees for many years to come.' I sympathised. I could have gloated over Fred but I did not, I felt sorry for him. I was not a union man and was a big influence in the factory staying free of unions. This incident only served to confirm my opinion of unions.

I knocked on Mr Tinning, the factory manager's office door, one day. I needed to see him about a problem over one of the machines.

'Come in.'

I did. Before I could speak he asked, 'What do you want?'

'Well seeing as you asked, how about a rise in pay.' Mr Tinning laughed at my cheekiness. I never really expected a rise; in fact, I was happy with my pay. I went on to explain what my problem was. Next payday I was dumbfounded to find that I had a rise in pay. I was delighted though and so was Gwen.

Those were five wonderful years of training that set me up for the future as well as the most money I had ever earned and God continued to work out his call in my life.

The grapevine in the factory always did overtime so everyone in the factory knew I was a Christian and a preacher. It is great to work with people who know who you are and accept you for what you are and to know that God has a major call on your life. When I stop and think about how much happened in those five years I am amazed and praise God for the fun of being alive.

This story touched my heart and I really feel to share it. Dennis was in charge of maintenance, and did not work directly under me. He had forgotten more about engineering than I would ever know. We were not bosom friends and stood at arm's length from each other. One night we were both working back on a late shift with a skeleton crew. One of my apprentices was turning around a huge plate of 7/8th inch steel with a mobile gantry, lifting and lowering as he went. He did not have it shackled correctly and it fell on him, trapping him from his thighs down.

Vince was screaming out more from fright than injury but that is easy for me to say. Everybody rushed to his aid, but it takes time to shackle up again. I was looking for a lever to lift up the plate when Dennis shouted, 'Seven of you guys, that's enough, put your backs in to it and lift it. Bruce, get ready to pull Vincent out when I say 'go.'

Out came Vincent, bruised and badly shaken.

With a few days off, he was back at work. His boot with a steel cap and heel that had a horseshoe fitted, had saved his foot from being crushed.

It was a lesson not to quickly judge a person. Dennis's quick thinking had saved Vince. I needed this understanding of human nature as my Call continued to lead me into many different pathways.

Yet another story illustrates what it means to follow

the Lord and stay in his call. The supervisor of the shed building arm of the factory was nicknamed Bing. He was a good friend of mine, and a nominal churchgoer. He came to see me one day,

'Bruce, somebody has put a shocking nude cartoon on the notice board. What shall I do about it? All the men and women have to eat their lunch having to look at it.' Bing whispered in my ear.

'That's easy, pull the thing down.'

'I couldn't do that, they will jeer at me.' Bing was horrified. He was a six-foot beanpole and I could not understand his fearfulness. I walked down to the notice board, pushed past the men eating their lunch, tore down the offending cartoon, and walked back to my work. No comment about the incident reached my ears.

'I wish I had that sort of guts,' Bing commented.

'It's Christ in me that gives me courage,' I replied. A boom crane and power lines became entangled one day. That day I was off work for some reason and Bing was doing my job. He died in my place by electrocution. He left a wife and children.

It could have been me. The time for the Call to end was not yet.

Chapter Twenty-Five

The Call Takes Another Turn

Grant Engineering was running into financial trouble. The factory grapevine said the machine side of the firm was closing down. Grantly was retaining the shed building section and moving back to Monash, a fruit block settlement, where he lived.

A young German engineer, very smart and innovative, had taken over the machinery arm and was moving it to Adelaide. A job-offer with the new firm in Adelaide came up but because so much was happening in my ministry, I stayed in Bamera.

It should have been a very distressing time for me but was exactly the opposite. The five years I had been at the factory was a crash course in many ways and I had become a competent welder and steel worker with a whole bundle of people skills. God had seen to it that Grantly had mentored me well as well as others in the factory.

'What are you going to do Bruce?' Everyone wanted to know, their curiosity ate at them.

'I don't know, something will turn up I expect.'

'Why don't you try John, he does big industrial steel

construction. He might want somebody,' a workmate suggested.

'Yeah, that's good idea,' I replied, and at the first opportunity I went to see John.

Regardless of the brief downturn in employment, my church activities were expanding very fast. It was obvious that God was moving in a very wonderful way and Gwen and I were smack, bang in the middle of it.

The Pentecostal movement was beginning to attract the attention of many local churches. They did not know whether to condemn it or condone it. Many people attended the meetings. Our little group were first to introduce Pentecostalism to the whole Riverland. It was a new experience as a pioneer; my background preparation had been outside of the organised church scene amongst the Aboriginal people. My experiences in the Holy Spirit and miracles were God given and inspired rather than in a Bible College.

Cliff Beard had been a great mentor in helping to start the Pentecostal work in the Riverland. By this time, his call had drawn him to Mildura and regions beyond. He has travelled the world with the message of Righteousness in Christ.

One of the first conferences I went to was held at the Christian Revival Crusade in Geelong, Victoria, 1964. Cliff and Helen insisted that I go.

'What are you doing at this Conference?' Another pastor was inferring that I had no right to be there. Helen was standing nearby, overhearing the conversation replied, 'Bruce is working under us.'

The CRC at that time consisted of 26 pastors throughout Australia. Today the movement has many hundreds across the world.

Regardless of the calling and anointing of God on my

THE MAVERICK'S ROUNDUP

life, there were voices that considered me a 'maverick,' simply because my Call had led in different and varied paths that were outside the norm. The term maverick was meant to be derogatory but I took it as a compliment. God had truly lassoed me back in my teens; it was man who hadn't been able to sling a bridle on me.

Pastor Harris was President and Founder of the CRC. He was a gracious man and when I was talking to him one day he suggested,

'Bruce, I'm running a refresher course for pastors at the Bible College. I wonder if you could come down for a couple of weeks. You might find it interesting.'

'Thank you Pastor Leo I would like that.' I'd had no formal Bible College training only by correspondence in my teens. This would give me a background in the CRC, I thought. I took time off from work and went to the refresher course. After about a week, You Know Who rang up, 'Bruce you'll have to come home. People are coming to Christ and we can't keep up with visitation and counselling.'

'Pastor Harris, I'll have to leave and go home. God is moving and people are coming to the Lord.' I explained.

'Yes, much as I wish you could stay, I hear the cry. I doubt if you will be back.'

He was right I didn't go to the CRC Bible College - alas I would continue to be a maverick as dubbed.

The annual Pastors' Conference had come around again. It would be nice to spend a few days being ministered to but getting there presented a number of problems. Money was limited and the tyres on the car were bald. Keeping a family of four including us fed clothed and educated needed miracles every day. In after years, some of the blokes who came into the church then have commented on my navy suit being old and shiny on the seat and elbows. I think Cliff Beard may have given it to me for I certainly never

ever bought one.

To attend Conference would need a miracle but we believed we should go and that God would provide.

Halfway across the Blanchetown plain we suffered a blowout. Now we had no spare tyre. We were a little despondent by the time we arrived at Conference. Cliff Beard was the first person to meet and greet us.

'I feel impressed to give you this,' and shoved a large sum of money into my hand. The despondency lifted, God knew our need and was caring for us.

Everyone at conference seemed to be asking,

'Are you full time yet?'

'No I'm still working.' I answered, wondering what constituted full time. I was full time, ministering in the church and working at a job. I felt irritated by their continued inference that a pastor wasn't successful until he was totally supported by his church.

'I've been full time and double time for years and years for the Lord.' I replied rather shortly.

'How big is your church?' was the second question on everyone lips.

'Why? What does it matter how big it is so long as people are getting saved?' I was tempted to reply.

Back in our room I turned to Gwen, grumbling, 'These people want to try pioneering in the country without a strong support base. They live in the city in cosy fellowships. What do they know about pioneering new churches?'

'Maybe they are just curious,' Gwen tried to calm me.

'I wonder at what stage Paul was asked by the other disciples if he was full time.' I continued angrily. 'How many leaders in the early church were worried about numbers when they were being persecuted to within an inch of their lives? Wasn't the main point then spreading the word about Jesus?

'Look, we are serving God not man.' Gwen replied firmly.

During a period of free time at the Conference, I went to visit my parents at Victor Harbour. Dad greeted me and then disappeared. He reappeared when we entered the kitchen and thrust a cheque into my hands.

'Here, I feel compelled by the Lord to give you this.'

I was speechless and then I shared with Pop our needs and the miracles that had occurred. He and I rejoiced together. Before we returned home I bought a full set of Michelin tyres and had them put on the car.

The CRC movement Australia wide was going through a time of great outreach and growth. The Riverland was just one place where the Holy Spirit was moving in the lives of many people.

I can never express my admiration for Pastor Harris and his incredible honesty of character and gracious acceptance of Gwen and me. I felt we had come home and were under a great covering. Pastor Harris's teaching on the New Creation teaching just confirmed again what the Lord had shown me over the years through the writings of E.W Kenyon, the Billy Adams Crusade and Cliff Beard. I praise the Lord for placing these men in my life at the right moment. I could call them mentors but they were more than that –fathers in the faith to lead and guide a son along the pathway of his calling.

Because of growth in our fellowship, it became clear that we must find another base other than the CWA hall. I discovered that the two divisions of the Lutheran church had amalgamated and were building a big new complex. In my capacity as a steelworker I became involved in building this great new church.

The small church that the Lutherans had been using came up for sale. It seated about 70 -80 people.

Old-fashioned straight-backed pews were used as seating but the location was excellent. So the team and I held a council of war.

'We should buy this Church. Its position is right on the corner of the block where everyone can see us and the noise factor will not annoy anyone.' I suggested.

'With what do we buy it?' a practical minded member asked.

'That's a good point. We only have ten cents in the bank,' our treasurer reminded us.

'But the building is going for a song. We should try and buy it,' another voice reasoned.

'The Lutherans are asking for a decision in two weeks time and they want a down payment,' I said.

'We'll tell them we'll buy the church and make the down payment,' our treasurer boldly spoke up.

'Let's go home and think about it and pray.' I suggested. That is what we did.

Later the treasurer worked out that at the time of declaring we could pay the deposit there was only ten cents in the bank. I don't know if Treasurer Ray's statement was holy boldness or stupidity but God came through for us.

We all thought about mortgaging our homes, perhaps selling a car? Taking out a loan? In the meantime, I thought to give Pastor Harris a ring. He broadcast our need through his congregation and one senior businessman became so convicted by the Holy Spirit that he offered $300.00 there and then. But in the morning after a restless night in which the Lord continued to speak to him he offered $500.00 - that was the down payment on the building.

On the appointed day when my colleagues and I were to meet with the pastors and elders of the Lutheran church to discuss the deal and make the payment, we were dressed casually and there was nothing to set anyone of us apart from the rank and file.

'Who is your pastor?' one of the Lutheran men asked, casting a critical eye over us. Maybe he was thinking what sort of cowboys are we dealing with here?

'Bruce is our pastor,' my colleagues pointed to me.

The surprise on their faces was a picture because I had been working on the steelwork of their new church. The idea of a worker/priest was inconceivable to their minds. I also found the situation amusing from another angle. Every time a Lutheran elder walked onto the site the general building crew, especially the brickies, would try not to swear and hush each other up. Yet I, a pastor, working amongst them was not treated to such respect - in fact quite the opposite at times. The perception was that a pastor could not possibly work as a labourer and be authentic, as I've said before the worker/priest concept was hard to accept.

After much discussion over the purchase of the church the question was asked by their treasurer, 'Would you be agreeable to a $500.00 deposit on the church,'

'Sure,' replied our treasurer confidently. We were up and flying. The fellowship became known as the CRC Centre, Berri.

Preaching was always my main calling, and since that day of revelation as to our position in Christ, when I had found the great life giving formula in the little book The Blood Covenant, the thrill of that same teaching found in the Biblical letters titled Ephesians and written by Paul, the Apostle, became ever more electrifying. A Chinese writer, Watchman Nee wrote a book titled Sit Walk and Stand, which emphasised these truths. His writings were brought to our attention at this time giving us a further impetus in our faith.

Soon after we had settled into our new church home

we met Stephen and Virginia Morphett from America. They arrived in Australia to set up Christian Children's Joy-time Clubs. We met them at a Conference in Adelaide and spoke with them over a meal,

'Where do you live?' Virginia wanted to know. 'Have you ever thought of running a children's Joy-time Club?'

'Well, no, I haven't.' I replied my mind turning cartwheels at the possibility. I was on for anything that would help us to reach the community for Christ.

'We could come to Berri and show you what to do and lead the meetings and tell the stories and other activities.'

'Ok you're on.' I said. We'll run a Joy-time club after school for a week under a tent at the church.' We hired an old army marquee and put it up on the church premises.

'You'll need to follow up with a Joy-time club to consolidate the kids,' Steve reminded us.

The Joy-time meetings were successful and so was the follow-up Club. Steve and Virginia used us as a platform to launch their children's ministry in Australia and show the need not to forget the role of children in church life.

This couple imparted all their enthusiasm, ideas and energy to our team of workers. This venture was the first of its kind in CRC and for us in the Riverland.

Virginia could certainly tell a story, and You Know Who brought out her accordion. The introduction of viewing cards and flannel board were great ways to tell a story and keep kids interested.

It was a huge success and the forerunner for children's crusades later for Gwen and me.

Because of our involvement in children's work Gwen and me were given honorary accreditation from the Morphett's Home College based in America. We accepted it as from the Lord.

To be honest I never really felt comfortable in

ministering to children but over the years the ministry was very blessed. I learnt children never follow a miserable person; another lesson learnt was to be a clown for Christ.

Adding the children's work to our outreach meant another building was needed, so the menfolk in our team got to work and soon there was another hall on the back of the existing church.

Children's meetings were extended to Lake Bonney in school holidays with Alan Bailey, a very gifted children's evangelist. He assisted us several times even though he belonged to another denomination of the Christian Church.

Many lives were changed by knowing the power of Christ. The meetings were alive with excitement and expectation at what God was doing.

Chapter Twenty-Six
On The Streets

On the streets we had learnt to work on a short attention span, with several speakers telling short stories and anecdotes that caught the interest. Preaching great long sermons was a no-no; nobody was allowed to drone on. I find it hard to be gracious to boring preachers. We might not have been the world's best singers but our singing and accordion music went with a swing.

The hoon drivers with their extractors roaring past us would lean out of the car windows and heckle us. We would loudly reply back, 'that's not the power; try the power of God in your life. That's the power you need.' All action must be bold.

There was one street meeting I vividly remember in Waikerie. A crowd of young men grouped around us.

'You don't know what you are talking about. We could do better than that,' the leader of the group told us.

'Ok, you're on. You come and stand here where we are and we'll stand where you are and listen to what you have to say,' I smartly replied.

'Come on Joe, you can do it. Have a go,' his mates urged.

Amid the clapping and encouragement, Joe strutted onto the footpath where we had been standing. He looked at us with a smirk on his face and opened his mouth to speak; not one word could he utter. He went down like a pricked balloon, after that incidence Joe dramatically changed.

One of the many incidents that caused much laughter was when Don, a member of our team was speaking. We were all listening intently when he suddenly spun around and addressed those of us standing behind him, 'What was I going to say?' Just as quickly he swung back and began to speak again. It seemed rather humorous at the time and the team dissolved into much laughter. We hadn't written his script and neither were we mind readers.

Taking the streets for Christ always creates incidents.

One night in Waikerie a carload of well-dressed young men from a particular Lodge came and spoke to us.

'We are going down to the river for a bit of fun. You've got the music and the girls. Why don't you join us?'

'We are Christians.' I said, wondering what the catch was.

'So are we. We don't drink and there will be no hanky panky. We just want to hear what you have to say.'

'Ok,' I put it to the team and they agreed and so we spent an hour or more talking to these young men and sharing viewpoints. There was no trouble at all.

Across the years my teams and I have sown a great deal of seed into people lives. Numbers of people today are crossing our paths again telling us how God stepped into their lives forever. I hadn't realised God had spoken to them.

In taking the streets for Christ, my team and I were

pioneers. Not many were actively involved in such a ministry. Often we would contact the police and let them know where we were working and with whom, because our team was visiting all the towns in the Riverland. It was in our best interest to do so. Often we would contact the police and inform them where we were working and with whom.

For instance, it was just another night in Waikerie, a street meeting had closed and the team and I were standing talking to a group of young people. They were firing questions at us and we were firing back the answers. The police, thinking a fight was about to break out drove up,

'What's going on here? You better break it up.'

'We are not causing any trouble we are just talking. There won't be any trouble either,' I assured the police.

'Make sure you don't block the street or you'll have to move on.'

'Please, just give us a go. These young people are not giving us a hard time.' I stressed to the police. They drove off down the street a few blocks and pulled up to watch. They were sure there would be a riot.

It was one of the most successful nights of question and answer with these young people.

Good, sensible questions by seeking young people. It is important to build a rapport.

Through our work on the streets we discovered that hundreds of teenagers gathered at a Shell Roadhouse in Renmark on Saturday nights after the pictures. So that's where we went – to the Shell Roadhouse - arriving about 10pm and leaving about 2am.

Among the first kids that we met were two early teen girls, very promiscuous. They became very friendly and introduced us to many of their friends. It could have been risky taking the teenagers in our group to these places but the team was very strong in faith and supportive of each other. The owners of the Roadhouse didn't mind us being there so long as we didn't cause a riot and stop trade talking about Christ. There would be crises like the time when we were getting ready to go home. A would-be tough guy swaggered up to one of the lads whom I was taking home and began to verbally abuse him. This lad was very slight, very quiet and would have appeared as a good target to bully, and because we were Christians that too was reason enough to abuse.

I was about to intervene When You Know Who stood up and very firmly told the would-be tough to go home. 'You aren't out of nappies yet and shouldn't be out here drunk. Go home to your mother.' The young tough went down like a pricked balloon and walked away; we piled into our car and took off.

So many kids going wild, with parents who didn't know what their kids were doing, wouldn't believe that their kids could do any wrong. Like the minister of a local church that wouldn't believe that his daughter was up at the Roadhouse drinking. He had to believe when one of our team, a member of his church took his daughter home.

Do you know where your kids are? Don't get too comfortable - go with them. The old saying, 'people who pray together stay together,' is very true. Don't allow the family to drift apart and then blame somebody or the Government for not doing something to help. Don't allow walls to be built in the family but keep open the doors of communication.

When we arrived at the roadhouse one Saturday night, we found the young people had decided to go to Martin's Bend that night. Martin's Bend was a few miles from Renmark, a favourite meeting spot for teenagers to misbehave.

'Why don't you come as well,' they invited.

'Yeah we'll come.' They thought we wouldn't of course. 'We've got the Bibles and you've got the booze.' It wasn't every day that people like us were invited to one of their parties. So we went. On the way I called into the Police Station,

'My team and I are going to Martin's Bend. There's a mob of young people going there and they've asked us to come.'

'I don't think it's a good idea to go down there with that lot. There'll only be trouble.'

'I don't think so, sir. We know them and we'll be careful.'

'We'll come down in case,' the police decided.

'Please give us a fair go. We're sure there won't be trouble.' I assured them.

We arrived at Martin's Bend. So did the Police but out of sight of everybody.

The kids sat around in groups and in twos and drank and necked. Our team sat amongst them while I spoke a few words about Christ. All was going well and friendly until a big Valiant full of shouting, abusing young men arrived.

They sat in their car revving the engine, surveying the scene.

'I'll go and get rid of that mob of wowsers,' one yelled and jumped out of the car. The first person he met was Basil who just loves to talk about what Christ did for him and is very good with his one liner statements. The young tough forgot to send us packing.

Another tough decided 'I'll get rid of them, you see if I don't.' Joy met him and engaged him in a conversation; he too forgot to send us packing. A third young man, 'You watch me deal with those wowsers.' He jumped out of the car and ran to the group. One of the group was there to greet him. He too became caught up in the discussions. Soon the whole carload was involved with the engine still running. The tension was so strong that it could be felt, however, the team didn't back off but boldly proclaimed Jesus and the power of the Lord just fell on those young men who wanted to fight only to end up asking questions and forgetting what they meant to do. It was a good night.

I went to the Police Station on the way home, 'Thanks, guys for not interfering.'

'Did you have any trouble?'

'No, we had some good talks to the guys, it was all OK.' I assured them.

Always during these tense moments Gwen and Gay would be around behind a car or bush praying and what was potentially a dangerous situation would dissipate and the words would be accepted. Our Saturday nights were spent among the teenagers until 2 am.

When we went out onto the streets we took with us an excitement, our listeners caught that enthusiasm and were intrigued. What was happening was bigger than us it was God at work in our midst.

To whom did Christ seek out? The people in the market place, the streets and the outdoors, wherever the people were, Christ was there.

It is recognised that a leader must lead; he or she must be in the front. It sometimes takes a lot of courage to lead from the front. Christ was leading us from the front he was going before us. I was taking my leadership from him and leading the team.

Unfortunately the establishment, be it the church or a business, will brand that person who takes the initiative to lead as a rebel and takes steps to stifle the so called rebel, the impetus of the establishment is lost reducing it to mediocrity. The so-called rebel is also shackled, unable to flow and be a fruitful person.

The eagle stirs its nest so that the young birds must learn to fly and leave the nest so God stirs our nest and hopes we will leave our comfort zone and learn to fly in uncharted skies with him.

Chapter Twenty-Seven
Building On Two Fronts

There were always two streams to my Calling, the day-to-day steel construction for a living and the leadership of winning people to Christ.

After Grant engineering closed and moved to Adelaide, I applied for a job with John whom I mentioned in an earlier story. I was successful in getting the job. John worked from a large uncovered yard, which I found different after working for five years in a shed. It was a bit of a shock.

It was John, my new boss who won the contract to build the Lutheran church on which I worked at the time of buying the redundant church building for ten cents. I was very involved in the building of the new church and the buying of the redundant building. This was the nature of my Calling.

As is usual in the workforce there grew to be a good-natured rivalry between the bricklayers and the welders. The brickies always complained that the welders burnt their string lines, though I didn't see it happen.

If in good fun we could play a trick on each other it would make the day more interesting, particularly if I was the butt of the joke. The bosses didn't mind so long as the work wasn't neglected. The brickies were a hard working, hard living bunch and I was a puzzle to them because I neither drank nor smoked; got on well with everybody, worked hard and was a parson as well. This gave me many opportunities to talk to the men during lunch breaks.

During one such break we were sitting down leaning against a wall of an existing building when somebody was heard bumping around inside.

'Sssh! be quiet, keep the cussing down, it maybe one of the pastors,' one of the brickies said.

'What about Bruce? He's a pastor, but you cuss around him?' One of my teammates laughed. Suddenly they saw how silly they'd been and wanted to know,

'What's a pastor? What does he do, Bruce?' someone asked.

'Why is he any better than other men?' another person wanted to know.'

I was able to get a message across to these men.

Swearing at me or around me doesn't upset me, but when the name of Jesus is used in a foul manner; I am then upset and will quietly take the person aside and explain why I object. Often an apology is made to me but it should be made to the Lord.

At the end of a particular building job, Lou, the foreman, and I couldn't resist playing a joke on the brickies. We took their two wheelbarrows and welded the handles together. It was several months before we heard of the outcome then one day I met Butch in the street and in the course of conversation, 'Bruce, you will get yours in due course,' he threatened.

One day I would get my come-uppance but in the mean time I couldn't resist another trick that would add to the already mounting tally. I was told to drag a welder up onto the highest scaffolding and weld a beam in place for a bell to hang on. With a lot of puffing and blowing I finally hoisted the welder up.

Having done the job and packing up to get the welder down again, I noticed a good pair of sneakers left behind and I had an evil thought. I took two welding rods and stripped off the flux and threaded them through the lace holes then welded them to the beam of the bell tower. I heard later that the scaffolding had been taken down and Butch had to get an extension ladder to get his sneakers.

The Lutheran church we built was beautiful. I felt proud of what we had achieved and wondered what it would be like to preach in every Sunday, but it wasn't part of my calling to preach in such beautiful surroundings. Even though I was preaching every Sunday the buildings I spoke in were just ordinary practical meeting places.

I felt sad in a way, people had paid large sums of money for a beautiful building to please the Lord and gain a right standing with him, ignorant that he had already given them a right standing through faith in Christ. It wasn't the beautiful building that gave them a right standing, all they needed to do was to believe and accept and live in the finished work of Christ's sacrifice.

If only it were possible to make people see what God has already given them but it's a truth that seems to only break across the mind as a revelation. Let me just use this quote: 'It is by grace you have been saved, through faith – and this not from yourselves, it is the gift of God – not of works, so that no one can boast.'

I must back track a little at this point. Ian the Kiwi had obtained a job at a new irrigation settlement, Sun-lands, Waikerie when he first came to the Riverland. He travelled each Sunday to Berri to worship at the CRC Centre in Berri of which I was now pastor.

Ian's life and witness made his work mates curious and amongst them was Kevin Hodges. The Lord spoke to

Kevin very clearly through Ian's witness so much so that Kevin decided to go to Ian's church, the CRC Centre, Berri and see for himself what Ian was talking about. Later Kevin was to say, 'I was impressed. The preacher sang with great enthusiasm even though he was out of tune. The service was very unusual but everyone was sincere. I felt that God was here.' Kevin and Jacki were convinced that Christ was their saviour and accepted him into their lives.

Kevin and Jacqui discovered completeness in their lives and couldn't stop talking about it to their best friends Basil and Joy Porter, who lived at the settlement of New Residence.

Because of Kevin's friendship with Basil and Joy, Gwen and I were invited to Basil's home 25 miles away for an evening of questions and answers. Basil and Joy raised all their objections, theories and questions. Thinking that the conversation was just going around in circles I said,

'It's getting late; I think we'll call it a day. Can I pray before we go?' I said wanting to do the spiritual bit. 'Yeah, that's fine.' Basil shrugged.

When I looked up from my unbelieving prayer and looked at Basil, he was crying his eyes out. I thought it was best to leave him to sort himself out and also I had to go to work next day.

A couple days later the phone rang,

'Bruce, can you come and talk to us. I'm still crying and so is Joy.' Basil was on the phone.

'Ok. I'll be there tonight.' I was eager to see them and answer their questions and offer counselling. The Lord really spoke to them and their experience was extra-ordinary and miraculous.

But there was a concern, Kevin and Jacqui voiced that concern about their three-year-old son and asked for prayer. Gwen and I joined their concern.

Bradley was taken to a specialist and diagnosed as autistic. In those days nobody knew very much about autism and Bradley and his parents were sent home to cope as best they could. They were distraught not knowing how to help their son.

Gwen and I didn't know either but to take pressure off Jacqui we decided to bring the toddler home with us for a couple weeks.

We would pray for him and over him and seek the Lord for a miracle.

Both Gwen and I prayed for wisdom and studied Bradley's behaviour and felt not to let him withdraw into himself but draw him out continually.

From the time he woke in the morning until he took an afternoon nap and again until in bed at night, Gwen, our four children and me never allowed him to be alone. At meal times when we were all sitting around the table we would get him to make noises and repeat them after him as if it were a game. We would praise him, telling he was a good boy for making the sounds then we would all add the words 'Mum' or 'Dad' until he eventually repeated it with us.

By the time he went home he could say several words. He still tended to want to go and stand with his face to the wall; however, Kevin and Jacki took over where we left off. Today Bradley has held a job for many years and lives a normal happy life though still a bachelor. The Lord gave us and the parent's wisdom and a miracle in what could have been a very sad situation.

The bottom line to the story of Kevin and Basil is they both became pastors in the CRC and pioneer associates of mine. Ian, the Kiwi, married and he and his wife spent several years in Papua New Guinea as missionaries.

There is another family, one of many, influenced by

the experiences of Kevin and Basil - the Kingsley George family. They were neighbours of Basil's. Kingsley vowed he was not going to get caught up in Basil's religion but one day when Basil was visiting, Kingsley complained of a bad back. Basil asked to pray for him and his back was healed. Kingsley and his family decided to go to Berri to the CRC Centre to find out what was happening there.

'Listen you kids, we'll sit right at the back and when the service is finished we'll make a quick getaway.'

'Ok, Dad.'

But the Lord spoke to Kingsley and his wife Marion, and they found themselves talking to the other people there. They too later accepted the Lord.

As all this was happening, another event occurred. No, I didn't backslide, or fall from a plane, instead the veranda of a fruit-packing shed that I was working on collapsed. The clip lock roofing came undone and twenty metres of veranda collapsed. Two mates and I fell three metres to the ground, breaking the heel of my foot.

My first thoughts were of my two mates and what happened to them. Lionel! He was an older man, was he hurt? I didn't seem to be hurt so I tried to get up and help him. I found myself being roughly pushed back down, 'Sit down and don't move.'

A passing crane driver saw the accident happen and rushed to the scene.

'I'm Ok, what about Lionel?' I protested.

'You sit there until someone can look at you. I'll check on Lionel,' he ordered brusquely.

I fell feet first and my heel was squashed flat as a pancake. I was taken to hospital and treated and sent home to languish for several weeks. I accepted my enforced rest as a time to gather my thoughts for whatever might be ahead. That rest was soon interrupted one Monday morning when

I heard an agoning cry;

'Bruce! Help' Gwen screamed from the laundry.

'What's wrong?' Thinking it must be bad if Gwen was screaming like that, I grabbed for the crutches and jumped out of bed but the crutch caught in the blanket and I landed on my hurt heel. The pain was excruciating and I fell to the floor.

I had to hope Gwen had survived her drama because, no way was I going to be able to help her.

She had caught her hand and arm in the wringer of the washing machine. She was able to push the release bar and her arm though red was not injured. She had heard the thump from the bedroom and rushed in to see me on the floor. Between us I got back to bed.

X-rays later confirmed that the fall had probably done more good than harm though rather drastic and painful. My foot had not been placed in plaster; it was thought it would heal better without. The fall had seated the heel fragments into a better position.

'You will never be able to climb again; your leg is a half an inch shorter than the other. You'll probable get arthritis in it as you get older,' the doctor warned.

'But I'm a welder and rigger. It's my job to climb,' I despaired.

'You'll have to get a desk job or something.'

'But what will I do? Where will I find that sort of a job?' I could see my life going south at a great rate of knots and made a decision that if possible I would get back the use of my ankle as fast as I could. It was another crisis that threatened to derail my life. Was this the way the Call was leading?

I have met many ministries who claim that God will lengthen legs through prayer. I have always been sceptical although I admit that many miraculous things have occurred. In my case my leg wasn't lengthened but I refused to let it hamper my work.

My boss, John, was very pleased to see me back at work and for a period of time I did light work at the base.

Finally, the insurance assessment was made allowing for compensation for my disability

'What can't you do now that you could before?' The doctor queried, looking at my foot.

'I can't walk a beam three metres or more off the ground. I can climb but very dependant on my arms. Oh, and I can't stand on my broken foot and put my trousers on.'

'You're mad,' the doctor exclaimed disgustedly, 'You should claim a much higher level of disability.'

'I can't tell fibs,' I protested. 'Besides I won't be beaten. I want to keep on with my job.'

'Well considering you will have to have another operation at some later stage, you will receive the sum of $1500.'

I've had lots of operations since but that promised operation was not one of them, praise to the living God.

My life continued northward unaffected despite the negative predictions of the doctor. I was able to follow my Call both in the work place and in the ministry.

The enforced period of inactivity due to my ankle was of great frustration to me. There was no work cover or help as there is today. I was not able to drive and Gwen became my taxi driver, just an extra chore for her to fit in to her busy life style.

She came home from shopping one day and sighed as she cooked some mincemeat for our evening meal.

'What's up honey,' I detected a discouraged droop to her shoulders.

'There was a nice chicken in the butcher's today, nearly

bought it. I thought how nice a change in our diet would be. I didn't think I could afford it.'

'Things will be better when I get back to work.' I tried to be cheerful but I was frustrated at being unable to work and ease Gwen's load. That night I had to go over to Berri to a church meeting. Gwen was the driver and I with my crutches drove from the passenger seat.

Almost into Barmera on our return trip, a truck passed us laden with vegetables and goods for the market in Adelaide the next day. As the truck pulled ahead of us something white fluttered to the ground caught in our headlights.

'What fell off that truck?' I said sitting up a bit straighter.

'It looked like a chook or something.' Gwen slowed trying to see what it was.

'It's a duck. Stop. We'll have that. A dog or fox will only get it.'

'Maybe we can find out if anyone lost a duck.' Gwen suggested.

'Pull over,' I was impatient with Gwen's slowness to act

Away from the headlights it was hard to see the duck and catch it in the rough scrubby side of the road.

'Catch it, Gwen, don't let it get away.' I was hopping up and down along the side of the car on my crutches. I was sure Gwen was going to lose it.

Finally she caught the bird and handed it to me while she drove us home.

Next day it was in the oven. Oh what a succulent duck it turned out to be, bigger and better than any chicken from the butcher and cheaper as well. The Lord had provided for us a little luxury. I remembered another quote: 'Before they call I will answer and while they are still speaking I will hear.'

Chapter Twenty-Eight
A Sense of Justice

When to react and when to let things lie is always an important question to consider in the work of the Lord. My ire is roused and I become very indignant when an individual is considered or imagined to be a lesser individual by another person. It's then I feel somebody must speak out and I usually do. Many times I've severely flouted authority over these issues.

Two members of the Aboriginal Welfare Committee were ministers of religion. My anger was roused by the lewd, filthy conversation of these two men. They must have been trying to impress the other members of the Committee with their broadmindedness. But they impressed me the wrong way. I quietly took the Chairman, Mr Jack Foote also a devout churchgoer aside,

'Jack, I've had it! If those two men continue with their filthy talk I will call them to task publicly to shut their filthy mouths.'

'Well I don't really like what they are doing either, Bruce.' Jack too, was a bit fed up but he was more diplomatic. He must have had a quiet word with them because never again did they indulge in lewd talk during our meetings. A confrontation was avoided thanks to the diplomacy of Chairman Foote.

Diplomacy didn't always come to the fore in my dealings with men. I objected to the boss's untruths and cruel accusations about me being a bludger in front of my work mates, this particular day. I went home stewing, talked to Gwen but I would not be calmed down. I had to go past his home on my way to a prayer meeting so I called in.

'Hello Bruce, come in,' his wife opened the door.

'No, I would like to see the boss out here, please.' I usually entered like one of the family.

The Boss came out, 'What do you want to see me about?' he had a very abrupt manner.

'Nobody talks to me in front of my works mates like you did this morning, It was very wrong as I was the foreman, and I'm not a bludger.' I blurted out just as abruptly.

'Aw, Bruce, I'm sorry. I say these things from time to time. I apologise. I talk to my sons like that sometimes and I know I shouldn't. I'm sorry Bruce,' the man stuttered an apology and excuses.

'Well, I don't want it to happen again,' I felt appeased by his back down and apology. I felt in a better mood as I reached the prayer meeting. Well, somebody had to challenge him.

Next morning we were well at work welding a big batch of roofing trusses when the boss rolled in with a great flourish.

'Stop work, everybody,' he puffed importantly. 'I want everybody over here, please.' When we had gathered around he said,

'I want to explain that I wronged Bruce yesterday when I called him a bludger. He is a very trusted worker and very reliable and honest. I'm very sorry for what I said.'

In standing up for my rights something changed between him and me from then on. Even though we sometimes went head to head on problems that arose, we worked through them. He never treated me in such a manner again. I believe that Christians don't have to act meek and mild, but as righteous children of the living God. Christians should stand up and be counted.

A very dangerous situation arose and needed some plain speaking when I was working to set a huge stainless steel wine tank into position at a winery. The jib brake on the crane wouldn't work and the boss was standing on the side abusing me in good round language. Thoroughly fed up I ran the tank up the jib clear of the ground, switched off the engine, leaving the tank suspended on the gears. I climbed down from the crane and said to the boss, 'That's it! The tank can stay as it is until you find out what's the matter with the brake.'

The bottom of the tank was of a conical shape and could not sit flat on the ground and would have been damaged if it had. It was worth a huge amount of money, so the boss ordered sleepers to be stacked around the base of the tank for support over night.

'Well, everyone, let's go home and Bruce, give some thought to why the brake won't work, please.'

'I think I've worked out the problem, Bruce,' the boss said when he greeted me next morning.

'What's the problem?' I was curious, because I was very suspicious.

'I serviced the crane the other day and I think I have wound the cable the wrong way on the drum.' It wasn't always easy for the boss to admit being in the wrong. So we headed for the Winery to fix the crane.

The boss looked at me sheepishly and barked, 'Get in

and drive it and if any big mouth shouts at you tell him to get lost.'

'Yeah, boss.' I agreed with a grin. The work mates laughed. The tank was placed in position easily after all that drama.

The boss was very black and white in his relationships so when he took a dislike to someone, he did it thoroughly. One of the young men whom I taught in Bible Class and a member of the CRC Centre was also a member of my work crew. He became a victim of the boss's dislike.

'That kid is a thief, I don't trust him,' the boss confided to me one day. He continued to give the young man a hard time.

'There isn't a dishonest bone in that young man's body,' I eyeballed the boss angrily. 'He's as straight as the day is long.'

The boss then did an about face and trusted the young man. Later when the young man left his employ, the boss presented him with a gold fountain pen. That young man eventually became a pastor in the Assemblies of God.

I don't believe in a meek and mild Jesus. The Jesus I believe in cleansed the Temple, confronted hypocrisy and evil front on.

The boss had won the contract to erect the steelwork of a new flash Catholic Church in Barmera. The usual bricklaying crew were there and we were reunited to build this church. I think Butch was sporting a new pair of sneakers but I wasn't asking for obvious reasons.

The design of the church was quite unique and called for three huge steel trusses right across the main building. I was again operating the boom crane. Of course, there was the usual comments and banter between the two trades.

It was Friday and payday,

'You better get down to the bank and cash this cheque

before closing time.' John handed me my weekly pay cheque.

'Thanks John, I'll do that.' I took it and put it in my shirt pocket. The heat was stifling and I was wearing a loose sleeveless cotton shirt to let maximum breeze through. I had just picked up a huge truss with the crane and was carefully driving around to the site when Butch jumped on the left hand running board of the crane, hose in hand spraying water full blast. I was soaked, cheque and all much to the delight of everybody in sight.

'Got him the *%@# at last,' Butch exalted.

'Well done, boys,' I laughed. I could only sit there and take the dousing and think how good the cool water was on such a hot day.

Several hours later I remembered the cheque. Then they all gathered around as I spread the cheque out and weighted it down on the crane bonnet. It appeared readable and when I took it to the bank, it was honoured.

The Brickies reckoned they'd had a win and were pleased. I agreed that I had received my just desserts. My pay was in my pocket and we all went home feeling justice had been done.

I couldn't help thinking that on a different level Jesus made sure justice was done by becoming the go-between between God and me; Jesus saw to it that justice was done by placing his life on the line or in this case - the cross.

I took the full brunt of Butch's revenge that I'd earned so with God I deserved his full wrath because I was unable to meet his standard yet Jesus came and stood in and saw justice was done so I could enjoy the presence of God with out blame. On this level everyone is happy - justice has been done.

Chapter Twenty-Nine
Going Full Time
(Beyond The Black Stump)

What is a workingman's world if he doesn't wet the baby's head?

'Bruce, the wife of the boss of another big building company has had a baby and he's putting on a keg after work to wet the baby's head. As my foreman, I expect you to be there,' John the boss said.

'I dunno John. I don't drink.'

'I want you to be there,' he insisted. 'I'll see that there is a bottle of soft drink,' and away he went. When I arrived the keg was opened and the beer flowing. John noticed me enter the shed and he muttered, 'Sorry' and dashed off. Next thing he's back with a bottle of Woodroofe's Lemonade, and in front of 60 –70 men he poured out a glass and handed it to me. I felt it was a stupid thing to do but John often did things without thinking. The foreman carpenter of that other firm immediately cut in to talk to me.

'I've never seen anyone with enough courage to stand out like that,' he said.

'I didn't get much choice in the matter, did I,' I replied. 'I was forced.'

'I admire your stand. I can't do that, I feel I must go along with everybody else,' he admitted as we went on to have a very good chat.

Amongst workingmen, I have never felt pressured to conform to their level. To use a quote from the Book of books, 'Do not conform any longer to the pattern of this world...'

As God moved in the church so there was a big move at work. John won some very interesting contracts. One was to build cantilever verandas along whole streets in the main shopping precinct in Renmark, taking out the wooden posted verandas. Also in Renmark I was employed on a three-month contract to erect new steel catwalks over a number of wine vats, replacing the old wooden ones. The manager of one particular winery came along one day,

'Bruce, knowing your position in the church you would be interested in coming and viewing today's bottling of Communion wine.'

'What's the difference between this and any other wine? I asked as I followed him to the bottling room.

'Nothing really, the wine is a good light red. Of course religious icons are printed on the label.'

So there you have it. I still don't use wine for communion nor does any church that I'm associated with.

God moved across to Loxton and into the Murray Mallee. To keep up I approached John for a reduction in time to three days a week, which he graciously accepted. Eventually I resigned. John in front of the workmen said, 'If at any time you want to return there is a place here for you. Even an hour or two a week, please come back.' He had changed immensely and I had learnt so much under him.

THE MAVERICK'S ROUNDUP

The area I travelled to minister to people was from Renmark to Waikerie and through out the whole Riverland and Mallee area. People were accepting Christ and the church was expanding.

One of the last jobs Lou and I did together was build a bell tower for the Greek Orthodox Church in Berri. Part of the contract was to repair the bell and cart it and the tower from our workshop base in Glossop to Berri where the church was.

When we had serviced the bell we were supposed to bag the tongue but the bag 'accidentally' fell off and the bell rang all the way to Berri. Christmas and Easter were wrung in and many other occasions as well. It was understood that the bell had to be tested…

I was also saying goodbye to a very rewarding phase of my life.

The Greek Orthodox Church had a lot of free advertising that day. But I digress. Interest in Christ was increasing in Loxton and I couldn't keep up with visiting and counselling.

Caught up in the move of the Holy Spirit was a car dealer who accepted the Lord through the witness of one of his salesmen. He opened his garage up for BBQ's and meetings. It was one of those garage meetings that Basil and Joy Porter first attended, and where Basil began to question what Christianity was all about along with many people.

I worked throughout the Riverland and it seemed God had worked with me and with the witness of dedicated people. I often regret that I didn't do more as a shepherd of the flock but I don't see how I could, the expansion was almost too big and too fast for me.

Our first service in Loxton was in a big tent and we invited evangelist Peter Allard as guest speaker. His message to put it in a nutshell was 'I am crucified with Christ nevertheless, I live but not I but Christ lives in me.' And another scripture,

'It's no longer I that lives but Christ that lives in me.'

We advertised extensively and bathed the event in prayer. It was a new experience for the town's people for they were very comfortable in their brand of Christianity.

The first night saw Peter preaching his heart out to a few faithfuls until a large number of young people arrived. They milled around outside and were quite disruptive and wouldn't come in and sit down and listen so Basil and I and some of the team that were not involved in the meeting went out to talk to them.

Gwen had set up a bookstall at the back of the tent to make available Bibles and books. She discovered a Bible had been stolen but had asked the Lord to bless it to the taker. Years later we met a woman and Gwen asked her if she had a Bible,

'Yes I have. Years ago there was a group held a tent meeting in Loxton and I pinched a Bible from their stall. It has been very precious to me.'

The Lord said, 'My word shall not return to me void,' and it hadn't.

So Peter Allard came and went and returned a second time, adding to what God was doing.

Into all this mix a rabbit trapper called Tex Bailey or is it Harry, arrived. By whatever name he used we knew him as Tex.

The impact that this man - who was God's man for the day and dared to be different - had on the farming community was incredible at the time.

Personally, the experience of seeing what God can do with a rabbit trapper who is committed certainly enlarged my thinking.

THE MAVERICK'S ROUNDUP

Tex was fearless in his witness and had no time for convention, but I saw how God used this man and tried to steer the people he contacted, into the fellowship of the church. There were many people without a church connection and from all manner of walks of life.

Tex would witness to a non-believing farmer and if that man would not listen, 'I'll be back next year in the middle of a drought,' he'd warn the farmer. Sure enough there would be a drought and Tex would be back to talk about the Lord to that farmer.

Entire families were baptised in the name of the Lord, all contacts of Tex.

This was why I quit work in an effort to reap the spiritual harvest. The salary was very small but my God was big and Gwen and I knew that we must move with God.

Tex had parked his caravan out in the scrub beyond Alawoona and I believed I should go and spend time with him. He knew how to trap rabbits. For him it was an art. He would set 300 traps in a night and in the morning there would be 200 rabbits in the traps.

'The rabbits belong to the Father,' was his belief. It was his policy to give new believers a good concordance Bible and the Dake's was his choice.

One gentle, gracious lady came to the meetings. She had become isolated from her church because of her drunken abusive husband. This man prided himself that he could get rid of every parson that came to see him. When I visited him he tried to be as abusive, argumentative and hateful as he could be.

'I'll see you next week Gordon,' I said as I left. I was determined this man was not going to win this round.

'I'll bet. That's what they all say,' he laughed gleefully, thinking that I wouldn't come back for a second dose of his abuse and that he had won.

'I won't be here, when you come next week,' his wife whispered as I went out the door.

'That's Ok. There might be some fireworks,' I expected Gordon to get really angry.

The day for visiting arrived and I called on Gordon, 'Good day, Gordon,' I called at the door, 'Have you got the kettle on?'

'Ha! I didn't think you would have any more guts than the rest of the namby-pambies.'

Week by week I drank many cups of tea, heard his stories, more than I wanted to but God won. It was a tough fight but Gordon was delivered from alcohol. He had been in an accident brought about by alcohol and was badly injured. Later he had a leg amputated.

The mallee farming area out from Loxton could be said to be beyond the black stump, it was so harsh and isolated. Rabbits had devastated the country. There were so many rabbits that a whole hillside appeared to be a moving mass of brown animals.

The farmers were incredible people taking up this type of land farming it and expecting to make a living.

It was Conference time once more and two of my colleagues, Mark Walker, Brian Howard-Jones and myself decided to travel south through this mallee country just to get a feel for the bigger picture. We stopped for a cool drink at the Alawoona Bakery owned by Irene Heinrich and husband Neil. He was the baker. Alawoona was the biggest little town in that area, a centre at that time.

We were always looking for God's next move and were intrigued to find that the Heinrich family had built a small hall down the side of their shop to hold parties and receptions in.

'Wow! This would make a good place to hold a meeting in,' we three looked at each other and grinned.

'Mrs Heinrich, what would you say about allowing us to hold a church service in your hall?' I approached this small, birdlike woman.

'I don't know,' she looked very surprised. 'I suppose we could. I'd have to ask Neil, my husband. He's asleep just now. He was up baking all night.'

'Ok. We'll think about it and see what might happen.' I said and we three men went our way, but that hall remained in my mind, I never forgot it.

Through the ministry of Tex Bailey, quite a number of people were interested in attending a service but the CRC Centre in Berri was too far to travel, so services were arranged and guess where, the Heinrich's hall on the side of their bakery. Faithfully, Irene attended the meetings but not Neil; he was supposedly sleeping after working all night.

I used to stand to preach near Neil's bedroom window, I doubt that he slept much but heard plenty. Later he accepted Christ. It was the Heinrich family that became involved in the move of God in that area and that hall was the centre.

Tragedy struck the Mallee community when Mr Johnson, respected farmer and church elder in the Uniting Church in Loxton, was killed when spotlighting. Only Neil could have known where Tex's camp was and where I was staying at the time. It was 2 am when Neil found me and took me back to the Johnson farm to be with Nan, his wife.

The accident occurred during a holiday period and the ministers were away so it was a very difficult time. Alawoona is a long way from where I lived at Barmera and that made funeral arrangements difficult. The decision was to have the funeral in Alawoona; however the only church in the little town was an Anglican. The covering priest lived in Loxton. He graciously came and opened the church and allowed me to conduct the funeral. The building seated about ten people and because I was unable to go beyond the altar rail I had to stand with my elbow on the casket. There were about 200 people attended the funeral, most had to stand outside. Mr Johnson was a very much loved and respected husband, father, church leader and farmer. I never had the privilege of knowing the man but came to know and respect Nan, his wife and family.

From tragedy there is always triumph and from that tragedy many people came into an experience with God.

I was more than busy visiting people and running meetings. A loose policy of having a service in Berri once a month was established. The other services were held wherever a group of people gathered and needed fellowship.

For a time we held services in an unused little old stone church somewhere in the Mallee. The acoustics were abominable, when I preached my voice bounced around the ceiling many times. When the congregation sang it sounded like all the choirs of heaven were singing.

'The singing is anointed,' Gordon the ex-alcoholic raved. 'I'll record the services so I can replay them during the week.'

'Well if that is how you see it, Gordon, but the sound bounces around the ceiling and I can't stand it.' I complained.

'Aw I've never been in a meeting where God's Spirit was so strong,' he was adamant.

'If you are blessed that's all that matters,' I smiled.

God is not governed by the tyranny of distance and he continued to move beyond the black stump to the tiny towns of Wanbi and Paruna. Thanks to Tex, there was a lot of interest in God a way out there because of some outstanding miracles. Tex had everyone asking questions about God.

THE MAVERICK'S ROUNDUP

Doug Whittaker was a farmer, with a large family, living at Wanbi. He and his family were among those whom God touched.

'Bruce, will you stay for tea?' Margaret, Doug's wife, invited shyly when I was visiting them.

'Yeah, that would be nice, thank you.' I replied.

While tea was cooking, Doug and his sons showed me around the sheds and over the farm, just bare rolling paddocks of sand. I thought we'd had it tough as kids but compared to the way this family lived, we were in paradise.

When we sat down for the meal, Margaret had cooked the usual spuds, pumpkin and meat. I must have looked a little startled because on my plate was a small lamb chop and everyone else had generous portions of steak.

'We didn't like to give you the steak, its emu meat and you might not like it.' Doug apologised.

'Thanks Doug, but now I'm curious, I'd like to try a bit, please.' I asked.

It was impossible for my false teeth to chew it at all. I learnt again not to make quick judgements and learnt to appreciate the circumstances of the less fortunate. I always felt guilty pulling into Doug's yard in my big Valiant that I had been persuaded to buy by the newly converted car dealer in Loxton, in comparison to Doug's old bombs. It was a revelation to me how these people could make a living out of that land.

Doug became the unofficial welcomer at the meetings because of his gusty laugh and shouted greetings. He helped organise a meeting in the Wanbi Town Hall where Pastor Harris was to be guest speaker. It was near impossible to get Pastor Harris into the country he too was flat out on Operation Outreach. However, he consented to come to this rally.

Pastor Harris arrived at Wanbi in his big Chevrolet

and was met and welcomed by Doug with his loud voice, hearty laugh and Aussie vernacular.

'Struth! It's the Boss,' Doug exclaimed, astounded, poking his head through the window of Pastor Leo's car.

'What's here at Wanbi that makes it a centre,' Pastor Harris asked. The vast distance and isolation amazed him.

'Oh that's easy,' laughed Doug, 'Wanbi's got the best watering-hole in the country.'

Pastor Leo looked around. Waterhole? Where is the waterhole? All he could see was rolling sand dunes being tamed to become farms.

That meeting was powerful. There were some great victories in people lives and several wonderful miracles.

A few weeks later I was talking to Pastor Leo,

'Bruce, when I was talking to that Whittaker bloke, he told me Wanbi had the best waterhole around. What did he mean?' Pastor Harris asked.

'Pastor Harris, Doug is talking about the one and only pub for miles around.' I laughed. That made Pastor Harris's day. He never forgot his experience beyond the black stump.

Doug lived 80 miles from the church at Berri but somehow the family used to attend church every week, rain or shine.

'Bruce, I think the car's given up the ghost. It won't go any more,' Doug informed me one day. I'd already helped him fit cord rings into the engine.

'Is that so,' I said, wondering how I could help this gutsy man.

'Yes, I'll have to skip church for a while until I can get some sort of transport.'

A big debate with You Know Who might throw some light on the problem, I thought. We had just bought a bomb for our daughter Diane to drive to her first job in Berri. The outcome of the debate was the little car was given to Doug. Another car was bought for Diane.

'Thank you, Bruce,' Doug didn't know what to say.

'Just thank the Lord,' I brushed aside his profuse thanks.

So Doug and his family didn't have to skip church and his hearty laughter continued to echo through the building.

It seemed that in finding Christ these people found a new zest and drive for life. They were real new creations in Christ with resolve and purpose.

The Centre at Berri was consolidating. A team of good men and women was emerging and leading the assembly. The Sunday services were well attended. With a building and regular services music was needed. A couple from Adelaide donated a lovely Pianola and Gwen became the musician.

We were becoming accepted by the other churches as the Pentecostal stigma faded after years of persecution and loss of our friends. The Charismatic Movement was about to take off and some of the local churches were daring to be 'charismatic'.

Baptism by immersion was practised for people who wished to demonstrate that they had become Christians.

One very incredible baptismal service comes to mind. At a particular part of the river where boats were launched became the venue of a baptismal service. Two tents were erected on the bank as dressing rooms for those wishing to be baptised. The only drawback was the water could not be heated, but nobody was worried. Whole families were baptised that day among them were several from the Uniting Church. The minister gave his blessing even attending himself.

'I would like to be baptised. My husband doesn't see the need to be baptised by immersion but he doesn't mind if I am,' a young woman explained after I had given both her and her husband instruction.

'It might be a good idea to wait until he feels it is the right thing to do.' I advised.

'But I really feel the Lord speaking to me about it,' she persisted.

'Well, let's leave the decision until Sunday and see what happens at the service.' I didn't want her to go against her convictions nor did I want something to come between her and her husband.

After baptising a number of people I glanced toward the bank to see who was next when I noticed this woman with tears running down her face. Beside her stood her husband stripped to the waist in his navy suit trousers. He had suddenly felt the need to be baptised and so joined his wife. The atmosphere was electric. Everybody was crying by now and there seemed to be more water on the bank than in the river.

Later, when filling up with petrol at the local service station, I noticed this man; he was wearing his shirt and suit coat atop a pair of my baggy brown shorts without embarrassment. He looked radiant. We all returned to the church for a mighty celebration of new life in Christ at a communion service. Twenty-two people were baptised that day.

It is always very hard work to get outstanding, powerful overseas ministry into the country areas or even top Australian ministry and that is often where good ministry is needed the most. Tex Bailey ignored this trend and contacted Ted Whitesall from America and paid him to come from his own pocket. I approached the State CRC Council about the integrity of this man and found they wouldn't stop me from inviting him to speak but were not keen to endorse his ministry. Tex and Pastor Leo had some meaningful discussions concerning Ted.

My team felt to give Ted a go regardless of what State Council thought, it is easy for leaders in the city to acquire good visiting ministry.

Ted's ministry and manner was very unorthodox but from his ministry came miracles and demonstration of the Holy Spirit. It was born home to me that God accomplishes great things by using 'bent sticks to float axe heads.'

One of the many outstanding testimonies from Ted Whitesall's ministry was when Tex Bailey met Len Mason. Len was suffering from stomach ulcers, his future was very bleak and he was wondering just what was ahead of him. Len didn't believe in anything but after Tex talked with him Len said,

'If the Lord will heal me he can have my whole life forever.'

The next service at which Ted preached and prayed for the sick Len was in the prayer line. He was healed. He went home and sat down to a roast meal something he had not been able to do for years. Len and his wife Ruby, wherever they went, they witnessed about Christ. Till the day they died the name of Christ was on their lips.

Len remained in the Berri Assembly supporting my ministry for several years until I moved to Whyalla.

I, with my elders, have taken risks using different people not always successfully, but sometimes very successfully in the release of people and great ministries that otherwise would have been lost to the Kingdom.

The question has been asked, 'What would you do if you had your life to live over again?' The reply is, 'Take more risks and help people into God's kingdom.' I agree.

Because Ted was unconventional, I have to confess, the follow up was hard work and I needed all my people skills to steer the fellowship onto firm ground.

Alan and Betty Nance, farmers from Paruna, another

couple to stand out as leaders in God's move in the Mallee. Our daughter Robyn later married their son Rodney.

The Nance farm, to my eyes was nothing but white sand. That this family managed to eke a living from such dry land is a tribute to their courage and cleverness. Knowing many people from this community enriched our lives by seeing how they handled themselves in such difficult situations. Today people think they have it tough. I sometimes wish I could take them back and show them what tough means. It was great to serve these people.

Chapter Thirty
Called To The City

Conferences seemed to have a certain effect on Gwen and me. It was at a CRC Conference in Melbourne that I was challenged yet again by the Lord when we heard that Pastor John Ridley of Whyalla was leaving. He had pioneered the church in Whyalla for ten years and for sometime had been asking for someone to take his place.

Due to family reasons he could no longer afford to stay and was leaving regardless of whether there was a replacement. Gwen and I were challenged to pull up stakes and move to take his place.

Our children were very reluctant to leave friends, schools and find new jobs and so the change meant much heart searching and seeking God to be sure the move was part of his Call on my life.

From the Berri Assembly point of view it would continue to grow. God had raised up strong men who needed space for their ministries to grow and my leaving would give them that space needed to flex their faith and talents.

Of course it was a wrench to leave friends and lifestyle.

GWENNETH & BRUCE LEANE

We had spent 8 years in Barmera beside Lake Bonney; our kids had grown up there. Gwen had built up a very profitable dressmaking business that she had to leave not knowing what was ahead of her in Whyalla. We had spent twenty-one years in the Riverland and with my involvement in the work force and the church it was sure launching into the unknown.

There were a number of disquieting comments that made our decisions harder:

'Why are you leaving when the church is going so well?'

'You are wrong to move.'

'You've got it made, why move?'

But God wasn't telling me not to move and from past experience, he had always made his will loud and clear.

From Whyalla there were no promises of financial security. We had no idea how we were going to live, as the Assembly was not a big one. All that was promised was a rented Housing Trust house that John had leased. It was a pioneering assembly though. There was a small hall, kitchen and toilet amenities.

Eventually the day came to move. Robyn's boyfriend Rodney Nance was not going to be left behind and he moved with us. Diane was soon to be married to Arnie Weir and so she stayed behind to board with members of the Assembly and for whom she worked. Robyn, number two daughter must find work and our two sons were still at Primary School. Our future son-in-law Rodney needed work.

To transport our furniture I borrowed a tri-axle trailer from Grantly, my former boss and a 4 by 4 Toyota truck from a member of the Berri Assembly. While I drove the truck our family travelled in our car towing another trailer with small tatty tarpaulins covering our goods. Thus we set off late one stormy afternoon, driving to Eudunda and pulling up under the canopy of a closed service station.

We tried to rest but the mosquitos were so bad I finally roused everybody,

'Come on, let's go.' So we set out again, reaching Whyalla about 8 am next morning after having driven most of the night. Besides the mosquitoes I drove the truck at least halfway before I was able to unlock the gears and release the four-wheel drive. Every time I got the truck above 40 kilometres an hour the trailer threatened to jack knife. On the back of our truck, just for fun I had tied a notice saying, 'Faith without works is dead, and here is the works.'

The Ridleys were moving out the same day but they expected us to be later and were not ready for us to unload our furniture into the house. The weather was threatening rain but it held off long enough for us to be able to unload important pieces of furniture and keep the rest dry and for the Ridleys to load their furniture without damage.

'One more thing before I go,' John instructed me.

'What's that, John?' I thought he was going to say something profound.

'Will you visit the people on this list and collect the money owing to me. I've taken photos of them but haven't been paid.' John too, had been supplementing his income as a photographer. 'Do you want to take over my clients and work as a photographer?'

'No, John, I don't.' Photography was not my cup of tea it would be bad enough trying to collect the debts but I don't think I collected one dollar for him, it all seemed so futile and I'm not a good salesman or a debt collector.

John and Elizabeth had been hard workers and faithful to the point of sacrifice and the difference between John and I must have sent shock waves through the congregation. John was an educated, English gentleman and I, a practical, down to earth, uneducated, Aussie. We were truly opposites. However the Assembly took our family and us to their hearts.

Our move to Whyalla was when the city was experiencing a boom in the 1970s. Whyalla, at the time, was considered to be the largest provincial city outside of Adelaide with a population of over 30,000 people. It was a comparatively young city and home to young families and young people. It was an exciting place to be.

Iron ore was mined, steel manufactured and the building of ships attracting people from every nation in the world along with all the social problems that go with such a society.

We didn't need to go overseas to be missionaries; the nations were on our doorstep.

Our daughter Robyn worked as a checkout operator in a supermarket; she was the only Australian on the staff.

We had always lived in rural areas; our friends had always been from rural districts. To live in an industrial city amongst industrial workers was a challenge. Rural people and industrial people have two differing mindsets and so we faced big changes and challenges. My Call was to lead me into some very strange corners in this melting pot of a city.

It took a while to settle into the city. I was on a part salary and Gwen had to start again in the dressmaking business. Our house was a typical brick Housing Trust home on a very big block where a couple of trees and lawn grew but no garden to speak of.

It was very hard to establish relationships, which I felt were very essential; many of the flock were English, and I was an Aussie. To cross the culture divide wasn't easy.

Rodney easily found work and so did Robyn; our sons settled into Primary School. I dug into my toolbox and brought out a pair of secateurs and began a round pruning fruit trees and roses. The pruning round grew very quickly but it was labour intensive and poorly paid. Old neglected apricot trees take a long time to reshape and don't respond in one year. People didn't understand this and didn't want to pay to wait. I built a round of 150 gardens to prune and clean up.

Out of the pruning job I saw an opportunity to dry fruit especially apricots. So as I pruned I noted the gardens and when the fruit was ripe would return and collect the unwanted fruit. Many people had huge trees in their big back yards and the fruit only wasted. Because of my time on the fruit block, drying fruit was a cinch. An elder in the Assembly, Bob Relyea caught the vision and came to my aid. One year we dried many kilograms of apricots.

Bob and his wife Francis are now missionaries in Peru the country where they met when Francis lived there with her Aunt and Uncle. Bob was a Peace Corp officer.

Since their family has grown up, they have returned to Peru.

Of course the pruning is only seasonal. In the summer I had no work, that's when I decided to enlarge my toolbox to include a chain saw. I began a tree lopping business removing unwanted gum trees. People thought I was mad, as trees in Whyalla were very precious. I paid for the saw in six months and developed a good business. The South Australian Housing Trust started giving me the trees that were too big for their gardeners to deal with.

Over the years I felled many huge trees without cranes or cherry pickers. This occupation proved to be excellent for my two sons, Philip and Raymond. They became very proficient apprentices. Working on big trees soon became its own advertisement. We had many exciting experiences. When I lived and worked in the Riverland I used to look at all the buildings and verandas I worked on. Now I often reminisce over the trees that I cut down.

One Christmas a dear elderly lady from the Uniting Church rang, 'Bruce would you give a quote to cut down two very tall Norfolk Island pines in my front yard?'

Big was the right word and there was no room to clear fell them. I had to cable them down a piece at a time using the Land Rover as a winch. Raymond was my assistant on this job. Very soon he was a favourite of the lady of the house who plied us both with cakes and biscuits, calling Ray, 'A sweet young lad.'

After felling one of the trees a bloke from across the road approached me,

'Excuse me, but please don't take that tree down before 9.30 am tomorrow. I'm a fisherman and I've been using these trees as a marker for my fishing spot for over twenty years. I have to find a new marker to replace the trees.'

'No problem,' I replied.

At the completion of the job the lady of the house said,

'I'm very pleased with your work. Here is a bonus for Christmas.'

'Thank you very much,' I rejoiced at the Lord's goodness. Christmas, that year, was a lot more lavish than was expected.

Talking about Christmas, God always goes on holiday at that time of the year. The offerings are always much less and so the pastor has less in his pay packet for his Christmas fare. However, God never allowed us to be deprived of anything; he always managed to find a way to provide for us.

One year we were going to take a much-needed holiday over Christmas and were planning just how to stretch our meagre budget, when Philip rushed up to us after the church service.

'Dad, we can't get in the car to go home.'

'Why, what's the matter? Do we have to take someone home or do we have a flattie?'

'Just come out and take a look,' Philip urged.

Wondering what had gone wrong I followed Philip out and received the shock of my life. The car and boot were piled with boxes of Christmas fare that we could pack and take on our holiday. Jean, bless her heart, had put a lot of thought into her purchases that would be useful for a camping holiday. Her generosity was beyond the call of duty. She will never know how much she did for us that Christmas.

But the Lord hadn't finished setting us up for Christmas that year. The next day we had a visitor. He was passing through Whyalla on his way to celebrate Christmas in Adelaide.

'I just thought I would drop off this cheque and say Merry Christmas,' he said as he passed me a slip of paper. After he left I opened the cheque and again I was overwhelmed by the Lord's provision. What is it the ancient writings say? 'He is able to supply all our needs according to his riches in glory.'

I have digressed from cutting down trees as I have one more story I want to share: Ray and I were coming home after doing a job and pulled into our street when we saw that a big pine tree had split in half. One half fell on the fence and the other half rested on the roof gable.

'Look there! I'll have that job.' I said to Ray. 'I'll go in and give them a quote right now.' So I knocked on the door and gave a quote.

'No, we'll get the tree removed ourselves,' the owner was rather cold on the idea.

'Well here's my phone number and if you change your mind give me a ring.' I drove home. In less than an hour there was a call to come and cut the tree down. The boys and I had fun proving our efficiency. Nobody could undercut my quotes, because my overhead operating costs were kept to the bare minimum. My competitors were always over equipped and had to quote high. They were not organised for a quick turn around. By now there were two chain saws in my toolbox and ultimately I finished with four. I couldn't afford to have broken down in the middle of a job. My life was too busy. My toolbox had turned into a toolshed.

Because the city was made up of young families, the number of kids was amazing. Gwen and I saw the size and number of schools across the city and saw an opportunity going begging. Fresh from our successful children's work in the Riverland it was obvious that we had a scheme or two up our sleeve to reach kids.

After debate with willing members of the Assembly and new contacts from several other Fellowships in the city, putting up a tent in the school grounds, if possible, might be the way to go. Welding I could do but sewing up a big tent was stretching it a bit, so I found a canvas maker in Adelaide who would make a tent according to my specifications, which were huge. I had to devise a way in which women and inexperienced people could easily help erect the tent.

The canvas roof was gabled and the sides made of blue plastic sheets reinforced. I mounted three big poles down the centre and placed three winches on them. The ridgepole was 2 inch steel pipe. The canvas roof would then be winched up the poles into place. I would be racing from point to point - advising people how and what to do. We learnt to erect this monstrosity and pull it down very efficiently and quickly in the end. It all took time to organise and I had many a brainstorm during the night in tent fabrication.

THE MAVERICK'S ROUNDUP

Preparing song sheets, making up flannelgraphs to illustrate stories, building a team of enthusiastic workers, teaching ideas and principles was part of reaching the multitude of kids.

Being a member of the Ministers Fraternal I invited the other ministers to be part of this venture. I pointed out that their Sunday Schools would grow. Even this carrot dangled in front of them didn't excite them. The idea was too way out. There were people from other assemblies who did become keen members of the team though.

Our first tent meeting for kids was held in the Hinck's Avenue school where our sons attended and close to our home and church. The Head master had known us from the Riverland and he was willing for us to put up the tent in the school grounds. Something not ever dreamed of today.

The tent in the schoolyard generated great interest amongst students and teachers. Our bright songs also sparked a musical revival as teachers brought out their own instruments and taught the kids songs at school.

Our rapport in the Hinck's Avenue school paved the way to opening up other schoolyards for children's meetings.

We would expect to start the first meeting with 100 kids and each day attendance would build to 240 children. We didn't use seating but spread old carpet on the ground and the kids sat on the ground enabling us to seat many kids. The meeting would last about one and a half hours of non stop songs, activities, stories and memory verse for five nights a week. Then a club would be formed as follow up. There were several couples that became club leaders.

The school ministry was not without many incidents.

One day four kids were seen sliding down the gable roof of the tent. It wasn't long and I heard about it. They were having a great time. I raced around to the school but

I was a bit slow and they got away from me. Fortunately for me, they left behind their very good jackets, just the right ammunition to catch the kids but how best to use it? I threaded some light chain through the sleeves and padlocked the jackets to the roof rack on the Land Rover when we went to the next meeting. After two nights, the owner of the best jacket showed up, 'Mr Bruce, could I please, have my jacket?'

'No. Not until you tell me your name and address along with an apology and promise not to climb on the tent again.'

'Yes, I'm very sorry and I won't do it again. Please can I have the other jackets?'

'No, tell their owners they have to get their own the same as you.'

The young miscreants came forward, gave their names and addresses and made promises not to do it again.

'Ok, if any of you climb on the tent again, I shall be visiting your parents and reporting you to the police.' No more trouble in that school.

At another school, a lad was spotted and recognised interfering with the tent. As I knew the headmaster reasonably well, I suggested,

'Why don't I put on my Security Uniform and revolver and if you would call him into your office I could then have a good talk with him.'

'Good idea,' the headmaster agreed and set up a meeting with the lad.

I gave the lad a good lecture and there was no more trouble at that school.

We ran these meetings over four years and about 4,000 kids came through the tent flaps. On top of the children's work were the usual two Sunday Services, day-to-day pastoral duties and meetings, making life very full.

The tent did double duty for other outreach meetings. During my Whyalla ministry I had been asked to go and spy out the need for an assembly at Alice Springs, which I did. Then later Pastor John Ridley and his family, Pastor Basil Porter and his family, Gwen and I and some of our family went back to follow up and have a holiday at the same time. Later Basil and Joy and family moved there and assumed leadership of the fledgling Assembly.

As pastor in Alice Springs, Basil invited me up for a campaign so I packed the tent, gathered up a team and returned for a campaign at Anzac Hill in the big tent. It also saw service in Port Augusta for outreach meetings. So the big tent saw a lot of service.

One of my regrets through the years of ministry is because the CRC was a young organisation there was not enough of a lifeline to feed the outreach ministries. These ministries sometimes foundered because there was no strong support.

I learnt during my time working on the fruit block that a new vine can be started one of two ways. One: Plant small vines and care for them day by day. The second is to bury canes still growing on the parent vine so that the parent vine provides life and sustenance to the new vine. The new vine starts twice as quick and strong. In those days the outreach lifelines were non-existent and the assemblies were slow to grow and sometimes didn't. Fortunately today some leaders are using the layering principle to plant new assemblies. It doesn't matter how far underground the cane is buried just so long as it is attached to the parent vine likewise the parent assembly needs to financially and spiritually nourish the new church.

With all the work and responsibility a little bit of light relief from the daily grind was needed. As a family, we decided that because Philip had successfully matriculated, I would take him and Raymond for a trip in our 15 HP Morris tourer that I owned at the time. We visited Chambers Gorge and were headed to Arkaroola camping all the way. The car was packed to the roof. All was well until I hit a cattle grid. Because the car had no clearance, the engine was torn from its mountings. The carburettor came through the bonnet. The wheels were stove in and the car looked like a humped back camel. I tied the engine down with wire and limped into Arkaroola. Two new tyres were scrubbed out over the remaining sixty miles.

'Good grief, how did you get that car here?' the garage owner was amazed.

'With great difficulty, anyway, will you lend me some jacks and welding plant so I can fix the car enough to get home,' I suggested to the garage owner.

'Yeees, I suppose so.' The owner was very reticent to allow a stranger to use his gear. I didn't blame him because I wouldn't either in his position.

Throughout the next day, I jacked, welded, heated and hacked, reshaping the car enough to get it home.

"What do you do for a living?" The garage owner was intrigued after watching me cut and shut the car.

'I'm a minister of religion,' I crawled out from under the car and pushed up my welding helmet as I answered him.

'What!' He looked as though I had two heads.

'Despite my dirty appearance, that is my official title.'

'Now I've seen it all.' He rolled his eyes for a confirmation from Heaven and looked at me in disbelief, adding, 'Look, I'm closing up shop and going home. Is there anything that you need?'

'Yes. Can you leave the arc welder out? The exhaust pipe is squashed flat. I will have to break it and re-weld it.'

'You can't arc weld an exhaust pipe,' the owner said

emphatically, 'but I'll leave it out any way.' I soon became a class exhibit as people dropped by to see the parson sort the car out. I did weld it and it stayed welded until we got home.

Next morning I started the car up for a test drive. There was no fifth or reverse gears. Turning the car needed an acre paddock.

'Ok boys, pack the car, we're going home.'

At the nearest town I stopped some way from the police station to report the grid. I didn't want the policeman to spot the car and decide to take a closer look at it. He might have put it off the road and left us stranded.

Thirty miles from home a bearing began to scream; I let it and drove into the yard and switched off the engine and there it stayed.

With the insurance I bought a Series 3 Land Rover, which became very valuable for carting the big tent from school to school and weekend camping trips and holidays with our sons. It wasn't a good run-about so I paid a visit to the car wreckers and found a many-painted Cortina. Its problem was the clutch had been assembled backwards. Because it was cheap I brought it home and fixed the clutch and it went like a charm. It certainly didn't look beautiful with its many-coloured duco.

I drove it to Adelaide for a Conference one time, pulling up beside a new Valiant.

'Bruce, what are you doing driving a car like that. It's a disgrace to the Lord.'

'That's all right, Pete, but it cost me less to come from Whyalla than yours would just crossing the city.'

I often thought about how Christ walked the dusty roads. He had no flash car or luxury conveyance.

Did people of the day chide him for being a disgrace to God for walking instead of riding a donkey? I forever marvel at the provision of the Lord to keep me moving. I was still only on a part salary at this time in my ministry.

Thinking of salaries the church treasurer treated us like we were not worthy of our wage. I had to ask for the cheque and You Know Who was a bit testy. A lot of hospitality was needed and sometime the larder was bare.

After several years I suggested that he present a Treasurer's report. He left town taking the books with him. 'I'll bring them up to date and send them back,' he suggested. But I never saw the books or him again. A funny thing happened, after he left the offerings soared. I had many questions in my mind as to the reasons why and they were not charitable.

Chapter Thirty-One
Chaplaincy

It was suggested that I might like to drive for a security company on weekends. I applied and got the job.

Every Sunday night after the evening service I put on a security uniform and strapped on a revolver and drove all night covering 80 - 90 businesses across the city. The only thing I ever shot was an injured dog that was hit by a car. No one ever questioned my action.

'How can a minister carry a gun?' People would continually ask me. I got the impression it was a sin.

'I would rather have a Spirit filled, child of God carrying a gun than any sinner I know.' I would answer. They would go away thinking about that statement.

One of the many incidents that occurred while driving for security happened on a Thursday morning. It was at a meeting of the Ministers Association of which I was Chairman at the time. During this meeting I wore the hat of a pastor, in the afternoon I became a security officer guarding the BHP payroll. I had to stand on the footpath with a repeater shot gun at the ready as well as a revolver on my hip, while the boxes of money were carried out to the armoured van. Coming toward me was one of the priests whom I spent the morning with.

'Good afternoon, Leon,' I greeted him cheerfully.

His eyes popped at my mode of dress and gun, and gathered up his robes and fled without saying a word, much to my fellow security officer's amusement. Throughout my life I have worn so many different hats that people are confused trying to fit me into the right slot.

Sergeant Bill of the Whyalla Police Force was a member of the Assembly and it seemed that many times our paths crossed during a time of crisis. Like the time I found a man lying on the median strip, moaning, doubled over in pain. I rang the police to report the man, when they arrived it was Sergeant Bill. I found later the man had gone to the deli to buy milk but he had recently undergone a vasectomy and had indulged in some horseplay too soon that had hurt him causing him to collapse. He came good when attended to.

I often found myself in the right place at the wrong time or should it be the other way around. Anyway this night I found the lights on in a supermarket. The premises were not on my list to visit but my gut feeling was that something was wrong. So I stood in the street in the middle of the city and fired three shots into the air, but no assistance appeared. The lights went off so back to work I went thinking it was not my business and all must be well.

Next morning a dear sweet lady from the church rang me,

'Bruce, could you please help my son, he and a friend broke into a supermarket last night and this morning the police found them under a bush counting the money. Would you be prepared to help him face the court later on?'

'Well. I'll go with him but I won't plead for him.' I warned her.

THE MAVERICK'S ROUNDUP

Many people have no idea about court procedure or how to act. My advice is to sit in the court for a few times before your time to appear and watch proceedings to be familiar with what happens and where to stand and how to act and how to address the magistrate when you are called.

Appearing in court is one thing but when you enter empty premises on a dark and stormy night it is very spooky. A footy club building down on the beachfront was on my list of premises to check and when I pulled up I thought I heard a cry. Way out in the gulf prawn trawlers were at work and their voices were carrying clearly to shore. After checking the premises and punching the time clock, I heard the voice again. So I swung the utility down the esplanade and shone the spotlight along the beach picking up what looked like an orange sleeping bag lying in the water.

I went to investigate and found a woman on her back with the waves washing over her. As I was pulling her out the waves, I asked,

'Did you call out?' I asked as I pulled her from the waves.

'No, she mumbled, 'only to my God.'

I called the Police and almost immediately two burley policemen arrived and rudely told me,

'Get lost, you aren't needed any more.'

I stood back out of the way but waited to see what would happen. When the ambulance arrived I heard the ambulance driver say he was the woman's brother-in-law. She had become very distressed because of family problems. Throughout a long night I cautiously kept a check making sure she recovered. I never met the woman again but knew she had recovered.

I remembered the words, 'his eye is on the sparrow', and rejoiced that God heard the silent cry of the woman and spoke to me. That is my God!

I have never adopted the belief that we have to put ourselves under the blood of Christ each day. With the way in which God has led me, sometimes in a crisis, there isn't time to put myself there. I simply trust God that I live in him and he in me. With this outlook, I can say boldly, 'If God is for me who can be against me.' Understand that righteousness is a living day-by-day experience.

It is all very well to expound on Christ being within you but in the dead of night, big engineering factories can be hair-raising experiences. I entered the premises of one such firm and found the lights on. Cautiously checking the premises I decided that nothing was out of place and sat at the manager's desk to write a note explaining what I'd found when something heavy landed on my shoulders. The hair on the back of my neck stood on end. I reached around, roughly to deal with 'it' and finished with a huge ginger tomcat in my arms. He purred me to death. I found a cat hole in the wall. The boss thought it a joke when I told him. I did too when my heart rate settled.

Such experiences test how truly we live out the statements of faith that we declare so glibly.

Fear, though, is still a warning system that God has built into us. We can walk in faith but we can still have the daylights scared out of us. A man is a fool if he is not careful.

When I first arrived in the city I wondered just how I would find the haunts of the young people, how I could discover what made the city tick. I was warned as part of my job not to become involved with people on the street. But I did befriend some of these young people and found out a lot of valuable information. So God used the MSS security to provide much needed finance as well as teach me all I needed to know about the city. Many doors of contacts were opened amongst the owners and managers of businesses.

Through the Ministers Association I came in contact with Chaplaincy in BHP and the Shipyards. Several of the ministers were already chaplains in various areas. With my background in steel and employment as well as pastoral ministry, they thought I would fit in. The BHP Company was desperately short of chaplains, which was an honorary position. The Shipyards employed 3,500 men and women, so I agreed to take up the chaplaincy, but in what section was the question. The two areas open were the Pellet Plant and the Rolling Mill.

'Don't go to the Pellet Plant,' one of my colleagues said.

'Why is that?' I asked

'It's absolutely filthy down there. Nobody wants to work there.'

'Ok. I'll go down there then,' thinking that that's where the greatest need would be. But when the Company was approached, they said,

'No, we want Bruce to go to the Rolling Mill and the Finishing End.'

So that is where I ended up. I had to wear a white hard hat with Chaplain and my name on the front of it.

Being a chaplain I had almost unrestricted access to a huge area.

The superintendents offered me their offices should I need to talk privately to any of the men. I loved it and was soon absorbed into the Company and the city.

The bosses and superintendents wore white hard hats and one day I approached a man working in a very demeaning job, hoping to get acquainted with him.

'How are you today, mate?'

'No good! Too many %$#@ white hats; aw, sorry Pastor, I didn't mean you,' he stuttered, when he looked up and saw who it was. Oh well, you can't win them all.

Another incident comes to mind, one of the men had approached me; we'll call him Joe.

'Bruce, could you talk to my boss?'

'What's your problem, Joe?'

'I've got a problem with alcohol and have been told that if I'm caught drinking at work again I'll lose my job.'

'What are you doing about beating the addiction?' I wanted to know if he was sincere in wanting to overcome the problem.

'I'm going to AA and it's helping me.'

So I went to see the Superintendent knowing that Joe's foreman was an even worse alcoholic. I'd been warned that the Superintendent had a temper and that when mad he threw his hat on the ground and jumped on it. After a very healthy debate Joe kept his job and the Superintendent didn't jump on his hat.

Another time a retiree from the Company spoke to me, 'Chaplain, would you please come to court with me,' at the same time pulling out a great wad of notes, 'I don't mind paying you.'

'What's the problem? What's happened?'

'Well, I've worked at the Company for twenty years without a blemish on my record either at work or in my private life. On my last day my mates had rolled out the alcohol and I drank too much. I was picked up for drink driving and abuse.'

'Ok, I'll come and stand with you in court and speak for you.' I felt a bit sorry for the bloke.

So I appeared in court with the man and pointed out to the Judge,

'This man's conduct in the community has been exemplary. It's a shame that he has to leave work and the community after all this time with a mark against his name because his mates were over generous with the alcohol at his farewell party.'

'Thank you, Chaplain,' the Judge said, 'I see your point and will take into consideration what you say. There won't be a mark against his name.'

Outside of the court the man said, 'Thanks very much Chaplain, I do appreciate you speaking for me, I was terrified.'

The roll of money didn't get another airing. I had lost a day waiting with him for his case to be called.

Because of my work as a Chaplain with BHP I helped many alcoholics and in due course became recognised as a bit of a patron saint to Alcoholics Anonymous. I thought it to be a dubious acknowledgement but from this association came the offer to be a guest speaker at the next annual meeting.

An hour before the meeting I got a ring from a lady to come quickly, her husband was threatening her and her daughter with a carving knife. Hurrying around to the home I found the husband off his head with alcohol and was very violent. So I grabbed a solid kitchen chair and moved in to disarm him. It was pretty wild for a few minutes but eventually he became the usual sad, crying, full of self-pity, wreck that alcoholics all degenerate into.

This man was the main contact person for Alcoholics Anonymous and anyone could call him for help. It was he who had arranged for me to be the guest speaker at the coming AGM meeting of AA. So I helped to get him to bed and then rushed home to change my clothes for the meeting. Also later that night I was rostered to drive for Security.

When I reached the hall where the meeting was being held, I felt very angry and steam was coming out of my ears at the double standard being fostered by AA at that time. I felt very strongly about the alcoholic's creed in adopting a power greater than themselves, but never calling that power by the right name – God, so I based my talk on the quote made by the Biblical hero, the Apostle Paul: 'He whom you ignorantly worship I declare to you.' The members at the meeting looked stunned but the leaders from Adelaide became very angry and asked me to leave.

It was time for me to go to work as Security agent anyhow but over the next hour and a half I kept sneaking back to hear the members droning on, 'I am an alcoholic…'

It is like asking me to say I am still a sinner but saved by grace. I may have been a sinner saved by God's gracious favour, but by believing in Jesus Christ I have been given a status above that of being a sinner. I urge readers of these words to stop trying to be good and accept the gift of goodness that Christ offers when he stood in for us at the cross.

It was interesting that in the ensuing week the local members came to visit me one by one and apologised, not that I needed an apology, but not the visitors from Adelaide. I never associated with AA again and I didn't continue to try and help the man in question.

After the alcoholic incident I became involved in a marriage that was showing signs of breaking up. A young English couple were having marital problems and had come to me for help. I felt we were getting somewhere, and then they asked,

'Pastor, can we ring the UK on your phone?'

'Yes, I'll give you fifteen minutes only,' I warned. It was during the day.

The call went on and on. I was becoming agitated. I could see the phone bill skyrocketing and was worried what You Know Who would say. I got them off the phone eventually. The call maybe served to stabilise their marriage.

THE MAVERICK'S ROUNDUP

After their departure I went to bring in the mail and found a battered envelope in the box. Ripping it open out fell $40.00 in notes wrapped in torn brown paper. There was no explanation or anything. I thanked the Lord for his provision in paying the telephone call. I truly hoped the couple would be able to get their act together after all that. It was then time to go to the Ministers Association meeting.

During the course of the meeting I was asked, 'Bruce, do you believe that miracles are for today?'

'Yes, I do,' I was remembering the letter and the $40.00.

'Have you seen any miracles lately?'

'Yes,' I said, looking at my watch, 'Twenty minutes ago, is that up to date enough?' I went on to explain what had happened.

Years later I met my old friend Doug and his now grown son from the mallee

revival days, I told him the story of the miracle of the $40.00. He turned to his son,

'Don't you tell this story to your mother.'

It was, as I suspected, Doug who had sent the $40.00 in payment for the car that I gave him all those years ago.

Amazing how God can be so on time with his provision and also challenge other believers in their faith.

'My God shall supply all your need according to his riches in glory.'

Chapter Thirty-Two
Significant Others

Pastors' wives are very unique people. Unfair demands and expectations are piled on them. They are measured against other pastor's wives or what is imagined to be the perfect pastors' wife.

'Oh the previous pastor's wife was so wonderful. She dressed so well and was so talented. What do you do?'

'When can I see the pastor? I've cooked a cake for him. I want to give it to him personally. He looks rather thin, don't you think?'

'He understands me more than my own husband does. You are so lucky to have him.'

'You are standing in the way of his ministry.'

I could go on forever with the comments aimed at pastors' wives. I want to pay tribute to all pastors' wives. They are unsung heroines, because it is always the pastor who gets recognition regardless of his wife's achievements.

My life with You Know Who has been a partnership. She has helped and shared my load in ministry. I could never have coped if she hadn't been beside me.

Every business project that she started has had to be

abandoned because my call moved us on, especially when we moved to Whyalla.

Arriving in Whyalla the sewing machine was unpacked and advertising went out to try to make contact with potential customers. An opportunity to take up industrial embroidery arose so there was a shift in direction as we launched out to buy an industrial embroidery machine and Gwen became a machine embroiderer.

It wasn't the automatic machine of today; it was hand operated using a hoop. I had to draw up the designs and then they were transferred to motifs for the sports clubs, motor racing clubs, T-shirts and whatever else was to be embroidered. The work was very repetitive having to repeat the same design up to two hundred times if a sports club had ordered that number of motifs.

As a mother and later grandmother, through many of my health challenges personally, and put downs publicly, Gwen has always been my friend and helpmate. We are still in love. We have laughed and cried together, prayed together. Gwen has been the prayer warrior. I am aware that most of her close women friends, either by death or movement of my ministry, have been lost. Rather than make waves and create trouble, she has resigned from positions in the Assembly and allowed another to take the lead.

It takes two halves to make a whole and anything that I say or have done comes from a shared ministry. I might talk about 'I' but it should be 'we'. Together, we will travel until we relocate to the Kingdom of Heaven and together hear the Master's words, 'Well done good and faithful servants.'

There is another group of people who are important in an assembly. They are often a Pastor's nemesis, but they also are his right hand men. They are the Oversight or Elders.

There are many wonderful men who have stood with me and I have felt bereft when for one reason or another, I lost one, as happened when I first came to Whyalla.

'Dad has had a heart attack and is in hospital, could you please visit him?' Elaine his daughter was on the phone.

George and his wife Grace were pioneers of the Port Lincoln Pentecostal Assembly and later in Whyalla. George was a steady, faithful family man and a pillar in the Assembly.

When I got to the hospital he was able to talk. His wife and daughters were there. So we prayed for him but I felt very concerned for him and for his family and though I had done the faith bit, praying for his healing, I had no conviction that he would get well and I felt a bit of a hypocrite but as I looked at him I felt strongly that it was his time to go home. In fear and trembling but with a strong desire to be practical for the sake of the family, I asked the question,

'George, do you have a will?'

'No! That's what worries me. Can you help?' he whispered.

I swung into action and rang my accountant; I had pruned his trees for years as payment for his services.

'Chris, can you dictate a will for me?' I explained the situation.

'Get a piece of paper and write down what I dictate to you.'

I handed the phone to Elaine and she wrote as Chris dictated. The Will was witnessed and signed.

Next morning George was in Glory. My advice is: make a will - don't put it off. The family can be left in very hard circumstances. Grace and her children would have had a hard time had that will not been drawn up.

A hole had been left in my Eldership at his passing.

THE MAVERICK'S ROUNDUP

Elders sometimes have hidden agendas; they are only human as is everybody else.

'How are elders appointed in the church?' a certain member approached me one day while living in the Riverland.

'The pastor appoints men who are proven to be honourable, trustworthy, with a good sense of business and love the Lord above all else.' I explained.

'I think I would fit the bill. I'll guarantee $25.00 a week to the church offering if you will put me on your oversight,' The Certain Member said.

'I'll have to think about it,' I hedged. I could see that he was angling to run the church as he did his business and that he was offering a bribe. It was tempting; it certainly would have fattened the church coffers. I remembered Ananias and Sapphira and knew that this was not of the Lord. When I gently declined he was very unhappy with me but I wanted to please God rather than man.

I am very aware that elders receive more scriptural comment than do pastors and wonder if there hasn't been a wrong emphasis placed on the positions of Pastor and Elder. I have grown to appreciate elders throughout my ministry and consider them the foundation stones of many assemblies. Any Assembly that doesn't have a God-called Oversight is structured to fail, even cease to exist; pastors very often move on but elders remain and stabilise the assembly in times of change. I believe that an assembly is only as strong as its Elders or Oversight.

Among the significant others is Doctor Geoffrey Bingham. His ministry and teaching left a deep impression on my life. For a number of years he was Dean of the Adelaide Bible College and before that on the mission field in India.

Geoffrey built a centre at Coromandel Valley in the

Adelaide Hills under the name of New Creation Ministry.

I believed that Geoffrey put the meat on the bones of the new creation message that was revealed to me so many years ago when reading E W Kenyon's books. He was one of South Australia's best-known theologians maybe throughout Australia.

Distance, finance and my own ministry responsibilities kept me from becoming more involved in the New Creation Ministry. However I did share closely with Geoffrey in a number of inter – church missions conducted by New Creation Ministry at Christies Beach, Maclaren Vale, Broken Hill, Port Lincoln and in Whyalla. It was thrilling to see how God reached through tradition and touched so many people's lives.

I have never seen equalled, the power and authority that Geoffrey exercised in preaching and teaching the Bible, as evidenced by the depth of conviction occurring in people's lives. Geoffrey had no use for manipulation and gimmicks often resorted to in ministry.

Geoff's knowledge and depth of understanding of the scriptures was awe - inspiring. I often wished that I could sit at his feet and learn more. But it seemed it was not part of God's call on my life for I was led into other streams of service. Yet I profoundly respected his ministry and contribution into the lives of so many people across the nation and the world.

Taking a safari holiday through the remote north of South Australia we invited Laurel, Geoff's wife to travel with us. It was memorable for many reasons one of which occurred as we approached a rail crossing at the ghost town of Farina. No train had rolled along the tracks for many years but the warning to look for trains and stop hadn't been taken down.

Our son Philip was driving his little Suzuki van ahead

of us and being young and wanting to keep the law, he obeyed the sign. Laurel was driving our Land Rover and I realised that she would never be able to stop the vehicle in time that we were going to run into Philip and yelled, 'Miss him Laurel!' She did! She swung the steering wheel, applied the brakes and headed for iron rail guards along the crossing, while Gwen and I held our collective breaths. However, she managed to miss the rails and Philip with no damage to either vehicle or us. Philip was oblivious to his danger and wondered what was going on as we shot passed him. We thanked the Lord for his intervention in a crisis. The Land Rover was a heavy vehicle, a prayer meeting could be held in the time it took to stop the vehicle.

I can only thank God for directing Geoffrey across my path and giving me a more complete understanding of what is popularly termed the New Creation teaching.

Chapter Thirty-Three
Building Bethel Centre

One thing became clear to me, I should build the auditorium and finish the church that John Ridley had sacrificially laid the foundations for a number of years previously and which now had become too small.

I knew it would be tough but my toolbox now housed a welder and other equipment; I had gained experience and skills needed to build it.

As I think about it and the many volunteers who donated many hours of work and finance to such a project, I am thankful that they came alongside and worked with me until the job was done. Hooray!

With great foresight, John had acquired land in a very strategic position in the city and built very good amenities and a small hall, which later became the foyer as John originally intended it to be.

I began the building with some trepidation, because I still had to earn a living as well. I don't think I'd advise any pastor to start a building project, pastor the church and earn a living at the same time.

The generous financial support by various members

showed their love for the Lord and sensitivity to his prompting. Bless them every one.

There was only one ticketed builder in the Assembly at that time. The Lord surely blinded the building officials along the way.

The foundations were laid in one day. I urged the contractor to supply more men and trowelling machines. But no – they knew best and so it became a race to finish the floor before it set. All praise to the men who helped that day but I was very unhappy with the contractor's end results.

Another testimony to God and the men was shown when the whole steel framework of the auditorium was erected in a day without a hitch, thanks to the plate cutters, drillers and placers.

Before the day of erection the steel beams had to be tacked up with three pin welders. A turbo welder was hired for one day only. It was a big job and meant a long hard day but the job was completed.

One of the members, Brenton, was a trade's teacher at a high school. He was able to open the workshop and he and I made the doors and window frames. As the building progressed each group of people swung into action; the carpenters, the painters, the carpets, trimmings and furniture were taken care of by the various groups of people.

The bricklayer was Les, Gwen's brother. It was his faithful plodding methodical work that saw the walls rise from the dust. Mortar mixer, brick supplier, scaffold builder, those were my jobs. Les only built one more house after the church, before succumbing to a brain tumour.

Putting the roof on was another day's work and thanks to the men of the regional churches the roof went on without a hitch. I didn't know at the time but the plumbers and builders in the city were watching how we put the roof on. Praying as to how to put the roof on in the middle of the night God gave me this idea on how to bow the roof and it worked.

The building took two years to complete leaving me very tired and stressed at the end. The hard work, sacrifice and a stressed out nervous system was worth it. Of course there have been many changes to the building over the years, additions to accommodate youth work and children's work and offices for the pastors.

A very fine Doctor and his family joined the Assembly and I promoted him to the leadership. He was a powerful speaker and helped with the ministry. I was devastated when he informed me he was leaving the Assembly to form another fellowship. A number of members followed him thus leaving the Assembly much reduced in numbers and financially crippled. I had taken a risk, promoted a gifted person to leadership and had been let down.

I loved this man and those who went with him. Many of them I had sought to release their personal gifts and talents, opening areas of service for them. Encouraging the gifts of men and women has been my life so how could I separate myself from trying to release these people for service. It is so much a part of me, of my Call, regardless of the hurt to me. The doctor eventually returned to England from where he originated.

To try and build an assembly and protect oneself from being let down is not the road to success. One has to take a risk and so I took the risk and was let down. But that is not to say I failed. The Bible says that if we try to save ourselves we lose ourselves but if we lose ourselves we find ourselves.

It was a time when I was extremely low physically and mentally. In fact I found myself with no more to give. I had given my all and it seemed it was not enough. As I look back from the pinnacle of hindsight it all seems like a bad dream. As I write this story I relive the hurtful emotions of that time.

I envisaged a youth centre and had acquired a large pool table

A shop front window was built in the front of the building to house a craft shop.

However the members wanted a sanctuary unsullied by the world of commerce or youth activities. I had to let my visions go.

I can only say my vision was before its time.

Today, ironically craft groups flourish in churches as tools for evangelism. Youth programmes including musical teams are part of church life as are also bookshops and meals. I can only say my vision was before its time. I pondered what my next step was to be and soon it was clear,

'It's time for a change, Bruce,' Kevin Hodges said to me one day,

'What makes you say that,' I became very defensive.

'You are very tired and need a change,' he continued.

'I haven't completed all that I want to here in Whyalla,' I objected, I didn't want to let go of an unfinished dream.

'Very often the Lord's plan is that somebody else completes the dream that we begin.' Kevin added.

'I admit I'm very tired,' I agreed.

'I have a plan,' Kevin said. 'I will come to Whyalla as senior pastor and you can become an itinerate pastor moving around the churches in the west coast and gulf regions. Each of the churches will contribute to your wage.'

'It sounds Ok,' I agreed. It was time for a change. While I acknowledged my weariness I was largely unaware of how mentally depleted I was.

The changes were made and Pastor Kevin Hodges,

who became a Christian in the Riverland Revival, and was pastor at Port Lincoln at the time, moved to Whyalla and took over the leadership of Bethel Centre, as it became known. I was released to take up an itinerant ministry covering Port Lincoln, Tumby Bay, Ungarra and other areas. I spent time visiting, encouraging, building bridges in relationships. I found myself working amongst farming people with whom I was familiar.

As I took up an itinerate ministry, I realised several things and said to Gwen concerning the great divide between country and city, 'It is hard to create understanding between city folk and country folk. The Executive committees of organisations based in the city seem to have no idea of the problems faced by pastors in the country.'

'Distance is truly an isolating factor and places a great demand on ministries.' Gwen too is aware of the tyranny of distance.

'There always seems to be the factor of them and us that is never solved.' I concluded somewhat saddened. As a roving pastor, I was able to bridge the isolation and give encouragement where needed.

It was a challenging time for Gwen and the family. She and I had never been apart for any length of time but I spent several months away travelling. I can say, though I went through much heart-searching and grief at this time - it was all part of the Call. The time of itinerate ministry was in the plan of God.

During the period of a roving evangelist, pastor, father confessor and troubleshooter around the north and west, living in my caravan, I eventually arrived in Port Pirie. Gwen was still living in Whyalla with our two sons.

Change was in the air in the mid north assemblies. Booleroo Ministry Centre in the Flinders Ranges had been an outreach of Port Pirie and when Pastor Peter Frogley moved to the area he became senior pastor of Booleroo Centre Assembly, which then became an assembly in its own right.

Two Christian Schools were operating at Port Pirie and Booleroo Centre under his direction and vision. Due to lack of teachers and students the Port Pirie School closed and remaining students were bussed to Booleroo.

Very soon after my arrival in Port Pirie as a roving ministry, Pastor Bert Darwin resigned from the leadership of the Port Pirie Assembly. Bert and wife June, with their two sons had pioneered - built up - and served the Assembly faithfully for ten years.

I was invited to lead the Assembly in the absence of a pastor. Because of the changes there was much hurt and heartache and it was my job to minister healing and harmony between the two assemblies by preaching from time to time in Booleroo. By this time it was now 1980.

It was a difficult decision for Gwen to make to leave the family and in particular our sons in the house in Whyalla, and move over to Port Pirie to be with me. Usually the kids leave home but this time it was the parents who left home. It was a very challenging time for the family once again. Families of pastors often find the ground moving from under them and they are left without support. It is not a good feeling for all concerned.

Chapter Thirty-Four
Lengthening The Ropes

There were two very Godly and faithful elders in the Assembly at Port Pirie and they became my very good friends and have remained so. Bob Palmer has since relocated to Queensland. Ray Beyer still resides in Port Pirie. They gave me their full support and that of the Assembly allowing me to still minister in an itinerate manner.

Port Pirie soon became the centre for outreach groups in Jamestown, Booberowie and as far south as Clare. In Jamestown the old Baptist church was hired for Sunday services so I parked my caravan beside the church and stayed over several days to do pastoral work.

God began to move amongst people in the area and the assembly there grew. Chris Flower and wife Jenny became the God chosen elders and on whom I relied heavily to shepherd the flock. Jamestown in turn was fast becoming a centre for outlying smaller towns. Chris Flower was a great leader and organised with Jenny some very wonderful social gatherings contacting many people with the gospel.

Kim and Valery Norton were part of the assembly in Jamestown but they lived in Booborowie a number of kilometres away. They came to me one day,

'Bruce because we live a long way from Jamestown and there are a number of young people who live in this area and are keen to know more about the Lord, can we have a mid week house meeting at our place?'

'I don't see why not.' I responded. 'Chris Flower can run the mid week meeting in Jamestown and I will come out to your place.' It meant a good deal more travelling with an ever-increasing workload but I couldn't deny these young people, they were so keen.

Kim and Valerie were newly married and soon their home was a centre for many young people whom they encouraged in the Lord. It was a delight to visit these home meetings and fellowship with the group of young people in their very formative teenage years. The group also met with the Jamestown Fellowship on Sundays. Although I drove a lot of kilometres to minister to this group it was like a breath of fresh air to talk, pray and have fun with them.

I needed help and I'd heard that Max Richardson and wife Michelle, members of the Port Lincoln CRC were enthusiastically looking to serve God and wanting to test their wings in ministry so I put my idea to Kevin Hodges,

'Max and Michelle are keen to move into ministry, how about they come here to Port Pirie - I need an extra pair of feet and it will give them an opportunity to grow.'

'Sounds like a good idea. If they go where they are not known, they will be accepted better than if they stay in Port Lincoln.' Kevin agreed. Max and Michelle moved to Port Pirie as my assistants.

A lot of development ensued from Max and Michelle's move to Port Pirie.

Max's testimony in the Lord was amazing and his enthusiasm was infectious.

Max and Michelle were very hospitable and their home

became a centre for young couples to hang out. As always, there were detractors against the new ideas and new people. Max's enthusiasm seemed to pressure people who were set in their old ways. I knew from the Riverland Revival that it was God at work. However, it took all my people skills to keep harmony between Christian people who had been in the Assembly since its foundation and the newer members who were so ignorant of the Bible and of God.

***

I remember coming home one day frustrated after talking to some long time members and saying to Gwen,

'Why is it older Christians don't allow God time to perfect the newer members?'

'Yes, the established believers seem to want the newer members to be perfect the moment they come to Christ. They seem to forget they were like that once and have taken years to be established in the Lord.' Gwen added.

I felt the need to add to the ministry team Mark and Marian Walker. I

Officiated at the wedding of this couple in Whyalla, a number of years earlier. Mark had pastored the Assembly in Port Augusta for several years before changing direction. When I became pastor of the Port Pirie Assembly he began to flow back into ministry again. He too became a good backstop in the ministry with the influx of new people.

As the new members flowed into the assembly they brought with them problems that sometimes created high drama. Gwen and I came home one afternoon after doing some visiting ministry to find a mother and five children barricaded in our house.

'What's going on here?' I said alarmed at finding our home occupied.

'Dad's threatened to shoot us. We didn't know where to go or what to do so we came around here. You weren't home but we thought you wouldn't mind if we came in for safety sake,' the oldest son explained.

'Where is your father now?' I could see I would have to go and talk to him.

'He's back at our house now,' the mother explained.

'What are all these knives doing around the house?' I was alarmed at how many deadly looking knives had been placed in strategic places around the house. Did we really possess so many vicious weapons?

'I put them there in case Dad came and tried to break in,' the son explained fearfully.

All my people skills were called upon to persuade the man to obtain medical attention and ensure the wife and children could return home and live in safety. They were among the people God had brought into the Assembly and who showed a desire to follow the Lord.

The father was diagnosed as suffering from a bi-polar disorder and received treatment. He then went back to his family. After being diagnosed and placed on medication he came to see me one day, 'Bruce will you keep my rifle and bullets for me?'

'I most certainly will,' I replied, relieved that he had willingly surrendered his firearm and ammunition.

'I don't trust myself, I might do something terrible,' he added.

I hid them on top of my wardrobe. However the situation was always volatile and we watched the family closely. It was downright scary, to think that we could have arrived home to find these people murdered, our own lives in jeopardy as well.

The house we lived in, also the manse was a beautiful 1920s design with stained glass windows, spacious rooms, and high ceilings. In the early days it had belonged to the Harbour Master.

The church hall was a school building transported from Murray Bridge and placed along side of the house so that the church entrance was on the sidewall and led right into the back door of the house, certainly no privacy for the family in the house. So out came my tool box and I cut a front door in the church building and rearranged the interior to cope with the influx of people and make the back of the house a little more private.

One dear widow from Crystal Brook used to ring up for a chat. I couldn't tactfully get her to ring off.

The doorbell in the house was so loud and shrill it almost created a resurrection; feeling very frustrated I took off my shoe and threw it down the hallway and drew Gwen's attention.

I signalled to ring the doorbell, which she did.

'Oh, look Mrs B…I have to go, I have a visitor.' And I rang off before she could get another breath and start again.

Our stay in Port Pirie was short lived.

'I'm going to leave the Crossroads Christian Centre. I believe God has called me to take up another ministry in Adelaide,' Pastor George Laslett informed his fellow pastors around the Gulf region of South Australia. There was no response from any other ministry and I felt the assembly should not be left without a pastor. So I spoke with You Know Who,

'There is a need for a pastor at Port Augusta. What say we move up there and take up the ministry to that church?'

'Who will take over here?' Gwen queried.

'Mark and Marian are well able to pastor this church,' I reasoned. I must say Gwen never faltered at a challenge.

When I saw Mark again, 'How about you return to the

ministry and pastor the Port Pirie Church and I will move to Port Augusta.'

'I don't know,' he said. 'I will have to pray about it and talk it over with Marian. I wouldn't want to take over the Jamestown Assembly. Who would cover them?'

'Well I suppose I could go over on a regular basis and preach until someone can be found to pastor the Assembly.' I considered the options and the amount of travelling.

'Ok. I'll pastor the Assembly in Pirie,' Mark agreed.

It meant that I would have to oversee Booleroo and Jamestown from Port Augusta a round trip of 150 miles on a Sunday. With all bases covered Gwen and I packed our worldly goods onto a truck and relocated to a small SA Housing Trust home over West Side, Port Augusta in 1983. Another chapter ended as the Call moved us on.

Chapter Thirty-Five
Our Resting Place

Young Captain Matthew Flinders, in 1802, was the first European to explore the area around Port Augusta.

Port Augusta also became known as a centre for outback distance education. The original School of the Air started in 1958 at the Royal Flying Doctor base. A year later, when it moved to its own headquarters, there was an enrolment of 100 students. Now this world famous education service for remote isolated children has taken to cyberspace, letting children and families learn and communicate in a virtual classroom via the Internet.

Port Augusta (population 14,000) remains a rail town, especially since the 2004 inaugural run of the long-awaited 'Ghan' Adelaide to Darwin rail link, and the continuation of the Pichi Richi historic narrow gauge rail from Port Augusta to Quorn. But the "crossroads" town is diversifying. Aquaculture is an expanding industry.

Placed at the head of the Gulf, Port Augusta was an important meeting place for many and diverse Aboriginal groups who gathered to trade and exchange knowledge and skills. Indigenous people still meet, exchange knowledge skills today centuries later as Port Augusta once again becomes a centre for Aboriginal culture and learning.

There was a different mindset to deal with and people to understand and befriend. Port Augusta is where the Call led and that is why we packed up and moved on.

Port Augusta is a place with almost no eucalyptus trees that are native to the area. John Zwar the city gardener, and also Churchill Fellowship winner, was a great botanist and greened the city by planting many thousands of trees, setting aside recreation areas of green lawn changing the face of the city.

It is back to renting a home again. I detest going cap in hand every week or fortnight with rent money.

I feel it to be demeaning and it doesn't sit well with me. I realise others take it as a matter of course.

Our house was a small SA Housing Trust home with a backyard the size of a pocket-handkerchief. But I managed to fit in a shed and a shade house along the back of the house, plant a couple of fruit trees. When the garden, if it could be called such was established and with no more room to do anything with, I discovered the trees and shrubs in the street were in need of some tender loving care. The dripper lines needed unblocking, shrubs were replanted and trees pruned, the street started to look as though someone cared.

A school building had been transported to Port Augusta from Murray Bridge and renovated into a church.

Tim and Carol Marsh had pioneered the Crossroads Christian Centre. Carol was the teenager we took into our home and Tim the hotshot young musician looking to make his mark for God in the Riverland. After leaving Crossroads they eventually went to America where they pastored several churches.

After being in Port Augusta for two years our desire

was to have a house of our own. We were now on a wage and paying rent but why not put the rent into paying off a house? We had received a small inheritance from my parents, enough to buy land. We heard of an acre block going cheap and started negotiations. It was just what we wanted. However the owner decided that he didn't want to sell after all. We were disappointed and abandoned our plans for a house.

Three months later the same guy knocked on our door, when I answered I was greeted with 'Are you still interested in buying my block of land?'

'What, have you got the block on the market again?' I queried, stalling for time.

'Yes, the land has been rezoned and I'm not able to build horse stables as I planned. Do you want the block?'

'Yes,' I said without hesitation, we felt the Lord had said, 'this is your land I have given to you,' and bought the land. We started searching for a transportable home and found a firm at Gawler who seemed reputable and whose workmanship and price pleased me.

'I have a house already built with carpets and all. The young couple had to surrender the house due to a problem. You can have the house for the original price as I need a turnover on the house,' the builder said as we looked over plans and colour schemes.

'That sounds a good deal. We'll accept your offer on condition that you insulate the ceiling and put mirror film on the front windows, it gets very hot in Port Augusta.' I insisted.

'Not a problem,' he agreed.

Logically, we would be in debt for many years to come unless the Lord provided a miracle. I visited the bank with whom I had dealt with for many years to apply for a loan. The manager was very doubtful owing to my small wage but as I owned the land he gave the loan at a certain rate of interest that I thought would be manageable. I also approached Gwen's brother-in-law for a second loan to which he agreed.

Meantime, 'I just want to make sure the loan is still available.' I approached the bank manager several times.

'Yes it is all in order. Just call in and pick up the cheque when the house arrives.'

The grand day arrived in November 1985, when the house was to be delivered. We were on the block watching and waiting for it to come up the road, negotiate the streets and place it on our block. Oh, what a feeling!

The house was placed on its blocks and I went to the bank only to find the interest payments were raised from what we had agreed to. I was upset at the increase but I had to accept the conditions.

'Mr Bank Manager, I will pay off this loan as quick as I can and close my account and never come back.' I didn't know how I was going to pay off the debt but I believed that I would get free of the bank.

'Oh now, Mr Leane, don't be like that, its how things happen.' protested the manager.

'Yes I will. You have put me in a real bind and I won't forget.' I was extremely upset. I felt I had been dealt a slippery deal. Our joy at having our own home was not dimmed. The connection of power, water, sewage and phone enabled us to move in just before Christmas. We had found our resting place and twenty-five years later we are still living our dream. Gum trees, shrubs, fruit trees and vegetables, great views and climate.

It's amazing! The things we learn to do in our youth often remain with us and in later years they are again brought into use.

The memories lay dormant until I discovered that a

pool of water formed after every rain along the rail line across the road from our new block. I decided to tap into it.

A two hundred-metre trench across the then dirt road was dug from my garden to the pool and a one-inch poly pipe was inserted. When it rained the water siphoned into my garden. I then realised that if the water was harvested quicker I would have more water so I re-dug the trench and laid a one and a half inch poly pipe but I wish now it was a two inch pipe. I installed two pumps and three tanks to give me storage for 18,000 gallons on my block. For the last ten years I have harvested up to 120,000 gallons of water a year from this depression. For every one ml of rain I can pump 1,000 gallons of water.

When I first started to harvest water it was thought to be a silly idea. But after years of water restrictions and rising cost of water, I am laughing all the way to the bank.

'How do you get away with it?' I am often asked.

'Well, the Railways and the City Council are aware of what I'm doing but they don't want to know.' I smile.

If I hadn't had to empty the wash water as a boy I might not have seen the potential to harvest the water. I have to say the idea was not only based on the past but God given.

Trees, both gums and fruit are planted along with many Australian natives that are suitable for the climate in which we live. Everywhere we travelled during our holidays over the next few years, from Queensland to Western Australia and from South Australia to the Northern Territory, I've collected seeds. Arriving home the seeds were grown. The acre block became my garden of memories or museum of plants.

Chapter Thirty-Six
The miracle of Opal

Conference time again and we were accompanied by our two Aboriginal friends Clara and Mona. Guess what? It was the signal for another change.

Both of these women had been taken from their families and brought up in Colebrook Children's Home, first at Oodnadatta and when the home there closed then at Quorn where the home was re-established and even later to Eden Hills.

Clara never saw her mother again after she caught the mail truck from Oodnadatta back to Ernabella. It was many years before she was able to find and visit the grave and grieve over what might have been.

During a free time at the Conference, Clara approached me, 'Mona and I are going to buy a miners' licence and rights, you and Gwen come along and get yours as well.'

'What would I do with a miners' licence?' I wondered

'You could come opal mining with us.' Clara grinned knowingly.

'Dream on,' I told her. After some thought and discussion with Gwen, I thought why not? It might come in handy.

Becoming involved with Clara and Mona meant sharing their heartache for the tribal people of the inland. I tried for some years to obtain a permit to take groups into the Lands but at that time it was hard for Christian people to obtain entry after the Government claimed responsibility for the Communities and sidelined the Christian Missions. I had thought maybe the Call was to return to working amongst the indigenous but the door had closed.

A huge gap had been created in the social welfare of the people that had once been undertaken by the missionaries. In spite of the millions of dollars provided by the Government many of the social problems have not been resolved.

The ability to access motorcars has enabled the people to move freely and visit the cities and sample city life. It has also brought the curse of petrol sniffing, drugs and alcoholism that have broken up the tribal family unit.

Christianity has been blamed for breaking up tribal life but I think the provision of social welfare has had a worse effect.

The grandmothers and older women have carried the burden of care for children and the upholding of a standard of living.

Alcohol is the biggest robber of good men and women that I have ever known. Do you wonder why my resolve not to drink alcohol has never weakened?

Opal fever was coursing through Clara's blood; she was eager to return to Mintabie and she was influencing Gwen and me.

Mintabie is an opal mining community within the Anangu Pitjantjatjara Yunkunytjatjara in South Australia. It is unique in comparison to other communities situated in the APY Lands, in that its residents are largely non-indigenous.

From the time Clara returned to her homeland as a schoolteacher at the re-opened Children's Home at Oodnadatta, she had holidayed in the Lands. So she knew the area like the back of her hand.

If one is a little mad, it helps when getting three women to agree where and how to peg a claim. To peg a claim four three inch square pieces of wood one metre long are driven into the corners of a piece of ground 50 metres by 50 metres square. If the claim was proven to be under or over the specified measurements the Mines and Energy Department had the power to pull the pegs and give it somebody else. The claim had to be surveyed from data points and the degrees of every corner carefully marked. So you can understand the trouble I had with my three female partners wanting to 'Peg here, Bruce.'

'No, peg over there, Bruce.'

After pegging we had to pay for someone with a drilling rig to drill several holes over four claims testing for samples of opal colour. It took several months for us to find out that our claim was not productive even though Clara was sure it was where her old Uncle had told her to peg.

'I'm wondering if we should peg again, Clara. We have almost used up our savings.' I explained to Clara. I was feeling very doubtful about trying again.

'Give it another go, Bruce. I believe the Lord will show us where to mine.' Clara had greater faith than I did.

'OK. I'll try once more and if we don't find opal that's it, I'm not spending any more money.' I relented.

Everybody was watching us because we were working with Aboriginal people and it had never happened before and also no Aboriginal person had ever taken out a claim before. Clara, her family and Mona was the first Aboriginal people to take out a claim. A camp was established at

Mintabie and Clara lived there for the time that we were mining up there.

When my annual holidays arrived, Gwen and I headed out for Mintabie. By now we had formed a company of six, Mona, Clara and two of Clara's children and Gwen and I.

While studying where to peg our claims the second time we met another Christian man who lived there.

'Where do you think would be a good place to peg some claims?' I asked him in the course of our conversation,

'There does seem to a lot of activity out at Grasshopper Ridge. It might be a good place to have a look at. In fact if I was pegging a claim, that's where I would be.'

'Well, seeing as you know the area', I said, 'I think that's where we'll go.'

'I'd like to ask Uncle first,' Clara believed implicitly in Uncle's ability to know where minerals were.

'But if we wait, we might loose a valuable position,' I was impatient to get started and afraid we might loose an important claim; also I had an assembly to run.

Grasshopper Ridge was a completely new area being opened up and not many people had taken up claims out there. So contrary to Clara we started measuring and pegging with everybody saying that a fault line ran here and there and we should peg across the fault line. It was recognised that opal formed in these fault lines. Next door to our claims other men were drilling and then they started rushing around using mulga sticks which was illegal, to peg their claims. They had found opal! We caught their excitement. We could have challenged the illegal pegging of their claims but we were not about to get mean.

Four claims were finally pegged, and registered, and then Gwen and I left for Port Augusta and back to being a pastor. Nine hours later at 2 am we arrived home. Clara stayed behind in the camp as overseer and pegged two more claims.

Clara engaged a driller to test our claims and after much frustration, some colour was found on Gwen's claim, which meant chasing a contractor and convincing him to work the claim. Being convinced by a tiny bit of colour and Clara's charm and prayers a willing contractor was found. The terms were 70% for him and 30% for us; to be shared between six of us or 5% profit each from the opal.

To work the claim meant removing two metres of red sand, then blasting the cap rock and pushing it out with a bulldozer as well as picking it up and transporting it another spot with a massive scraper. The actual opal level was 15 metres down. Many, many months of dozing and scraping just to get down to the opal level occurred and then we had to employ a spotter to follow behind the dozer backward and forwards across the claim day after day watching for any sign of opal.

Is opal mining a gamble? I think betting on horse racing is a more certain bet. Or maybe cross lotto. But I don't gamble so how would I know. All I knew was that I was a pastor mining opal and going broke by the second.

One of my colleagues from the city made the comment, 'Bruce, you have no right to go opal mining. Your responsibilities are to the church.' The man who made that comment is no longer ministering in Australia, isn't that interesting?

It may have seemed I was diverted from my Call but if the events leading to the venture were anything to go by, mining was somehow part of the Call. We met some Korean Christian miners who came together every Sunday to worship. They invited us and any other Christians to share. They conducted their service in Korean but the hymns were the same so we sang in English and they in Korean. They even invited me to preach and they translated.

A tin shed was built and used as a church for quite a while. Even in Mintabie I could not escape the Call to preach.

My son Philip and I went up one weekend and enlarged Clara's campsite; we put a roof over the van and camp area to keep out some of the heat so it was more comfortable for Clara.

When the contractor finally reached opal level, Gwen and I took our annual holidays and went up there and camped. It was in the middle of summer when the heat reached 50 degrees down the cut.

Surrounded by snow-white walls the heat bounced off the sides of the claim. There was nowhere to go to cool off.

Nobody works in the summer up there and Mintabie becomes a ghost town. The populace goes south where it is cooler. But our contractor was broke and so he kept working. We would start work at 7 am when it was cool and also when there was enough light to be able to spot the gleam of opal. We would work until midday and then knock off and try to find a cool spot if possible. Living conditions were not exactly the Ritz. No power, fans, air conditioners; showers were taken by heating a bucket of water over a fire and filling a bucket perforated with holes hanging behind a screen and standing under it.

Tough times, tough people, no trust and no truth were ever spoken. Our contractor was adamant that we not tell anyone that we had found opal for fear we could get robbed or worse. At one stage Gwen and the spotter's wife were locked up in the contractor's home sorting opal with a loaded shotgun at hand with orders to shoot if an intruder should pay a visit. Opal was stored in a forty-four gallon drum with a lock down lid.

One night the contractor was down the pub when someone approached him,

'I hear you have found a good deal of opal?"

'Where did you hear that from?' The contractor was livid.

When he saw us next day he was on the war path, 'Which of you has talked about finding opal?'

No one of course admitted to having a loose tongue but we were trying to think where we'd been and whom we'd talked to.

'Don't you realise my wife and I have to live here. We could be robbed or worse,' he shouted. 'If I hear of anyone talking again, I'm finished. Find another contractor.'

'Bruce, did you find opal?' People always ask.

'All miners are liars. No we didn't.' I reply.

We battled over three years before I finally called a halt. I wasn't going to lose that which we had gained by fighting to get more and more.

'Can you tell me how much I owe on my loan?' I was finally able to approach my bank manager.

'You are in arrears by so much, Mr Leane,' I was informed.

'The debt owing on the house, how much is it?' I politely inquired. After a few minutes the sum total was announced.

'I will now clear my account and close it at the same time.' It was with much satisfaction I counted out the right amount of cash and was at last free from the bank. That really created a fuss. The teller called the manager and I was called into the inner sanctum.

'Why are you closing your account, Mr Leane?

'I said I would pay you out and quit this bank because of your raised bank interest when you quoted otherwise.' It felt good to be out of debt, because I also was able to repay my brother-in-law his loan.

It was amazing; the Lord had allowed us to clear the

debt of our house exactly. Then the opal seemed to dry up and we didn't find any more. We believed we were greatly blessed with a miracle of finance.

'Bruce, let's go back and mine for opal?' Several friends have urged me to help them since.

'No, that's it. We are not throwing money away. Our need has been met not our greed,' I said. We have found our resting place and have created our dream and are following our Call.

Chapter Thirty-Seven
Another Fifteen Years

I came to know John Zwar very well over the years, doing some tree lopping for the Council. John was in charge of Parks and Gardens in Port Augusta at the time. Cherry pickers and other machinery used today take the drudge and danger from lopping trees wasn't used very much then. Due to his influence I acquired many trees to plant along the footpath surrounding my block. Several of the neighbours caught the vision to plant trees and our particular corner is known for the many trees.

At that time my two sons and I bought another ten acres of land next to the aerodrome on Westside. This land was to be a get away for our sons and their families. Gwen and I thought we might build out there. So I planted up the sand hills with trees and shrubs. But in the end, we were too entrenched and not at all inclined to move, believing that what we had was given us by God for our retirement. Later we sold the land. It is with a source of pride that I drive past and realise my trees are still growing there.

'Old age – What is it? I'm not sure when one is supposed to become old.' I often say to Gwen.

'If you don't use it you lose it,' she replies.

Even if I felt like vegetating, You Know Who will never retire. She has no intention of slowing down yet for many years.

Due to the years spent in bed as an asthmatic, my spine and thigh joints have stiffened up and arthritis set in.

That I am still moving and manage my patch of ground and actively involved in the community and church is due to the miracle power of God and modern medicine.

'Why am I so tired? I can hardly stagger around the garden these days.' I complained to Gwen. It seemed as though having resigned from the church my whole being just collapsed.

'You need to see a doctor for a check-up.' Gwen was matter of fact.

'Your heart is not happy,' the doctor was matter of fact as well. 'You'll need to see a specialist.'

'You need a by-pass operation,' the specialist was matter of fact as well. Before I knew it I was sent to the Royal Adelaide Hospital for a heart by-pass.

'What will you do if I don't come back, honey?' I said to Gwen the evening before the operation.

'Oh, I shall live it up,' she tried to laugh.

'I've run the race and kept the faith,' I ignored her attempted flippancy.

'Do let's look on the bright side,' she gave me a peck on the cheek.

'I'm ready to meet the Lord. I know where I'm going and I'm not afraid. I never expected to live beyond seventy due to ill health.' Running through my mind was a quote from the Bible - that book that I had believed all my life to be words from God and never had reason to disbelieve, 'No, I will not abandon you or leave you as orphans in the storm...'

The operation was traumatic as all operations are. It

was a time when my mortality was challenged and I can say with a quiet confidence that I was ready to face my Lord.

'You should get another fifteen years out of your heart,' the specialist said.

'Thank you for giving me back my life,' I said. It is now quite a few years since the operation. It was clear the Call was still beckoning me on. It hadn't left just because of a hiccup over my heart.

God willing, Gwen and I will celebrate sixty years marriage. Gwen says I can't kick the bucket before the wedding anniversary.

I spent many years on the CRC State Executive in Adelaide representing the northern and western country churches of South Australia.

'I don't know, Gwen, but I feel tired. I am going to retire from the CRC State Executive.' I had just returned from a meeting.

'Well, it is your decision, honey,' she answered.

'Younger men will come forward and pick up the baton if I am not there. After all I am sixty-eight.' I looked back over the years of serving the Movement as well as God as faithfully as I could.

'It's true moving aside will make room for other ministries to arise,' Gwen agreed.

'The Call to preach still burns in my heart, I am rostered to preach at Crossroads Christian Centre. I believe the Lord has lifted part of the Call, that is, the responsibility and involvement of church politics. I no longer have the heart for such.' I was at last admitting that the Call had led me to a place of rest.

I could look back and know I had delivered all that the Lord had required of me.

'I have resigned from the CRC State Executive Council, what now?' I said to Gwen.

'I have often thought it would be good to be involved in the Friends of the Australian Arid Lands Botanic Garden,' Gwen said.

'Yes, that would be a good challenge. The Garden is still in its infancy. We might be able to help as well as learn.'

'You know John Zwar because of the trees you cut down for the City Council. He's the President of the Australian Arid Lands Botanic Garden,' Gwen pointed out.

I had hardly become a member when at the Annual General Meeting my name was put forward as Vice President.

'Do you wish to stand for the position?' the President John Zwar asked.

'Ye-es,' I was a bit reluctant and then thought why not, 'Yes I am happy to stand for nomination. After voting John announced, 'Bruce you are Vice President, I'm happy to congratulate you.' I was also on the Working Committee for the Garden for a number of years in the planning and developing of the Garden. Gwen accepted the position of Secretary for a number of years.

During a committee meeting I expressed my thoughts, 'It's

obvious that a nursery growing arid plants is needed to stock the Garden itself. The public need to be educated on the beauty, versatility and need to grow arid plants to save water.'

A big discussion ensued; some members were for it and others against it.

In the end with the help of a number of Friends volunteers with enough expertise and vision I set up a nursery. My toolbox was out again with a cement mixer to mix up potting soil and tools to build shade houses and hardening up areas.

Leading a bunch of volunteers was no different from

pastoring a church. As a motivator, it was not hard to motivate people who were retired and looking to do something useful for the community in their retirement.

Gwen and I committed every Wednesday morning to the propagation of plants along with twelve or so volunteers for at least ten years. Gwen became the seed - planting lady.

The Friends group at that stage was struggling financially and thanks to the nursery became a very rich organisation able to supply tractors, trailers and equipment needed for the Garden.

'Bruce and Gwen, will you come forward, please?' John Zwar had called out our names along with two other couples.

John proceeded with a speech of thanks for our support and hard work in the AALBG and then presented us all with a gold brooch of the AALBG emblem and certificate of Life Membership. It was a great moment.

'Whew, I've turned eighty,' I said to Gwen one day after returning from our Wednesday morning stint at the AALBG nursery, 'I feel like it too. I think it's time to hang up the snips and gloves and retire.'

'If you say so,' Gwen didn't really believe me; she had heard all this before.

'Yes, it's true. It's time I took a kick at myself and acted my age.'

After the involvement in the garden and the knowledge learnt, there was a gap in my life. So I bent Gwen's ear again,

'Why don't we set up a nursery and grow and sell arid plants?'

'Why not,' Gwen's eyes sparkled with enthusiasm. Maybe she too was missing working with plants.

'We know how to take cuttings and grow them. I'll build another heat bed and nursery,' the adrenalin was running hot, my fingers were itching, the toolbox was opened and soon a shade house was standing in the back yard. A heat bed was set up in a corner and stands for boxes of plants built. Cuttings were soon placed in the heat bed and told to grow. By the end of 2009 Gwen and I were attending markets selling our own plants.

The cuttings and seeds were all from our own garden, thanks to our earlier desire to grow Australian natives on our patch of ground. We are again emphasising the Eremophila family of plants. Eremophilas range from trees to groundcovers in a range of colours. They are very beautiful and drought resistant. We have named our nursery The Leane and Greane Nursery. Is the nursery part of the Call? It would seem so.

Philip and his wife Vanessa, our son and daughter-in-law are involved with Allan Manzanella and wife Cleofe of Cebu Island, Philippines. Through Philip and Vanessa, we became aware of the great need in the Philippines and Allan and Cleofe in particular.

We met them when they were in Australia for conference 2010 and became aware of the hardships that they operate under. In comparison we pastors in Australia have it so good.

Enter the Leane and Greane Nursery that has developed quite nicely. Gwen and I soon saw a place for the Nursery and in prayer prayed that whatever profit came from the Nursery would go to the support of Allan and Cleofe and their ministry. I rejoice in being a co-labourer with Allan and Cleofe.

We have many beautiful arid plants and regularly attend local weekend markets. The sales have been good but we also have made some great contacts for the Lord as well. The markets have proven to be an outreach for the Lord.

THE MAVERICK'S ROUNDUP

We don't expect to visit the Philippines. I would rather send the finance to Allan for him to use 100% on his ministry needs than to be a burden on him and a tourist.

Years of experience growing plants at the AALBG in has come back to bless us and we have been able to reach beyond our shores without having the upheaval of travelling in a foreign country. The Call has taken us in strange directions yet used every part of our life and being.

The Call made us a prisoner from which we cannot escape until we have relocated to be with the Lord in person.

Chapter Thirty-Eight
Jack and Jean

Many times I have been asked about the Call on my life, I answer with a quote from that ancient book which I use every day: 'I have not called you as a servant (to do this or that) but as a friend. You have not chosen me but I have chosen you and ordained you to bear fruit and your fruit shall remain. Whatsoever you shall ask of the Father in my name he will give it.'

Under these terms life never seems to slow down, for to live under the dynamic of God is to live to the full.

Gwen and I were driving home from Port Augusta to Stirling North when I drove through a red light. Of course it wasn't my fault. Right at the wrong moment Gwen asked, 'What do you want for tea?' She was speaking into my deaf ear.

To add to the confusion a great bully of a semi trailer that dwarfed even our 4x4 drew up on my left braking suddenly at the lights. My view of the lights on my left, were blocked and I sailed straight through. There is a camera at these particular lights.

'Bruce, I think you just ran a red light,' Gwen pointed out.

THE MAVERICK'S ROUNDUP

I sweated for weeks waiting for my unfair fine of $300.00, mumbling about being a poor pensioner and not being my fault. I was careful to not tell anybody, being too ashamed. Six weeks passed without that letter and I started to breath easy.

Breaking my silence, I spoke to somebody about the incident, at that instant I received a great revelation: the car was registered in Gwen's name and the fine would come to her and any point deduction would be against her name not mine. My record would be unblemished; all that anguish and condemnation for nothing when all the time I was covered.

That is exactly it – it's what Christ did in giving up his life. He covered our failures before God so that any judgement from God would not be held against us but against another, Christ who would take the blame. That shifts us right outside of any self-loathing and condemnation to living in an exalted position as a child of the King. More than that, he promises us, 'your fruit shall remain.'

There comes to mind one last story I must share, Jean and Jack, not their real names, were a couple who asked me to come and visit them when I lived in Whyalla.

We were sitting over the usual cup of coffee around their kitchen table amidst the cigarettes, matches and cigarette fog. Cutting my way through the smoke haze, when counselling, has always been a bit tough due to years of asthma.

'Bruce, we can't find the victory in Christ that you talk about and practise. We keep stumbling. Why? Please help us.' There were tears of frustration in their eyes.

'You need to realise that Christ has you covered; you are trying to fight the fight that he fought and finished for you,' I explained.

'Sounds easy, mate, like you tell it - but not so easy in

real life. Tell us more,' Jack was dubious.

I silently pleaded for divine wisdom as I drained the last drops of my coffee and plunked it down on the table.

'Jack, toss me your matches, please,' I asked.

'What, you want a smoke now,' Jack laughed he wondered if I might be living a double life.

'No, I don't,' I was very blunt. 'I want to demonstrate something to you.'

I took the matches and placed them under the coffee cup, saying, 'the matches represent me; the coffee cup represents Christ covering me. The cigarette packet here represents God the Father looking on. He says to Christ, 'How is Bruce getting on?'

'He's absolutely fine,' says Christ, 'I've got him covered.'

The Father smiles at Jesus and me because he can only see the perfection of Christ between him and I. I am no longer accredited with being below par.

Christ is our absolute covering for our substandard lives.

The timeless words from the Bible declare that 'we have an advocate with the Father (who is) Jesus Christ the Righteous.' Christ's giving of himself in death covers us so when God the Father looks at us he sees Christ the good one, not us the substandard one.

Those things we wish we hadn't done, or shouldn't have been said, a past that abused us, broken relationships that hurt us, are all covered by Christ and they are swept away as far as the east is from the west and God doesn't see them let alone remember them.

Christ has given us the right to say, 'I'm clean from the abuse, and I'm healed from the broken relationship.'

'Jack and Jean, you have the right to say I am in Christ and he in me and we no longer live under condemnation,' I said to the couple.

'But what about when we fail to live as we should?' Jean spoke up, she was very aware of how easy it was to slip-up.

'It doesn't mean to say we won't slip up but those slip-ups are under the covering of Christ.' I explained, adding, 'It is so profound it seems too easy. But it is so liberating.'

Jack and Jean were lit by an inner light as this truth burst across their minds.

I remembered the words of a song, 'I am covered over with the righteousness Jesus gives to me.'

'My words to the couple, 'Stop trying to improve yourselves, that's religion. Accept the covering of goodness given to you by Jesus and by believing you are good, that's Christianity.'

GWENNETH & BRUCE LEANE

Gwenneth Leane

Gwenneth began her writing journey in the 1970's when she enrolled in a Creative Writer's Course through TAFE gaining a Pass 1. Gwenneth added to her achievements by doing a correspondence course at Australian College of Journalism gaining a Diploma of Freelance Travel Writing & Photography.

Submitting work to a number of short story competitions Gwenneth was awarded three firsts and two second places. Gwenneth has had work published in numerous anthologies. Articles printed in magazines: Town & Country Farmer and Grass Roots and worked for a brief period as journalist for the local paper, The Transcontinental.

Gwenneth have self-published two biographies, and worked as editor for three books. She is a contributor to projects sponsored by ABC Open.

GWENNETH & BRUCE LEANE

Bruce Leane

Life for Bruce has been a rich adventure inspiring not only his family but all who came in contact with him.

Bruce's story is of a man who overcame illness and lack of education to follow the Call of God.

The Call led Bruce into Aboriginal camps situated along the River Murray in South Australia, Victoria and New South Wales.

He was encouraged to try his hand at opal mining in the remote north of South Australia,

From toolbox to pulpit Bruce has needed to think outside of the box which has led him to be nicknamed the Maverick.

Bruce came to rest in Port Augusta but the Call has not left him, instead God has 'strengthened his stakes and lengthened the cords of his dwelling place and he finds himself extending aid and ministry outside of Australia.

THE MAVERICK'S ROUNDUP

Bruce Leane

Late for Bruce has been a rich adventure inspiring not only his family, but all who came in contact with him.

Incredible story is of a man who overcame illness and lack of education to follow the Call of God.

The Call led Bruce into Aboriginal camps situated along the River Murray in South Australia, Victoria, and New South Wales.

He was encouraged to try his hand at opal mining in the Coober Pedy of South Australia.

Ill-health took its toll upon Bruce has needed to think outside of the box which has led him to be nicknamed the Maverick.

Bruce came to rest in Port Augusta but the Call has not left him. Instead, God has strengthened his stakes and lengthened the cords of his dwelling place and he finds himself extending aid and ministry outside of Australia.

www.ingramcontent.com/pod-product-compliance
Lightning Source LLC
Chambersburg PA
CBHW010447010526
44118CB00021B/2526

9780994438263